FILMMAKERS SERIES

edited by
ANTHONY SLIDE

STANLEY DONEN

by

Joseph Andrew Casper

Filmmakers, No. 5

The Scarecrow Press, Inc.
Metuchen, N.J., and London
1983

Library of Congress Cataloging in Publication Data

Casper, Joseph Andrew.
    Stanley Donen.

    (Filmmakers ; no. 5)
    Filmography: p.
    Bibliography: p.
    Discography: p.
    Includes index.
    1. Donen, Stanley. 2. Moving-picture producers and
directors--United States--Biography. I. Title.
II. Series: Filmmakers (Scarecrow Press) ; no. 5.
PN1998.A3D592 1983   791.43'0233'0924 [B]   83-2913
ISBN 0-8108-1615-6

For M. S. K.

CONTENTS

ACKNOWLEDGMENTS

A book, like a Donen movie, is a collaboration, and I would like to thank the people involved: Co-chairmen Russ McGregor and Mort Zarcoff of USC's Division of Film and Television for encouragement; Tom Cooper for his splendid retrospectives at the Vagabond Theatre in Los Angeles; Jim Farquarhson for locating prints; T. A. Bridget Kiley for legwork; USC graduate students Gay Studlar, Joanna Yeck, and especially Mary Whitley for materials; Dr. Robert Knutson and Ned Comstock of USC's Special Collections for the use of the Freed, Edens, and Warner Brothers files; Dr. Arthur Tilford for his top-notch photography; Luther Davis, Dennis Lee Galling, Betty Garrett, Leonard Gersche, Jane Powell, Charles Walters, and, of course, Stanley Donen for conversations; and, above all, Arthur Knight for delousing the manuscript as well as for speaking eloquent and kind words.

EDITOR'S NOTE

Stanley Donen was a chorus boy turned choreographer who became, possibly, the finest director of film musicals of more recent vintage. A listing of his credits from the late '40s onward reads like a history of the modern American film musical. From the cult classic Singin' in the Rain through Movie Movie, Stanley Donen has displayed an originality and vitality in his film musicals unequaled since the cinema first learned to talk, sing, and dance in the late '20s.

Joseph Andrew Casper is an assistant professor of cinema and television at the University of Southern California who has taken the time and effort to document the career of Stanley Donen, as he did so meticulously in his 1977 volume on Vincente Minnelli. He not only analyzes the work of Donen, but also puts it into perspective against the background of a rapidly changing American film industry. Donen's own comments make a valuable addition to the text, as do Casper's detailed chronology, filmography, and discography. All in all, neither the reader nor Stanley Donen himself could ask for a better evaluation and documentation of what has been and continues to be a long and glorious career.

Anthony Slide
Series Editor

vii

FOREWORD, BY ARTHUR KNIGHT

I have never ceased to marvel at the versatility of
American directors. One can immediately identify a Bergman film, a Fellini film, a picture by Jean-Luc Godard. Not
only do they have a "look," but they have recurrent themes,
ideas, characters, and images, making them ideal subjects
for any auteur-oriented study. But what do you do with the
Americans? They may turn from a straight drama to a musical, a film noir, or a western. Their work seems to em-
brace just about every genre and style. Of all the noted
Americans only the late Alfred Hitchcock was totally identified with a certain kind of filmmaking--but of course he re-
mained essentially a European right up to the end.

And yet is it really as simple as all that? Is a director to be identified solely through the stories that attract
him and lend a unity to his work? I think not; and neither
does Joseph Andrew Casper, as this provocative and insightful
study of the career of Stanley Donen emphasizes. Although
coming from the musical theater, and quickly establishing a
reputation as a talented and inventive creator of movie musicals, Donen's widening interests inevitably carried him on
to light comedies, a plangent fantasy, even a taut and effective mystery melodrama.

What Casper has contributed in this penetrating exe-
gesis of Donen's collected works is an approach to auteur
criticism that embraces yet transcends subject matter, and
leads us on to an appreciation of the style that is the man
(which, I suspect, is the true purpose of auteurist analysis
in the first place). To be sure, Casper never slights the

story side of Donen's works.   The literary aspects of each
film are discussed thoroughly and insightfully.   But then he
moves on to something that has rarely been attempted--cer-
tainly not, at least to my knowledge, in the study of the entire body of films by a single director.   With great precision,
and a vivid writing style that makes it all possible, Casper
analyzes in detail the use of camera, editing, and sound in
each of Donen's movies, and how he sets up his scenes.   And
what comes clear as the book progresses is that there is a
Donen style, a fluidity of movement, a sense of composition,
a feeling for tempo and rhythm that is distinctively his own.

        Not all of the Donen films, of course, have been
equally successful.   In some cases this can be traced to
dubious material, in others--as Casper frankly reveals--to
inimical working conditions.   Like many American directors
Donen often accepted an assignment simply to complete a
contractual commitment.   In effect this book is a refutation
of the oft-quoted auteurist doctrine that "the worst Jean Renoir film is better than the best Jean Delannoy."   The worst
Donen films have been pretty awful and the best have been
mighty good.   The important thing is to understand why--and
this is the task that Casper has set for himself, even though
it is hardly likely to please those auteur-oriented critics who
feel that they have merely to look at the credits to know if
a film is good or bad.

        On the other hand, I have always questioned the as-
sessment of quality simply on the basis of who was the director, just as I would question any other unproven assump-
tion.   To be sure, the auteur theory has provided us with a
valid and valuable approach to film criticism--but only when
used in the nonjudgmental, scholarly fashion implicit in these
pages.   Though Casper writes with a strong sympathy and
obvious enthusiasm for Donen and his movies (why else would
he undertake such an exhaustive study?), rarely does he permit affection to color his insights.   Donen, for example, was
understandably reluctant to have this book conclude with
Saturn 3, not one of his greatest hits, but Casper insisted
on keeping it in.   He felt it to be an important part of the
study.

        This book adds a new and important dimension to
auteur criticism--an assessment of the pressures and restraints, the compromises and special circumstances, surrounding every film.   Without these any auteurist writing
is not only incomplete, but probably invalid.   I suspect that
Stanley Donen is destined to become a seminal extension of the
auteur theory.

PREFACE

Like other veteran Hollywood directors, of whom he is the youngest and most active, Stanley Donen has practiced what he preached: "Entertaining people is, to me, the bottom line."[1] Even in the late '50s, '60s, and '70s, when most of his Yankee confreres were pursuing "reality," "art," or "the visceral" (and often slipping into the bog of didacticism, affectation, and tastelessness), Donen still made 'em like they used to: light, energetic, direct, lean, and decorous. As a matter of fact, his movies were as real as the "message" pictures in their awakening of our primal feelings and putting us in contact with them, as artful as "highbrow" cinema in their display of wit and invention and their command of the expressive properties of the medium, and as effective as any sensory massage in their transporting us to a realm of make-believe closest to heaven--rather than hell--on earth. As such he has fashioned one of the most enjoyable and stylish bodies of work in the American cinema. And, like all the best entertainment movies, his polished entertainments are riddled with the power of meaning. Furthermore, Donen's divertissements changed the face of the American film musical--a change that just happened to be the genre's crowning development--and gave American film comedy a good deal of sophistication, verve, and handsomeness.

In making these movies Donen has repeatedly acknowledged the importance of collaboration--a refreshingly honest admission when so many American directors have succumbed to "auteuritis," especially off the set.

True, in his contract days the collaborative aspect

did on occasion squelch his individuality.   But rarely if ever
did it interfere, then or later, with his overseeing every
part and ultimately shaping the whole to such an extent that
there emerges from his house pictures, as well as his independent productions, a distinct Donen signature, a signature
that has thus far been overlooked.

Though Donen's is still a work in progress, a critical
analysis and evaluation of his twenty-six films and dozen bits
and pieces and a review of his career seem in order.

The focus of this essay is on the films themselves:
their origin, production, and especially the aesthetic choices
that Donen and his cohorts employed to enable us to enter
his recreative world, with its oblique referents to our own,
so that in the end, we return to the real one saner and perhaps a bit wiser.

This look at Donen's style begins with the traditions
that have influenced his work and ends with a chronology of
his personal life, filmography, textual notes, bibliography,
and discography.   Throughout the text Donen himself speaks,
as recorded in a series of interviews with the author.

It is hoped that some readers will be inspired to
refine and expand this sketch of a pop artist's style and
slice of Hollywood history and that others--many others--
will be encouraged to see and enjoy, more deeply or for the
first time, Donen's movies.   Finally, this book exists to
thank Stanley Donen for gracing my life.

STANLEY DONEN

1. APPRENTICESHIP: 1940-1949

Columbia, South Carolina

My childhood wasn't very happy. It's a long, grim
story about being a Jew in a small southern town,
being a minority in a place where Jews at that particular moment were thought of as some sort of
people with horns. I felt apart from the rest of
the people. Therefore, I withdrew into myself.

But there were things that alleviated the discomfort
of growing up in Columbia, South Carolina, during the '20s
and '30s and satisfied, in part, the urge to live in another
world, a pleasant one.

I was fascinated with holding movie film in my
hand and photography. My father got me--I wanted
it, I guess--a little hand-cranked projector and a
short. I used to hold the strip of film up to the
light and see fire engines going down the street and
moving against the background, cars bumping into
each other, explosions. I also had an 8mm camera
which I loved to take in the car and, as the car
was moving, photograph the highways, trees, and
signs passing by. There was a huge flood, and I
was absolutely fascinated in photographing these
waters in the street. I was fascinated also by the
placement of the camera in such a way that I could
make something appear to be gigantic in the frame
when it might be minuscule in reality. I didn't
have the discipline to edit the films.

3

The boy ritualistically queued up at the nabe, where
monsters, clowns, gangsters, lovers, and cowboys delighted
him.   In 1933, however, at the age of nine, delight became
enchantment as Fred Astaire carioca'd across the screen in
Flying Down to Rio (Thornton Freeland, 1933).   Besides
rocketing Fred and Ginger to fame, giving the budding genre
some class with a score by Youmans, Eliscu, and Kahn, and
prefiguring the dance musical, Rio was the turning point in
Donen's life.

> I didn't know there was such a thing as a musical
> till Rio.   I sat there day in and day out watching
> that movie.   I must have seen the picture thirty or
> forty times.   I was transported into some sort of
> fantasy world where everything seemed to be happy,
> comfortable, easy, and supported.   A sense of well-
> being filled me.   This experience was created much
> more by Astaire than the other musical parts.   He
> seemed to me a most remarkable achievement:
> without gravity, possessed of a perfection of move-
> ment, and full of grace.   This led me to study danc-
> ing in my hometown as well as New York.   (My
> father managed some ladies' dress shops through-
> out North and South Carolina and Tennessee, and
> every summer he returned with the family to the
> company he worked for, which was located in New
> York.)

Dancing, then, was tap dancing because it was what
Astaire did.   Soon, the adolescent discovered the make-believe
of greasepaint, amber and pink spots, and costumes by working, during high school, in the Town Theater and by seeing,
during the summers, all the Broadway musicals.

Broadway

As soon as he was handed a high school diploma
Quixote headed for Broadway, much to the chagrin of his
father, who wanted him to study at the state university.   He
had just turned sixteen.

PAL JOEY (1940)

That fall of 1940 the naive teenager landed a job in
the chorus of the watershed musical Pal Joey.   John O'Hara's

sardonic book about a vainglorious entertainer who allows
himself to be patronized by a married socialite while pussy-
footing with her secretary; Gene Kelly's amusing lead performance and startling hoofing; some of Rodgers's most lilting melodies and Hart's incisive and scabrous lyrics; Robert
Alton's contextual choreography; Jo Mielziner's visual design;
John Koenig's clothes; and director George Abbott's legerde-
main all took the fledgling's breath away.

> I suppose I danced well enough. Yet, in retrospect,
> I really can't imagine why they chose to have such
> a child as one of the people who even wandered
> through Joey's life. I had a thick southern accent
> which made people laugh when I talked and I was
> very awkward too.

BEST FOOT FORWARD (1941)

The critically controversial show Joey was too sophisticated for its day.[1] Not so Best Foot Forward, the new
Abbott production that press and public welcomed the following
fall. John Cecil Holm's feeble libretto, set at Winsocki Prep,
dealt with the complications resulting from a famous screen
star's acceptance of a shy student's invitation to the prom.
Exuberance was in high supply: the neophyte cast included
June Allyson, Nancy Walker, and Gil Stratton Jr. ; Hugh
Martin and Ralph Blane wrote the rousing songs; Jo Mielziner designed the look and Miles White the uniforms; and, above
all, Gene Kelly and his assistant Stanley Donen created the
unflagging choreography. Kelly's protégé also danced in the
chorus and functioned as assistant stage manager.

> It was very unusual for a star to choreograph a
> show. Well, Gene needed some help. He knew me
> from Joey and thought I was energetic and ambitious
> --Gene had a great respect for hardworking people
> --and asked me to work with him. I thought him
> a unique talent.... When I got a job and saw what
> went on in a show, I was attracted by it all and
> drifted into the putting-on-the-show department. I
> never thought I was very good as a performer.

During the summer of 1942 the seasoned youth enrolled
at the University of South Carolina for a ten-week session,
taking all psychology courses.

BEAT THE BAND (1942)

In the fall, with the thought of college gone up in smoke, the quick study executed the same chores as assistant choreographer and stage manager in this third Abbott show, Beat the Band, which plugged into the big-band craze. The insipid book by George Marion and George Abbott involved a temperamental bandleader (Jack Whiting) who has subleased a penthouse from a man whose orphaned god-daughter promptly arrives from South America to learn about life in the big city. John Breen and Marion created the commonplace score, David Lichine and Donen the dances, Samuel Leve the scenery, and Freddy Wittop the costumes. Except for the "spirited" dances, the critics drubbed the show and consequently chased the patrons away.

Kelly's influence on Donen was evident already in this production and would be in all of his subsequent work. Donen, like Kelly, utilized a performer's specific talent in constructing a number, as opposed to the arranging of abstract patterns that was, in the main, what stage choreography came down to in the '20s and '30s. (Kelly's Joey opened with the protagonist auditioning for a nightclub job, not with a line of fifty leggy blondes, three years before Curly jumped over the backyard fence to tell Aunt Eller about the "beautiful mornin'. ") The numbers' pervasive athleticism was also a trademark of Kelly, whose dancing was athletic rather than balletic. Here, too, Kelly was an innovator, since the vogue on Broadway in the late '30s was for ballet and dream sequences. Kelly, however, would incorporate ballet in his dancing style in the second half of his film career. And Donen, following Kelly's example, staged even the songs in choreographic terms.

Working for three shows under Abbott, the theater's reigning regisseur, also had its effect. Donen saw that Abbott attacked a piece on a gut level and immediately dispensed with the inessentials--a procedure contributing enormously to his perfect sense of timing. This would also be Donen's approach. Abbott avoided fakery and thus made sure to motivate action and business. Psychological accuracy would be just as important for Donen. Abbott constantly ransacked his mind for what was interesting and surprising; so too, Donen. But, most importantly, Abbott taught Donen how to keep a piece together. If you are involved in a collaborative art, such as the musical theater or film, Abbott contended, someone must be in charge. Without a leader there is anarchy. But a leader was someone who opened up and listened to others, accepting or rejecting what they had to offer.   Abbott's notion of a director as the ultimate shaper of a collaboration was an ideal Donen strove for and eventually achieved.

Shortly after Beat the Band played its sixty-seventh and last performance former songwriter Arthur Freed, now MGM's musical impresario, purchased Best Foot Forward. Donen, the eager beaver, invested in a one-way ticket to Hollywood.   Movies, after all, were his first love.   And besides, his mentor and colleague Kelly was now working for this man Freed and for Joe Pasternak, another musical producer who had just moved to MGM after a host of Deanna Durbin hits at Universal-International.

Donen would return to Broadway only once more.

CALL ME MISTER (1946)

> Lehman Engel, the musical director, and Melvyn Douglas, co-producer with Herman Levin, were having problems with Call Me Mister, and I went back to stage some numbers.

This army revue victoriously marched down the Great White Way in the spring of 1946 with Maria Karnilova and three of Donen's future players: Betty Garrett, Jules Munshin, and Bob Fosse.   Director Robert H. Gordon saw to it that Harold Rome's score, John Wray's dances, Lester Polakov's sets, and Grace Houston's costumes supported Arnold Auerbach's satirical sketches.

> I came close to working again in New York when Steve Sondheim sent me his first effort and asked me to direct it.   It was called Saturday Night.[2]

Hollywood

MGM 1942 was the right place and time for an optimistic, gifted, and indefatigable musical nut, since there and then the musical was undergoing one of its most significant periods of development.   The studio housed three musical-production units (Jack Cummings's in addition to Freed's and Pasternak's) and a splendid array of musical talent.   The Freed contingent led the way with its crystallization of the "integrated" musical (in which a strong, coherent plot and consistent characters

enacted with care dictated the film's visual look and numbers) largely through the efforts of director Vincente Minnelli, the apple of Freed's eye.

> Why Arthur made such a big contribution to mu-
> sical movies was because he was singularly equipped
> to do so.... Nobody else had the musical back-
> ground, the Broadway background, the film back-
> ground, the appreciation for what was good in
> musicals, and love of film, the love of people who
> created musicals. And Arthur just had some sort
> of instinct to change the musical from a backstage
> world into something else. He didn't quite know
> what to change it into, just that it had to change. 3

BEST FOOT FORWARD (1943)

Through his own persistence, and Kelly's prevailing
on the graciousness of choreographer Charles Walters, Donen
wound up in the dancing chorus of "The Three B's" number
in Best Foot Forward (1943), a stodgy screen adaptation by
writers Irving Brecher and Fred Finklehoffe and director
Edward Buzzell. Lucille Ball as the star, Gloria De Haven,
and Harry James and his orchestra joined the stage originals
Allyson and Walker.

> Metro gave me a seven-year contract, an actor's
> contract really, which also stated that they had
> my services in other capacities too.

COVER GIRL (1944)

While Donen filmed the college musical, Kelly, once
again deferred from active service, went on loanout to Columbia to co-star with its reigning queen, Rita Hayworth, and
Phil Silvers in Arthur Schwartz's production of Cover Girl
(Charles Vidor, 1944). Kelly asked his former assistant to
join him on the project, and Donen also went on loanout.

> The picture had been in production some months
> before Gene was employed, and a lot of the mu-
> sical numbers that he wasn't in were already photo-
> graphed. [Cover Girl started shooting without a
> male lead. Studio boss Harry Cohn wanted to
> make the film with Columbia contractees and kept

Best Foot Forward: Chorus boy Donen (left center) with arms encircling Gloria De Haven's legs--June Allyson is the other girl--in "The Three B's." Copyright: Metro-Goldwyn-Mayer.

resisting the producer's suggestion of Kelly.]
When he asked me to work with him, we first ran
the numbers Rita had already done. There was a
fashion sequence ["Cover Girl"]. Some were flash-
backs ["Sure Thing"; "Poor John"]. Phil did one
["Who's Complaining?"]. Another had a small-
time chorus introduce the nightclub ["The Show
Must Go On"]. I thought these numbers [choreo-
graphed by Seymour Felix and Val Raset] appalling.
Part of Gene's Columbia contract included the right
to be able to guide his own musical numbers....
We tried to come up with something novel for him
to do. We then developed the idea of the sequence,
arranged the transitions in and out, and mapped
out the camerawork and lighting. Very rarely did
I tell him about dance steps. We next arranged
the music in such a way that it would help to or-
ganize the staging and camera movement. During

the actual filming Gene worked in front of the camera, I behind.   There was no director on the set
except us.   Then we checked to see if it was photographed properly and supervised the editing.   A
curious thing about the photographing and editing
in those days was that you never shot more than
exactly what ended up on the screen.

The enlisting of Donen and Kelly was the best thing
to happen to Cover Girl, which, despite a no-expense-spared
treatment and a host of able craftsmen, was turning out
rather undistinguished.   For one thing, Virginia Van Upp's
story--about a new "face" who, when chosen as Vanity Magazine's "Golden Wedding Girl," leaves a Brooklyn boîte where
she performs with her boyfriend but at the eleventh hour has
a change of heart--was, even in 1944, neolithic.   (Only sidekick Silvers's zany quips and magazine coordinator Eve
Arden's deadpan acerbities enlivened the tired situation--
characters that are surely the first cousins of Singin' in the
Rain's Cosmo and Funny Face's Maggie.)   Furthermore,
Rudolph Mate and Allen M. Davey's Technicolor photography
and Lionel Banks and Cary Odell's designs, which Fay Bab-
cock implemented, were pretty show-offish at times.   The
Kern-Gershwin score was no great shakes either.   (E. Y.
Harburg supplied the lyrics for "Make Way for Tomorrow";
H. E. Pether and Fred W. Leigh wrote the music-hall ditty
"Poor John.")   And there was little lyrical feeling in Vidor's
direction.   Offsetting all this mediocrity, however, were the
Donen-Kelly numbers, which displayed an originality in concept, performance, technical inlay, and handling.   Presaging
the shape of things to come in the genre, they gave Columbia's
first spectacular musical and first color film its true distinction.

The freewheeling, celebrative "Make Way for Tomorrow" takes Danny (Kelly), Rusty (Hayworth), and Genius
(Silvers) from spinning around on restaurant stools to duck-
ing inside their apartment door to avoid the cop who thinks
they're just a bit touched.   In between they dance through
the eatery's doors, onto the wharf's packing boxes and sand-
bags, along a sidewalk, and up and down several stoops,
while turning almost every prop into a musical instrument.

Right from the start the Donen signature is there: the
pally threesome, the gospel of joy, the animation of the decor
through dance, and expansive geography--which necessitated the
removal of a wall between two sound stages.   At midpoint a

Cover Girl: "Make Way for Tomorrow's" palsy-walsy trio--
Gene Kelly, Rita Hayworth, and Phil Silvers.   Copyright:
Columbia.

suspicious policeman, twirling a baton, makes a sudden appearance from frame left with his back to us--the first of
Donen's playful and suspenseful uses of the frame's edges
and yet another instance of thinking cinematically.   The situation anticipates "Singin' in the Rain. "   The startled trio
scamper round the corner, where with undiminished spirits
they tease a couple kissing, encourage a milkman to join
the fun, help a lush (the inimitable Jack Norton) to the door,
and pilfer a red geranium from a window box while catching
a pot of pink geraniums falling from above, obviously meant
for their heads not hands.   The dabs of bright color in the
somber blue and brown set are eye-popping and foreshadow
Donen's superb orchestration of color.

        During this solidly structured and psychologically mo-
tivated yet lunatic sequence the performers' index fingers
are as expressive as their marching and tapping toes and the
in-step camerawork and cutting.

In the "Alter-Ego Dance," the picture's smartest four minutes and another example of a cinematic number, Danny's reflection steps from a dusty shop window onto the sidewalk, where it engages him in a choreographic tug-of-war over whether to let Rusty slip from his life. Throughout, the camera's lateral pans and vertical tracks and the two dozen cuts accentuate the fury of Danny's tap on a deserted street in the wee hours, as befitting a battle with the self, always the most vigorous and private kind.

> I can remember the goose bumps when I got the idea. It occurred to me straightaway that a dance with two people was more powerful and fun to watch than a solo. ... We used a fixed-head camera for the necessary precision and then synchronized the two dances in the editing.

Val Raset was largely responsible for the design of Danny and Rusty's pas de deux, "Long Ago and Far Away"; Broadway's Jack Cole fashioned Danny's stage number "Put Me to the Test." The latter song's reprise, the work of Donen and Kelly, serves as Danny and Genius's entertainment for a truckload of GIs returning to camp, as well as a patriotic nod. Rear projection of a highway being traveled makes for an imaginative backdrop and motivates the farcical finale of the vehicle's sudden stop and the servicemen toppling over the felled performers.

ANCHORS AWEIGH (1945)

Cover Girl's success made Kelly a star. He now was able to control his musical numbers on his home lot, which is exactly what he and his partner Donen did on the Pasternak production of Anchors Aweigh (George Sidney, 1945).

Isobel Lennart's scenario from Natalie Marsin's short story, "You Can't Fool a Marine" concerns two sailors who, on a four-day pass in Hollywood, each fall in love. Joe Brady (Kelly) pairs with Susie Abbott (Kathryn Grayson), an aspiring singer working as a movie extra, Clarence Doolittle (Frank Sinatra) with a girl from Brooklyn (Pamela Britton), waitressing at a Mexican restaurant. The musical is also a Navy recruiting poster, with its subplot of Susie's orphaned nephew wanting to join the war effort, and a studio advertisement, with its showcasing of pianist José Iturbi, MGM's "artist in residence." Robert Planck and Charles Boyle photographed. Surprisingly, the Hollywood Bowl sequence was shot on location. Cedric Gibbons directed the art and Edwin B. Willis and Richard Pefferle dressed the sets. Lyricist Sammy Cahn and composer Jule Styne penned half of the numbers--mostly songs, since Pasternak preferred singing to dancing--while the other half was an amalgam of pop and classical standards by various composers. Like most Pasternak products, the film is an overwrought (140 minutes), fits-and-starts affair, the starts resulting from the work of Donen and Kelly. The partners had the same type of working relationship as they had on Cover Girl.

The film's first two shipmate numbers contain some nifty camera maneuvers. In "We Hate to Leave" the camera races before the two protagonists barreling through the carrier's corridors and swish-pans from one mugging face to another. In the equally ironic "I Begged Her" it sails, in an effective low-angle, over a series of cots (actually trampolines) on which the duo bounce their way toward us. The third shipmate number, "If You Knew Susie," in which the salts unravel an indelicate yarn at the livingroom piano to shock Susie's straitlaced suitor into leaving, boasts lyrics fractured by Donen.

The three Kelly-Sinatra duets are pleasing, but it is Kelly's three solos that stop the show, especially the ingenious "The King Who Couldn't Dance."

> I had the idea for Gene to do a number in which he would be live action and the other characters would be cartoon. From that came the story we wrote together.

Recess period in a grammar school, and Susie's nephew begs Joe to tell him how he got his medals. "Imagine the most beautiful day," Joe begins as a square image of him in U.S. Navy blues dissolving to him in the Pomeranian Navy whites appears on the boy's forehead and spreads to the frame's edges. (The uninspired transition device must be forgiven Donen, who was still feeling his way.) Slow motion makes the sailor's gambol over the green hillside even more carefree and lyrical. The sailor falls into an Alice in Wonderland hole, whose bottom appears to be a tunnel's beginning. A dissolve plants us at the tunnel's end (this elimination in narrative continuity will be one of Donen's favorite accelerating devices). The sailor exits the passageway and enters another world, its otherness compellingly

Anchors Aweigh: Donen's love for special effects: Gene
Kelly in the animated wonderland of "The King Who Couldn't
Dance." Copyright: Metro-Goldwyn-Mayer.

wrought by animation and colors made vivid by the high-
saturation dyes used to tint the animation cells. Animals
appear to shush the sailor and his flute-playing. An owl
explains that the king who lives "in yonder castle" has out-
lawed song and dance. The fast motion of the angered sailor
racing up the tortuous road and the dissolve of him scaling
the castle wall are additional time-savers. "A king has to
do everything his subjects can do, only better," the ruler
expounds, "so I hadda' pass the law because I didn't know
how to sing and dance." In a perfect correspondence with
the reality frame, the sailor turns teacher.

> We thought either Mickey Mouse or Donald Duck
> would be a wonderful dance partner. The studio
> said yes if we could get Disney's permission and
> if he would lend us his facilities. Gene and I
> went to see Disney and told him about our idea:
> live action and cartoon. We had never seen this
> on the screen before. Disney said that he, too,
> had had this thought and showed us some uncom-

pleted parts of a picture he was doing where this
had already been achieved.   [Disney's experiments
resulted in the feature-length The Three Caballeros,
1945, in which Donald took a whirlwind tour of
Latin America.   Disney used in the film both animated characters against real backgrounds that included people and real people against animated
backgrounds that included animated characters.
In neither case, though, was the synchronization
very close.]

Disney refused.   So we decided to use Jerry
the mouse as the king and Tom the cat as the
king's manservant.   These cartoon characters were
in the Metro shorts.   After extensive storyboarding
the dance was photographed first, then the mouse
was animated frame by frame, then the two figures
were linked optically.   Some 10,000 frames had to
be synchronized with Gene's movements.

Gene enlisted in the Navy.   I spent a year
working on that sequence with Metro's cartoon and
optical departments.   The picture was held from
release while I finished it.   The studio kept saying:
release the movie; forget about the cartoon sequence.

The dance that follows "The Worry Song, " by composer Sammy Fain and lyricist Ralph Freed, is developed
along psychologically accurate lines.   After imitating the
sailor's prances, glides, and cakewalk, for example, the
king begins feeling his oats by jumping on the sailor's right
bicep, which, Popeye style, flips him over to the left one,
which flips him back again.   The synchronization throughout
is perfect and the details extremely sensitive, such as the
reflections of the real-life mentor and his animated student
on the hall's shiny marble floor, or the animated medals
that eventually appear on the sailor's blouse.   The finale's
rhymed dissolve of the king on the sailor's knee to the
schoolboy on Joe's is a deft transition out.

In the folksong "Mexican Hat Dance" Joe tries to forget his anxiety over being in love with his pal's girl by dancing with a Chicano gamine (a bronzed Sharon McManus)[4] on
Olvera Street, a mecca of Mexican shops and restaurants in
downtown L. A. [5]   Each section of the huge prop-laden set is
worked into the dance: their waltz and handclapping around
the central fountain, his tap solo in triple-time flamenco and

then in swingtime, which is accompanied by his drumming
on various articles outside the shop on the right, and their
polka around the fountain and the huge, free-standing candle
in the background. The camera's pans and dolly outs, all
respectful of the varying moods, alternately treat the spatial
parts as separate entities and as a whole, all the while
strengthening the dance movements.   And the six cuts preserve the dance's continuity and energy.   The restaurant
across the way (behind the left frame), where Clarence supposedly is with Susie, stops Joe's smooth waltz steps, and
the camera, in a typical Donen flourish, pulls back to a
touching high-angle overview of the child standing dumbstruck
on the fountain's rim while the sailor retreats into the background of stalls.

        "The Bandit Chief Ballet," a practice exercise for
The Pirate ballet (Vincente Minnelli, 1948) and Singin' in the
Rain's "You Were Meant for Me," occurs on a studio set of
a Spanish Colonial villa with trees, parapets, and billowing
drapery.   Here Joe is tongue-tied by Susie: "I hear myself
saying words that have nothing to do with what I feel....
What I feel comes out of Romeo and Juliet, The Three Musketeers....   They go with this world of cloaks and swords,
that house...."[6] While the appropriate lights flood the deep,
exotic red, black, and yellow set, the camera cranes up
from them under a balcony and stops to frame Susie, now a
princess in jeweled mantilla and gown, looking lovingly from
her balcony upon Joe, now a black-caped brigand in the court-
yard below who throws his inamorata a rose.   It is one of
the screen's most magical shots, transporting us from the
present to the eighteenth century.

        Kelly's buccaneer ballet includes a sensuous tango to
"La Cumparisita" and a swing across the set on a hanging
drape in a forty-foot arc.   The ending is as miraculous as
the beginning: the lady drops the rose as the camera cranes
down to catch Susie and Joe kissing under the balcony set
and comes to rest on the rose.   This image will inspire the
frame of the An American in Paris ballet (Vincente Minnelli,
1951).

THE B MUSICALS AT GOWER GULCH

        With Kelly overseas the wunderkind seesawed between
MGM and Columbia, lending imagination and verve to musical
sequences.

> Columbia made a series of inexpensive musicals.
> I worked on six or seven over a year and a half. [7]
> Though they were ground out like sausages, the ex-
> perience was valuable. I practiced my craft, work-
> ing with music, track, and photography. I often
> directed the sequences. I always tried to have an
> original idea about how to do a musical sequence.

HOLIDAY IN MEXICO (1946)

Across town Pasternak and Sidney, delighted over the
lucrative Anchors, insisted that Donen be on hand for an over-
long Holiday in Mexico (1946). In Isobel Lennart's cloying
screenplay, based on a story by William Koslenko, the pre-
cocious teenage daughter (Jane Powell) of the American Am-
bassador to Mexico (Walter Pidgeon) runs their motherless
home. Out of jealousy she makes a pitch for José Iturbi
when her father ignites an old flame (poseur extraordinaire
Ilona Massey) and fails to show for their bedtime duet of
"Goodnight Sweetheart."

Although uncredited, Donen inventively composed Iturbi's interludes, ranging from Rachmaninoff to boogie-woogie,
and Xavier Cugat's band numbers. ("I Love You Very Much,"
in particular, is an effervescent montage that has even his
chihuahua warble a line.) While appearing in Freed's musicals only occasionally, the "big band" was a Pasternak staple.

> In all honesty, Pasternak held me in higher regard
> than did Freed ... although I held his pictures in
> utter contempt. Even after I proved myself with
> On the Town, I was still second banana in the Freed
> unit.

NO LEAVE, NO LOVE (1946)

No Leave, No Love (Charles Martin, 1946), well below
the Pasternak standard, followed. Martin and Leslie Kardos's
story of a marine (Van Johnson) who falls in love with a radio
singer (English newcomer Pat Kirkwood) was given a shot in
the arm by a "Cugat Specialty," which Donen, again uncredited,
fashioned into a fiery montage cut to a rhumba beat: swish
pans of a gourd, marimba, and bongos, white C-U-G-A-T letters appearing successively and diagonally across the black
frame that opens up to catch the man himself, the high-angle

diagonal dolly out of the entire orchestra in the nightclub setting, the dolly into hands playing a keyboard, the lateral pan
of the vocalizing señorita shimmying across the floor, a 180°
convex pan of the piccolo players, the dolly out from a xylo-
phonist, and the lively tracking of the corybantic Garcias.
Throughout the number runs a gag in which the senorita grabs
Keenan Wynn's drink at a ringside table and places it on her
dancing partner's head, where Cugat grabs it to swig it down
at the finale.

LIVING IN A BIG WAY (1947)

After his return from service Kelly went into Living
in a Big Way (1947).   Screwball master Gregory La Cava co-
scripted with Irving Ravetch and directed this Pandro Berman
comedy, which Harold Rosson shot in black-and-white.   La
Cava's My Man Godfrey (1936) hovers over the entire enterprise: its romance of veteran Leo Gogarty (Kelly) and rich,
spoiled Margaud Morgan (Marie McDonald) intertwines with
the topicality of the postwar housing shortage, its description
of a pixilated family, the butler's (Clifton Sundberg) droll
asides, and McDonald's Lombard imitation.

After the picture had been completed, studio chief
Louis B. Mayer asked Kelly to interpolate several dance
numbers to meet the public's expectations for a Kelly film
and to shore up the commerciality of this dull rehash. Donen
joined Kelly to create and direct the inserts, which, happily,
do not have the feel of inserts.

The team chose "It Had to Be You," the 1924 standard
by composer Isham Jones and lyricist Gus Kahn, for the opening sequence, a flashback of sorts.   Leo and Margaud's fox-
trotting in a crowded ballroom on the night before his unit
pulls out segues into a torchy adagio on a deserted tiered
terrace.   As silky as the camera movements and cutting are
during this Astaire-Rogers homage, it is the seamlessly interwoven dialogue throughout that is the number's notable aspect.

Donen and Kelly's next interlude, "Fido and Me," an
original by composer Lou Alter and lyricist Edward Heyman,
finds Leo with a terrier as partner (both have been kicked
out of the house).   They address their mistress's opened bedroom window and then engage in some big-top routines.   In
the number's second movement Leo courts a huge alabaster
maiden, whom he names "Miss Smogarty" (the garden statue's

haughty imperiousness has much in common with Margaud's),
with a parodic waltz, Apache dance, flamenco, and jitterbug.
The stationary camera, which at one point records an extended execution of some intricate tap steps and pirouettes
by Kelly, and the unmotivated dance styles (is he showing
off before his girl and if so, why the tongue-in-cheek tone?)
render this half just as lackluster as the first.

The creators redeemed themselves with the pippin
"Ring Around the Rosie: Children's Medley," in which Leo
interrupts his work on the apartment complex's stark frame
structure to play with the neighborhood children. Football,
hopscotch, seesaw, marching, bouncing balls, and rolling
hoops give way to strenuous acrobatics that cleverly incorporate sawhorses, metal rings, platforms, railings, lumber
piles, pulleys, ropes, and stepladders, all strung out on ju-
venile jingles. Pushups on rooftop rafters through which the
awed moppets can be seen three stories below (thanks to a
high-angle overview), a sprint across an unfinished rooftop,
and a swing on the top of a plank across a chasm of two in-
completed structures are standout bits.

THIS TIME FOR KEEPS (1947)

While Kelly essayed The Pirate for the Freed unit (which
Donen wasn't invited to collaborate on), Donen worked on Pasternak's This Time for Keeps (Richard Thorpe, 1947). It was
based on a story by Erwin Gelsey and Lorraine Fielding, with
a vacuous script by Gladys Lehman about the romance of an
aquatic star (Esther Williams) and a singer (Johnnie Johnston,
MGM's own crooning Crosby). The film was stuffed with seven-
teen numbers: water ballets, ballads, arias, Durante's antic
piano routines, and Cugat's ensembles, as well as some picturesque location shots of Mackinac Island.

Donen, credited, conceived and staged the aquacade
extravaganza, the film's one exceptional sequence. While
strutting in spiffy evening clothes around the sides of a mammoth triangular pool set in a nightclub, Durante tosses off
"Take Off the Proper Amount" and some perfectly timed
asides ("I hope Gene Kelly saves his money") while Williams
strips to swimwear. A circular island with a piano on top
floats them to the pool's center, where it rises on a column.
She dives off. The groupings of Williams and belles, both on
and under the water, are arresting. The howling windup features the column with Durante at the keyboard sinking and

<u>This Time for Keeps</u>: Jimmy Durante and Esther Williams about to "Take Off the Proper Amount." Copyright: Metro-Goldwyn-Mayer.

Williams popping out of the water in Durante's top hat and then reaching below to pull out the famous schnozzle. (Donen's people seem particularly prone to water accidents.)

KILLER McCOY (1947)

Donen was next assigned to <u>Killer McCoy</u> (Roy Rowland, 1947), producer Sam Zimbalist's remake of the melodrama <u>The Crowd Roars</u> (Richard Thorpe, 1938). In this hokey screenplay by Frederick Hazlitt Brennan, from a story and screenplay by Thomas Lenon, George Bruce, and George Oppenheimer, Mickey Rooney plays a tough kid who climbs the pugilistic ladder of fame while doting on the daughter (Ann Blyth) of a big-time gambler who owns his contract. The film is noteworthy only for Rooney's coming of dramatic age and "Swanee River," a soft-shoe routine by Rooney and James Dunn, his drunken old man, who sits around waiting for vaudeville to return. Donen, again credited, wrote, staged, and directed the number.

BIG CITY (1948)

Donen was back with Pasternak for Big City (Norman Taurog, 1948). This lachrymose tale by Whitfield Cook and Anne Morrison Chapin was based on a story by Miklos Kutner about a foundling (Margaret O'Brien) raised by a Protestant minister cum social worker (Robert Preston), a Jewish cantor (Danny Thomas), and an Irish Catholic cop (George Murphy). Donen, credited, handled the solos that launched Betty Garrett's screen career. Throughout "You're Gonna' See a Lot of Me," a mock strip first delivered onstage to a cardboard 1890s lifeguard and then reprised among the club's patrons, Donen's sassy camerawork misses not one of the chanteuse's alluring above-the-waist actions and her admirers' drooling reactions, especially the dummy's electric-lit eyes and levitating frame. On the other hand, Donen's flavoring of her novelty song, "Ok'l, Baby, Dok'l," in the presence of the foundling at a rehearsal, is surprisingly uninspired.

A DATE WITH JUDY (1948)

"Dance director" Donen went on to concoct "Mulligatwany," a production number involving some high-schoolers in a gym, for the Pasternak bonbon A Date with Judy (Richard Thorpe, 1948). It was excised before the film's release, however. Carmen Miranda's malapropisms and musical cavortings, which included teaching Wallace Beery to rhumba, and Cugat's swing were deemed enough decoration for Dorothy Cooper and Dorothy Kingsley's account of teenagers Jane Powell and Elizabeth Taylor vying for Robert Stack's attention.

THE KISSING BANDIT (1948)

The Kissing Bandit (Laslo Benedek, 1948) was Donen's final chore for Pasternak. Isobel Lennart and John B. Harding fashioned a flat burlesque, set in California of the 1840s, about a timid graduate of a Boston business college (Frank Sinatra) who inherits his father's inn and his role as desperate highwayman and bold womanizer. Donen's "dance direction" came down to conceiving and staging Sono Osato's fiery "Whip Dance," in which she attempts to draw the bandit's attention away from the governor's daughter (Kathryn Grayson). This amusing sequence, with its reversal-of-the-sexes conceit (Osato extinguishes the candles with her fingers, no less, and

cracks the whip around the kitchen as he cowers in a chair),
along with "The Dance of Fury," a specialty for Ricardo
Montalban, Ann Miller, and Cyd Charisse designed by Robert
Alton, are the only moments when the film comes to life.

TAKE ME OUT TO THE BALL GAME (1949)

Together again, Donen and Kelly presented Freed with
a story of baseball players who are also vaudevillians. Take
Me Out to the Ball Game (1949) was set in 1908, when the
sport was becoming America's favorite pastime. Their idea,
of course, was an excuse to reunite Kelly as short stop Eddie
O'Brien with Sinatra as second baseman Dennis Ryan. Thrown
in for topical color was Leo Durocher, eventually replaced by
Jules Munshin, as first baseman Nat Goldberg--another buddy-
buddy trio on display. Esther Williams subbed for an ailing
Judy Garland, whom Freed wanted in lieu of Kathryn Grayson,
as C. B. Higgins, the club's owner and Kelly's love interest.
(This change forced Harry Tugend to rewrite George Wells's
script and composer Roger Edens and lyricists Betty Comden
and Adolph Green to replace Hugh Martin and Ralph Blane's
score.) Betty Garrett played former moll Shirley Delwyn and
Sinatra's mate. Although Donen and Kelly wanted to direct
Take Me Out to the Ball Game, Freed assigned it to Busby
Berkeley, who was down on his luck at the time. They were,
however, allowed to create and direct all of Kelly's musical
selections. George Folsey photographed, Cedric Gibbons and
Daniel Cathcart designed the American Gothic look, which Edwin B. Willis realized.

The title number by Jack Norwood and Harry von Til-
zer is O'Brien and Ryan's heel-kicking tap in a Midwest
vaudeville house and a dry run for Singin' in the Rain's "Fit
as a Fiddle": the duo's "Yes, Indeedy," set in a ballpark
during practice, echoes "I Begged Her."

The trio's "O'Brien to Ryan to Goldberg" double-play
combination boasts a dazzling face-forward slide on the restaurant floor (effectively caught by Donen's extremely low-
angle camera) and a human pyramid atop a table. Actually
the dance contains little of the sport's characteristic movements and veers off into a celebration of the characters' respective cultural heritages by sandwiching O'Brien's Irish jig,
Ryan's Scottish fling, and Goldberg's hora and Yiddish monologue between the baseball dance metaphors.

Take Me Out to the Ball Game: The movement within the
frame of Esther Williams, Frank Sinatra, Jules Munshin,
Gene Kelly, and two unidentified chorus girls is part of the
energy of "Strictly, U.S.A." Copyright: Metro-Goldwyn-
Mayer.

        The secret behind the energy of the production number
"Strictly, U.S.A.," with the five principals and chorus at a
clambake at Getty's Landing, is the constant movement: the
choral background during the vocal, the isolation of the most
expressive sections of the dance, the lively processions up
and down the multileveled set, the dollying in and out camera,
and the jump cuts.

        Kelly's "The Hat Me Dear Old Father Wore upon St.
Patrick's Day," by G. Schwartz and W. Jerome, is an entertainment at the clambake in which he taps, jigs, marches,
and Cohanesquely struts as an Irish patriarch taking a stroll
down memory lane.   Before the climax the soundtrack goes
silent except for his a cappella whisper and the faint sound
of bagpipes, given an echo-chamber cast.   The number's subtle mood shifts are remarkable.

Kelly's duet with Williams, "Baby Love," was shot
but went unused since Williams looked klutzy during the dance
routine.

In addition to Kelly's segments, Donen on his own conceived, staged, and directed the rollicking "It's Fate, Baby,
It's Fate." In this number Shirley stalks Ryan outside his
locker room, chases him into the stands, and finally trails
him up the bleachers, where she pulls him off the back wall,
lifts him over her shoulders, and, for the payoff, catches
him in her arms at the bottom of the slippery handrail.

This choreographed song, built from Garrett's aggressive zaniness and Sinatra's dreamy voice, is a compendium
of Donen touches: the inventive conceit, the metaphorical as-
sociations drawn from the player's movements and/or decor,
the solid structure, the psychologically accurate development,
the knockabout humor, the farcical finish, the expansive geography, the smooth in-and-out transitions, the expressive camera, the deft pace, and the beat-conscious cutting. Special
effects and montage buildup are not on parade this time.

>   Ever since Rio, I kept watching musicals. I loved
>   Clair's musicals, Lubitsch's, Mamoulian's, the Gar-
>   land and Rooney ones. I thought there were some
>   interesting things even in Berkeley's pictures. I
>   didn't like Minnelli's musicals, except for Meet Me
>   in St. Louis (1944), because of the soppy stories.
>   They had no sting, zap, energy. I was fascinated
>   by the musical things Disney had done--the skeleton
>   dance, for example. [The Skeleton Dance, 1929,
>   was the first of Disney's Silly Symphonies, in which
>   music and animation were combined.]

After about fifteen years of watching stage and screen
musicals and learning musical traditions and film techniques
by doing, the twenty-four-year-old was aching to shape, in
exciting and innovative ways, not only parts but the whole.
What's more, he was ready.

2. MGM CONTRACTEE: 1949-1955

ON THE TOWN (1949)

At the Ballet Theatre, during the spring of 1944, Fancy Free, a collaboration of composer-conductor Leonard Bernstein and choreographer Jerome Robbins, played to standing ovations. Set designer Oliver Smith suggested that this ballet about three gobs on a twenty-four-hour shore leave in New York[1] be expanded into a Broadway musical. Bernstein's friends Betty Comden and Adolph Green, writers and nightclub performers, jumped on the bandwagon as lyricists, librettists, and performers, playing Claire and Ozzie. Nancy Walker, Sono Osato, John Battles, and Chris Alexander rounded out the cast. And director George Abbott brought up the rear.

MGM purchased the screen rights in a preproduction agreement for $250,000, which enabled the show, rechristened On the Town, to hit the boards that December. This musical, innovative in its atmospheric score and thematic dancing, ran for two years. The work, however, confused the stodgy studio brass, who, regretting their financial support, placed it on the shelf.

Abbott, out West in 1948 to direct a musical at Freed's invitation, proposed On the Town. At this point Kelly got Freed's ear. He himself was itching to direct and star in what was essentially a dance show. Besides, his partner Donen, with enough experience under his belt, wanted a crack at a whole picture. Responsibilities would be shared. The male trio of Ball Game (which was receiving excellent preview notices) could easily fill the caps and bell-bottoms. Freed finally let the gadflies have their way--almost. And the theater wiz Abbott returned East.

> Metro renegotiated my contract, this time a direc-
> tor's contract that also ran for seven years....
> We were very excited. We had a five-week rehear-
> sal period but after four weeks, we were ready....
> Co-direction came down to working with Gene and
> doing as much in collaboration as we could. By
> the time you hash it through from beginning to end
> ten million times, you can't remember who did
> what except in a few instances where you can re-
> member getting an idea. Gene is responsible for
> most of the dance movements. I was behind the
> camera in the dramatic and musical sequences.

Comden and Green, with Donen and Kelly peering over
their shoulders, rewrote the script to fit the players' personalities and talents, reduced the show's numerous ballets,
which had carried much of the plot and characterizations, and
stressed the camaraderie of the trio, as in their other Donen-
Kelly collaborations: Ball Game, Singin' in the Rain, and
It's Always Fair Weather.

Comden and Green's libretto genius lay in their counterpointing of bright satire and roistering slapstick with pathos.
This beautifully modulated piece had humor and a humanity as
well. Comden and Green's smart writing immensely appealed
to Donen.

The film razzes, among other things, the ritual of
shore leave, the musketeering of male buddies (and, in a
sense, Donen and Kelly's togetherness), small-town mentality
intimidated by that of the big city, predatory females, the
pretension of artists and intellectuals, tawdry Coney Island,
and New York's hot spots, where Puerto Rican, black, and
Chinese chorus lines are stirred in the melting pot of Yankee
show biz to emerge identically. Also joshed is the musical
form itself, which thrives on coincidence, as when we cut
from Chip (Frank Sinatra) telling Gabey (Kelly) that his chance
of finding Ivy (Vera-Ellen) in a city of four million is nil to
the girl herself putting a coin in the slot just a few feet away.
These jabs, along with the museum mayhem, the Empire
State charade, the car chase, and male transvestism, mix
with the sadness of time running out, the desperation of trying to have a good time, the loss of Ivy, the discrepancy between appearance and reality, the suddenness and finality of
good-byes, and, especially, the character of wallflower Lucy
(Alice Pearce). Much of Lucy's poignance, as Lina's in Rain
and Madeline's in Weather, arises from her status outside the
group.

The anachronism of the males hits another plaintive
note. These hicks adrift in a sophisticated metropolis are
also out of joint with the times. They act as they would
have acted before the war, when they and the country were
younger and more foolish. True, the sailors are part of the
optimism that pervaded postwar America--a mood that per-
meates the film--but they are oblivious to the uneasy transitions America was also then experiencing, which the film
subtly sketches. For one thing, and an important thing,
women had come a long way. Ivy is a workaholic: she
takes dance instruction by day and pays for her lessons by
working in a risque profession at night. She basks in Gabey's
illusion of her and, in a sense, uses and manipulates him to
bolster her ego. Hildy (Betty Garrett), a cabbie, is a woman
at the wheel. When Chip wants to take in many of his grand-
father's favorite landmarks, she sets him straight: "Don't
you realize that in a big town like this things are constantly
changing?" Claire (Ann Miller), a graduate student of anthro-
pology, surpasses the men intellectually. She is sophisticated, too. She knows that Ivy is a "nobody"; what's more,
she doesn't care. These women are aggressive, savvy, and
responsible. They carry the romantic ball. Hildy and Claire
tip the waiter to secure a table for the group and to fuss
over Ivy. They raise money to pay for the damages at
Coney Island and see that their fellows return to the ship
on time. The men remain children, unaware of "the wind
and the rain"; and the film's cyclic structure indicates that
others are to follow in their ways: the poignancy is thus
rendered even more resonant. This subtext must wait until
Weather to see the light of day.

Once again Kelly, Sinatra, and Jules Munshin (Ozzie)
each brings his own individual talents as dancer, singer, and
farceur to the whole. In particular, it is a treat to see
Sinatra actually convince and charm us as the shy bumpkin
who has never been out of Peoria, and Munshin contort his
plastic face and body in even more wondrously comic ways
than in Ball Game.

Vera-Ellen's Ivy wears two faces throughout: sweet
and petite outside, yet sly and robust inside. Discovered by
Sam Goldwyn for his Danny Kaye romps, this grinning ingenue
with magical feet did two Fox confections before MGM part-
nered her with Kelly in the sizzling "Slaughter on Tenth Avenue" for Words and Music (Norman Taurog, 1948). That ac-
claimed cameo got her the role of Ivy.

As good as these performers are, the picture really

belongs to the other women: Betty Garrett as the carnivorous cabbie Brunhilde Esterhazy, who has become, along with Travis Bickle, the screen's most notorious taxi driver; Ann Miller as the glandular anthropologist Claire Huddesen, whose guardian all too erroneously thought that her objective study of man might desensitize her subjective pursuit of men; Florence Bates as Madame Dilyovska, a dipsomaniacal ballet instructor who haughtily boasts that she taught everyone "from Nijinsky to Mickey Rooney"; and finally Alice Pearce, repeating her stage role as Lucy Shmeeler, the horsey odd girl out.

Donen and Kelly, believing musicals were landlocked in studios, fought to have the film shot entirely in New York. (This trend toward realism, part of the postwar climate, was felt in all the arts.) Though rejecting the idea, the studio gave the parvenus a consolation prize of a week's location shooting with the principals, which the directors blew on the picture's opener and finale.

The combination of location shooting and the studio stylization of art director Cedric Gibbons, who supervised the work of Jack Martin Smith (and about fifteen other art directors) and set decorators Edwin B. Willis and Jack D. Moore gave Town its schizophrenic look, which Harold Rosson rendered in MGM's customary high-gloss photography. Visually original, however, is a white-lettered time strip running across the bottom of the frame at intervals, in the style of the old New York Times billboard, that encapsulates the motif of time running out, conveys the city's feverish atmosphere, and bridges the episodes.

Spilling over into the straight passages are the montage-structured scenes and the choreography of action (that is, the rhythmic movement of players, animate objects, and the camera within a shot cut to the music's beat)--two techniques that Donen used in the direction of musical sequences throughout his novice days.

Both these devices, as well as the time strip, the casting of six principals who are constantly in motion within the frame, and the prevalence of dance, create the film's effervescent pace, a hallmark of all Donen's work. Only Kelly's ballet brings the tripping tale to a standstill for a while.

The Musical Sequences

Notwithstanding the directors' protest, the original

On the Town: Frank Sinatra, Jules Munshin, and Gene
Kelly bolting the Brooklyn Navy Yard in part of the location-
shot "New York, New York" montage.   Copyright: Metro-
Goldwyn-Mayer.

score was gutted.   The songs had to be more popular to
moviegoers; besides, the studio had composers on staff to
create new material and its own publishing outlet.   By taking this in-house route more coin could be secured for MGM's
coffers, Freed contended.   Consequently, Comden and Green's
not-so-sharp words were wedded to Roger Edens's accessible
airs, except for "New York, New York," "Come Up to My
Place," a sentence from the opening recitative "Sleep in Your
Lady's Arms," and the dance music for "Miss Turnstiles"
and "A Day in New York."

When it came time to hand out romantic interludes,
star consideration reared its egomaniacal head, and Ozzie
and Claire were left empty-handed.   "Prehistoric Man," although essentially Ozzie and Claire's number, does not satisfy in this regard.   Such an omission as this causes a lop-
sidedness in structure and characterization.

In contrast to the new tunes and their distribution,
the staging and execution of practically all the numbers measure up to those in the original show.   All but one number

involve dance or choreographic staging, as we would have
expected from Donen and Kelly, dancers and choreographers
who were bent on making dance musicals. Donen, especially,
believed that movies were essentially stories told in movement. And, too, the numbers parade every conceivable
dance style from burlesque to classical ballet and display an
integration with the book of steps, staging, photography,
track, and cutting more remarkable than in any previous
film musical.

"New York, New York": This showstopper, a landmark in Donen's career and the genre's history, begins
calmly enough. A red sun rises over the city's gray sky-
scrapers; a 5:57 a. m. tape floats across the screen; a burly
hardhat, with a lunch pail in one hand and a jacket slung
over his shoulder, shuffles along the deserted Brooklyn Navy
Yard to his post at a nearby crane while yawning a recitative, "I feel like I'm not out of bed yet. " But presto: a
destroyer's whistle pierces the silence: a 6:00 a. m. tape
scurries across; and a battleship explodes with slaphappy
sailors. Among them are Gabey, Chip, and Ozzie, who
strut right up to the camera (a familiar Donen ploy) shouting
the city's name.

A pell-mell, kinetic transpatial montage of the skylarking trio among the town's actual tourist spots feeds the
fire. In addition to sporting a different setting, each jump-
cut finds the trio in various movements: walking, biking,
hopping on a subway. The players and camera move to the
cacophonous melody's driving pace while each brief shot--
and there are dozens of them--starts and stops on the song's
jagged rhythms. The contrasting screen directions between
shots increase the dynamism, magic, and fun of the complete
tour of the town in three minutes. (The niftiest example involves a 360-degree pan of the gobs atop the RCA Building
followed by a vertical tilt down of the structure to them on
the sidewalk below.)

The number hits every dramatic base as well: developing plot, describing the setting while conveying its gal-
vanizing atmosphere and manic mood, introducing and deline-
ating character by detailing each sailor's idiosyncrasies, and
creating the feel of the boundless joy of friendship and of
people temporarily reprieved from duty.

"Miss Turnstiles Ballet": For this, one of the few
daydreams in his repertoire, Donen, with Kelly, chooses

form, color, and sound rhymes for the smooth in-and-out
transitions.   Gabey's dazed face cuts to Ivy's poster face,
which in turn, dissolves to her real visage.   Poster script
on pale yellow cardboard becomes enlarged black letters
superimposed on a gamboge cyclorama--the beige-white-
yellow of the abstract set repeating the representational poster's colors in a brilliant key.   Gabey's reading the type out
loud in the subway becomes a voice-over during the reverie,
providing a continuity device as well as the number's clever
conceit, in which Ivy's every movement and action takes its
cue from Gabey's voice-over poster prose.   For example,
on the words, "She goes out with the Army," Ivy, in a lus-
trous brown sheath, quickly departs the high-society whirl
by spinning behind one side of a partition and out the other
(an invisible cut), in a full brown-and-white cotillion gown,
to take an army officer's arm.   The camera, which has
been tracking before her, remains stationary as she marches
up to it and frames her smiling countenance.   Then, on the
words, "But her heart belongs to the Navy," Ivy suddenly
backs away from the camera, still marching, only this time
on the arm of a naval officer.   Too bad more was not made
of the conceit's inherent humor.

The moderately paced montage allows Kelly to survey
the history of dance and Donen to try out some camera and
editing tricks and to rib media hype and the mind's powers of
projection.   It also provided Vincente Minnelli with a blueprint
for Henri's daydream of Lise in "Embraceable You" in An
American in Paris.

"Prehistoric Man": Tossing off her picture hat and
an occasional double entrendre ("I love bear skin") in the
midst of her thesis on primitive man, Claire parts the front
slit of her green skirt to thrust out her long, silken legs in
a peppery tap.   With Claire lighting the fire, a bacchanal,
in which the quintet appropriates ancient African artifacts,
erupts ironically in the airless Museum of Anthropological
History.   (Never has Freud's superego-id construct been
given such a corybantic send up as this.)   And finale flou-
ishes do not come any better than the number's collapsed
dinosaur.

"Come Up to My Place": Brazen Hildy and bashful
Chip's debate over whether to visit her apartment or the
city's landmarks occurs in her cab's front seat in a mid-
Manhattan traffic snarl.   The melody, a parody of Offenbach,
conveys his nervousness, her passion, and the antagonism

in the situation, as does the business of having the vehicle
repeatedly come to a screeching halt (Hildy can't keep her
eyes on the road). Her sudden stops take their toll on Chip
--he is thrust forward and backward, almost hits his noggin
on the dashboard, and slides on the floor--while Hildy has
the steering wheel to brace herself.

The directors' mise-en-scène, in which Hildy and Chip
are framed from the front in a tight medium shot, with the
camera where the dashboard would be, and then from Chip's
side so as to catch Hildy's every agressive prank and his
own aggrieved glare, is immaculate.

"Main Street": Ashamed of his "big shot" approach,
Gabey confesses, "Us small town guys must sound pretty
silly to a native New Yorker like you. Back home in Mea-
dowville, Indiana ..." Ivy asks him to talk more about his
hometown. So, in the abandoned dance studio, he takes her
on an imaginary walk with an occasional dip down "Main
Street, " pointing out the corner where the boys hang out (she
primps to catch their attention) and introducing her to a cop
whose last arrest was in 1903. Gabey becomes the cop before whom Ivy proudly displays a ring on her finger. The
cavalcade of small-town characters and sites curiously stops
just as it gets going. The situation of country boy bringing
city girl home is fraught with dramatic, lyrical, choreographic, and, in this instance, ironic (since the girl hails
from the same hamlet) possibilities, which the number never
explores. Also, the little we do get is confusing. Is it an
engagement or a wedding band? And if she is spoken for,
why did she flirt with the boys?

The stroll builds to a soft-shoe routine with little variety or mood change. Its lackadaisical tone is reinforced
by the camera's pans. And the ending, with each on the other
side of the rehearsal piano, is genteel and trite.

Approximating rural Americana with its unadorned
lyrics, folksy melody, simple steps, and unwavering tone,
the number does furnish a striking contrast with the film's
other musical passages, all of which have an urban flavor.

"You're Awful": Atop the Empire State Building with
a starry indigo night above and twinkling Manhattan below,
Chip and Hildy replace debate with duet, staccato with andante.
(The impressive set, an emblem of their romantic transcend-
ence, was built in a ninety by ninety foot pit, ten feet deep.)

The stationary camera, no doubt, is shamefully revering the clever series of equivocations of Sinatra's star ballad.   "You're awful--awful good to look at. . . .   You're boring--boring into my heart. "

"On the Town":   The middle section of this number, in which the boys feign "the shore leave blues" is thematically silly but technically astute.   It dampens the celebrative song's spirited pace and pulsating rhythm (which, by the way, are enhanced by its skyscraper-top location and ensemble delivery).   This allows the number to catch its breath before revving up again as the three couples head for the elevator.   The modulation permits the directors to sustain the number's élan.

The camera really gets into the swing of things as it pushes everyone into the elevator by furiously tracking behind them, cuts to a close-up of the floor light on the elevator's lintel indicating the descent and then steps back to make room for the group emerging arm in arm on the crowded sidewalk below, and vigorously marches alongside the revelers.   The magic of that momentary descent of almost a hundred floors, besides being an inspired and psychologically right transition from top to bottom (time flies when you're having fun), is another dash of delirium.

"Count on Me":   Gabey and Lucy's mock tango and her typhoon of a sneeze, which sends the table upon which the group is sitting to kingdom come, are two special moments in this hillbilly ode to friendship.

Throughout, Donen and Kelly insist on Lucy's character as well as showcase Pearce's comic flair: she claps out of rhythm, sings extraneous lines, whoops at inappropriate moments, topples clumsily to the floor, and gets her head caught in Claire's skirt.

"A Day in New York" Ballet: A theater advertisement on a fence of a construction site--"A Day in New York/A Comedy in Three Acts/With Music"--sets Gabey's daydream in motion and needlessly summarizes the film's last hour. There are several striking things about the ballet: the dance studio correlative in which Ivy engages Gabey in an erotic pas-de-deux around a barre, with a canted camera off to the side catching the dancers and their full shadows on the wine backdrop and thereby energizing the frame with the appearance of four people; the red-lettered 11:30 P.M. time-strip flashing in the frame's upper-left corner to signal Ivy's exit; and the zoom-out to a high-angle overview of Gabey clutching a poster.

Still, the redundant narrative line and seven-minute length render the interlude ponderous.   Kelly insisted upon this ex-crescence--after all, the ballet had served him well.   He would commit this sin again in An American in Paris.

Following the theatrical tradition and bucking Freed, who believed the change would bewilder the audience, profes-sional dancers substituted for the Chip, Ozzie, Hildy, and Claire characters.   Carol Haney, Kelly's head dancer and assistant, danced one of the girls.   (Kelly's other assistant, Jeanne Coyne, became the first Mrs. Donen in 1948 while On the Town was in its conception stage.)   Some critics faulted the film for this choice, since the substitution, they felt, was distractingly obvious.   Yet the anonymity contributes to the dream's abstract quality and, in one sense, emphasizes Gabey's love because Ivy, unlike the rest of the group, is really Vera-Ellen and a vividly lifelike impression in his mind.

> I felt that the ballet was an interruption to the
> film's main thrust.   I equally felt the "Broadway
> Melody-Broadway Rhythm" ballet was an interrup-
> tion to the main thrust of Singing in the Rain.

"Pearl of the Persian Sea":   This Coney Island tableau features the gobs as Persian princesses advertising their charms on a platform before the customers.   A Charleston-cooch that causes Ozzie's skirt to descend, revealing his bell-bottoms, brings the attraction to a farcical close.

The critics were unanimously ecstatic about On the Town, especially the English, who felt that the Hollywood mu-sical had finally put on long pants.   The film won an Academy Award for Best Scoring of a Musical.   The public response was equally gratifying, much to the studio executives' sur-prise.   Today the film is regarded as a turning point: the first bona fide dance musical that moved dance, as well as the mu-sical genre, out of the theater and captured it with and for film rather than on film; the first to make a city an important char-acter; and the first to abandon the chorus.   On the Town also featured some location shooting and moved to contemporary, rather than period, rhythms.

> It has a certain amount of invention which was dif-
> ferent from other musicals.   The whole idea of the
> story is interesting and fresh for a musical, even
> now.   ... It was an expensive production for its
> time, costing a bit over two million.

ROYAL WEDDING (1951)

Donen, Kelly, and Comden and Green promised each
other that they would team again.   They would keep in touch
about possible ideas.   But first there were other commit-
ments to keep.

Kelly immediately took off to co-star with Judy Garland in Summer Stock (Charles Walters, 1950), for Pasternak,
and prepare An American in Paris, Freed's most costly and
prestigious production thus far.   Donen was set to steer
Pagan Love Song (1950), a Freed trifle with Esther Williams.
But the star, who had had such an intimidating time on Ball
Game, nixed Donen, and Robert Alton assumed the reins.
About four months later Freed's production of Royal Wedding,
a Fred Astaire backstager about love threatening a brother
and sister act, faced a replacement problem or two.   After
a week of rehearsals a pregnant June Allyson, the female
lead, gave notice.   When Judy Garland was named to substi-
tute, director Charles Walters announced that he could not
undergo the strain and strife of working with Garland again.
(They had both worked on Easter Parade [1948].)   So Freed
put Donen on the picture.

> Judy wouldn't come to rehearsals.   Undoubtedly,
> what Arthur [Freed] finally said to her was, "Stan-
> ley says he can't go on with the picture; we've got
> to change you ... not that you're not doing your
> job, Judy; but we've got to change you."   Then she
> slashed her wrists because she was fired.   The
> press called me and said that I fired her.   I didn't
> know she was fired until she was replaced by Jane
> Powell.

Inspired by Astaire's life--he started in a vaudeville double act with his sister, Adele, who later married Lord Cavendish
and abandoned the stage--as well as the approaching nuptials of
Princess Elizabeth of England to Philip Mountbatten, Alan Jay
Lerner's first scenario, like his later original An American
in Paris, is an artifice of thematic and visual rhymes.
Donen's direction sharpens them to heighten the humor, as in
his split-screen handling of the twin agent's transatlantic
calls.   It's all an extended gag really, which at best is
mildly amusing and at worst dispiritingly cute--nowhere in the
the class of On the Town.   And, too, a Lerner script flirts
too sedately and infrequently with satire, so most of the pre-
ceedings lack tang.

From time to time, though, Lerner, at Donen's insti-
gation during the production, does manage some crackerjack
ironies, as when blaring bagpipes from the street below turn
Ellen (Powell) and John's (Peter Lawford) first serious romantic moment into a shouting match. And Tom and Anne's
(Sarah Churchill) meeting is a screwball gem: standing before a haberdasher's window, Tom addresses not Edgar
(Keenan Wynn), who has since walked on, but Anne: "Do
you use that shaving cream?" Donen invariably starts his
lovers out on either an ironic or farcical foot.

The material, which was not really up his alley to begin with, was pretty well set before Donen entered the production.   Nevertheless, his industrious direction is edifying.
(Donen's ability to throw himself into the heart of the material even when it is not to his taste will remain with him
throughout his career.) Donen, at this time, had to prove
that he could direct an entire picture on his own.   Furthermore, he was directing an idol.

At age fifty-one, Astaire, as brother Tom, is as impeccable as ever.   Powell's turn as sister Ellen marks a departure in her career.   By helping her pitch a comic line
with the precision of a Claudette Colbert, Donen taps the
spice underneath all that sugar, turning MGM's reigning musical teenager into a woman.   Also a delight is the Astaire-
Powell team in four remarkably performed numbers; in these
she elicits more gallantry than usual from the gentleman as
he carefully watches over her, while he elicits glee from the
debutante as she admirably completes her steps.

Peter Lawford as John is, as usual, a handsome piece
of decor.   Fortunately, whistling a refrain is as far as he
gets musically here.   (Donen had the good sense to delete his
reprise of "Every Night at Seven" to Powell.) His presence
is too stuffy and manicured for musicals, yet he did pop up
in five of them during his contractee days.

Moira Shearer of the Sadler's Wells Ballet, who had
recently gained international film recognition as the lead in
The Red Shoes (Michael Powell, 1948), was set to portray
Anne but was vetoed by Astaire--perhaps the inspiration for
Astaire's reaction to the ballerina Cyd Charisse in The Band
Wagon (Vincente Minnelli, 1953).   Sarah Churchill, the Prime
Minister's daughter and Whitehall's answer to the White House's
Margaret Truman, who was at the time appearing in Los An-
geles in a road company of The Philadelphia Story, was signed.

Royal Wedding: Fred Astaire and Jane Powell's zany "How
Can You Believe Me?" Copyright: Metro-Goldwyn-Mayer.

Her lady of class is a refreshing figure in a genre that favors
the brassy dame.   Unfortunately, she's slighted musically.

As the brothers Klinger, Keenan Wynn, MGM's top
supporting player, assiduously explores every nook and cranny
of the stereotypic Yankee and Limey to droll effect.   And, as
the irascible Ashmond, estranged from his wife and the U.S.
because of a war debt (a Yank still owes him ten pounds, ten
shillings), Albert Sharpe etches an unforgettable variation of
Shaw's Doolittle, who must have been in Lerner's mind even
then.

Into Gibbons and Smith's pedestrian musical locales
and Willis and Albert E. Spencer's equally pedestrian executions of them--only the pub exudes a truly English atmosphere--
are inserted the Rank Organization's documentary of Elizabeth's
wedding and some stock footage of London.   Two romantic interludes in this airless musical, however, hauntingly occur on
foggy nights in parks, one graced by a lake--a setting that

Donen will consistently invoke for romance. In these two instances, Robert Planck's soft, impressionistic camerawork,
which Donen had suggested, is a welcome relief from the
rest of the film's sheen.

The ninety-three-minute running time never lags due
to Donen's penchant for simultaneously staging two or more
incidents within the frame, his gift for movement-within-
movement continuity, and the cornucopia of musical interludes, nine in all.

The Musical Sequences

The strong score was the collaboration of Burton Lane,
composer of numerous screen and stage scores (Babes on
Broadway [Busby Berkeley, 1941] and Finian's Rainbow [1947])
and Lerner, neophyte lyricist fresh from a moderately successful The Day Before Spring (1945) and the triumphant
Brigadoon (1947) on Broadway.   Their paths would cross
again in 1965 with On a Clear Day You Can See Forever.

All but three songs are performances, firmly motivated but only tenuously related to the text. "Every Night
at Seven" foreshadows the royal wedding, "I Left My Hat in
Haiti" describes a type of revue number, and "Sunday Jumps"
serves to relieve Tom's tension. "Open Your Eyes" is a
metaphor for Ellen's delirious state of falling in love. "The
Happiest Day of My Life" conveys her elation over John.
"How Can You Believe Me?" obliquely comments on the sib-
lings' touch-and-go personal affairs.

These numbers have the feel of star specialties inserted into the piece, a feeling intensified by their division
into four duets, two solos apiece, and one solo for co-star
Wynn. Undoubtedly, Donen's absence at the production's
start had something to do with this disruptive sense as his
musical sequences had more or less been attuned to a dramatic idea, while manifesting a predilection for the outdoors.

"Every Night at Seven" and "I Left My Hat in Haiti":
The old chestnut of bored royalty (Tom) flirting with the vivacious maid (Ellen) is dipped in the scarlet, gray, and gold colors
of a contemporary throneroom. In "Every Night at Seven"
Astaire dances an impish king, whether desolately perched on
the throne's arm with both feet on the seat and crowned head
cradled in his hand, or seductively pinning the maid in the
throne's corner with his elongated leg and torso.

In "I Left My Hat in Haiti" Astaire sambos his search for a lost hat with native girls (Powell among them) in a Gauguinesque marketplace.

In both instances Donen emphasizes the theatrical context. He does so in all his stage numbers without being stagey, however.

"Sunday Jumps": To soothe his frayed nerves over Ellen's tardiness for rehearsal in the liner's gym, Tom places a metronome on a stool, sets it going (frame right foreground) and beats time with his hands and legs (left middleground), an eloquently composed shot. This only increases his exasperation because the beating out of time concomitantly involves its running down--something he would rather forget just now. A glance at the clock in the background, and he huffily heads toward the door. About to exit, he absently grabs a clothes tree. Realizing that a bird in hand ..., he uses it as a partner. The gym's pulleys, parallel bar, sidehorse, balancing pins, and punching bag are interwoven into the warm-up routine to accentuate the dance movement. (The utilization of props for such an effect is part of Astaire's dancing style.) The number is noteworthy for its psychologically true unfolding.

"Open Your Eyes": The farcical conceit of a particularly rough night at sea, inspired by a similar incident in 1923 when the Astaires were on the Aquitania sailing to appear in Stop Laughing, informs this ballroom-dance performance during the Captain's dinner. (Ballroom dancing is the basic ingredient of Astaire's "outlaw style," which also includes tap, jazz, ballet, and exotic. Here, it is given an affectionate tweak.)

Donen and choreographer Nick Castle build the gag ever so gradually: the floor tilting during their waltz (by means of pneumatic jacks), their sliding and bumping into a post, her shoulder strap slipping off, their toppling upon a couple on a sofa, and spilling a bowl of fruit. A respite is necessary to build again, even higher this time, so the couple get back into the swing of things on the dance floor, carefully avoiding the oranges and apples now rolling across the room and brushing a stray table and chair away. With Ellen's fall the slapstick begins to build again, as they valiantly try to work the ship's lurching into their act. A sofa hurtling at them from frame top to bottom, upon which they gratefully collapse, provides a neat punctuation of this rollicking musical paragraph.

Donen's clean and controlled gag construction, which crystallizes about this time, is a throwback to the golden age of comedy.

"The Happiest Day of My Life": Supposedly a rehearsal, this time in the hotel suite with Tom at the keyboard (frame right) accompanying Ellen (frame left), the ballad is delivered to John (frame center). Donen's horizontally staged mise-en-scène is tension-filled, visually encapsulating the movie's conflict and counterpointing the mellifluous track.

"How Can You Believe Me When I Said I Love You When You Know I've Been a Liar All My Life?": Everything is deliciously zany during this tough, brassy duet between a gangster and his moll argued against a city-street canvas curtain: their gaudy canary-yellow, tomato-red, sky-blue outfits; his chest-climbing pants and pavement-licking pocket handkerchief; her costume jewelry, spaghetti shoe straps, brunette wig, and Ginger Rogers beauty mark; the illiterate wisecrackese patter delivered in nasal twang; the kicks, shoves, and belt in the gut interpolating the staccato tap; the role reversals; and especially the in-character bows (she drags him back onstage; neither smile despite the hearty applause; and then she pushes him toward the wings).

"Too Late Now": Donen's Ophulsian camera traipses over a stone bridge before the lovers, steps down to the lake and walks beside its edge, approximating the headiness Ellen feels at confessing her love to John. Her gray satin gown and his white tails in the bucolic setting echo the sureality. A dolly out to a high-angle overview of her facing the water with her back toward us in the background and of him resting on a bench facing us in the foreground, Donen's wise finale is a needed cooling off after so much intoxication. It is also a visual paraphrase of the lovers' quandary. The ballad was nominated for an Oscar but lost to the peppy "In the Cool, Cool, Cool of the Evening" (Here Comes the Groom [Frank Capra, 1951]).

"You're All the World to Me": The idea of Anne's photograph setting off Tom's explosion of joy on the furniture, door, walls, and ceiling of his suite might be Astaire and Lerner's, but its execution was Donen's.

> It was achieved simply by putting the room inside a barrel as in a funfair. Everything in the room had to be tied down hard and the room turned inside this barrel and the camera turned with it.

"What a Lovely Day for a Wedding": This street number, in which Edgar rejoices with other British subjects as he and the camera wend their way to the Bowen suite, is undeveloped: it should have climaxed with the Bowen's response.

Though it charmed Royal Wedding audiences, the critical reception was but fair to good.

> It's weak. Fred's incredible, and Lerner and Lane wrote some wonderful songs. But you don't care about the story.... It was moderately expensive, in the $1.5 million range.

LOVE IS BETTER THAN EVER (1952)

> Wedding finished production at the beginning of October, 1950. Rain was in the talking stage but its production was far down the road [June 18, 1951]. I had some time, and producer Bill Wright asked me to do this comedy. I felt some responsibility. I was paid week in and week out, several hundred dollars a week. The salary escalated a few hundred dollars every year. The raise depended upon the pictures you turned out. And I thought it was a neat idea to do a movie about a dancing school. Ruth Brooks Flippen, who wrote it, was in fact a small-time dancing-school teacher married to a comic (rather than agent, as in the script).

The agent's wisecracks couched in show-biz lingo and some needling of Broadwayites and suburban dancing academies occasionally freshen up this stale situation of country lamb inveigling city wolf into marriage--Donen's first exposure to the battle of the sexes.

Larry Parks is good as Jud, the glib ten-percenter with show business in his veins. He would have been better had Donen halved his mannerisms, obviously left over from his Jolson impersonations (The Jolson Story [Alfred E. Green, 1946] and Jolson Sings Again [Henry Levin, 1950]). After completing the picture in January 1951 he admitted to HUAC his membership in the Communist Party and was indicted. The studio then shelved Love Is Better Than Ever, Parks's last lead role, for over a year until the air cleared.

As the instructor who boasts that her school of 408
pupils had twenty-nine more than any other in New Haven,
Elizabeth Taylor is dewily beautiful whether in Helen Rose's
taffeta full skirts or tutus that reveal the shapeliest legs next
to Grable's. At age eighteen, she was just making the transition from junior miss to romantic ingenue both on screen
(Conspirator [Victor Saville, 1949], The Big Hangover [Nor-
man Krasna, 1950], Father of the Bride [Vincente Minnelli,
1950]) and off (the dissolution of her first marriage, to Nicky
Hilton, was in sight). Love's a shaky crossing, however,
for her voice is still a Margaret O'Brien hush and her expressions only makeup deep.

Josephine Hutchinson nicely understates the mother's
determined and distracted manner, never descending to caricature. As the unassuming father Tom Tully does a variation
of Spencer Tracy's Father of the Bride. And Ann Doran
never fails to allow us to see the steel-like ambition behind
Mrs. Levoy's wagging tongue and sniffing at half-opened doors.
Also on hand is Gene Kelly, in a cameo appearance as himself.

The house designers and decorators provide Donen
with authentic recreations of New York landmarks and suburban archetypicalities. Against these, as is his wont, he sets
dialogue and action and culls details from them for atmosphere, mood, and characterization, all the while impishly
noting the context's inherent ironies or even creating them.
To be sure, Donen's own familiarity with Love's milieux, and
working again with Rosson, this time in black-and-white,
helped enormously in this regard.

Jud's behind-the-scene hustling of the manager is a
case in point as well as an example of Donen's witty use of
film within film: it parallels the on-screen robbery (which
is hustling on a grand scale). Later on, a TV baseball game
parrots Jud and Stacy's game before it. Love crystallizes
Donen's penchant for introducing local color whenever possible
and inaugurates his film-within-film maneuver.

Donen relies too heavily on title-card scene connectives
in this film (and in Royal Wedding and Give a Girl a Break),
though they do have the effect of driving on the action. Most
of these, happily, wink at us, as the marquee advertising the
stage acts and the flick City in Danger, which perspicaciously
comments on Jud's presence in New Haven, or the "Anastacia
Macaboy Dancing School's Fifth Annual Recital" poster, with

Love Is Better Than Ever: Donen's staging of the romance
of Larry Parks and Elizabeth Taylor against local details.
Copyright: Metro-Goldwyn-Mayer.

every credit that of Stacy, thereby making her out to be a
suburban Oscar Jaffe.

Scene-structuring montages also keep the film's eighty-
two minutes taut, as do the musical numbers amply sprinkled
throughout. (Donen's comedies, as Shakespeare's, will continue to be festooned with such interludes, most of the time
suggesting that in the midst of all the fuss and fracas, there
must be time for song and dance.) The location-shot opening
montage of Manhattan, captioned by Jud's voice-over mordan-
cies, is an abbreviated straight version of "New York, New
York." The gleefully inventive "week in the big city" montage,
however, is something new from Donen. Here, "on the town
with Jud" shots, in which the locales become more serenely
intimate, alternate with the relay of mother's phone messages,
whose tone builds to a madly insistent pitch.

Most reviewers dismissed the film as a companion

feature in dualers.   The public stuck to their TV sets.
Whether Parks's leftist leanings had anything to do with the
picture's failure is hard to say.   Nevertheless, Love showed
Donen's adeptness with a straight comedy and was a rehearsal for the future.

> It wasn't good.   When I say a picture is good or
> not good, I'm talking about the quality of the
> script.... It was made for practically nothing.

SINGIN' IN THE RAIN (1952)

Kelly's Paris wrapped on January 8, 1951; Love exactly two weeks later.   Now Freed's court jesters could give
their undivided attention to their next collaboration with Comden and Green.

> Betty, Adolph, Gene, and I knew we wanted to make
> a movie about the transition from silents to talkies.
> The Arthur Freed-Nacio Herb Brown catalogue was
> going to be the music.   We had decided what those
> songs would fit into was quite obviously a movie
> about this changeover.   We looked at a lot of movies
> based on early talkies.   One was Bombshell (Victor
> Fleming, 1933) with Jean Harlow.   We even con-
> sidered that for a while.   Comden and Green felt
> they could write a plot that would work better.
> Gene and I loved it.   Whatever thoughts we had for
> additions or deletions were incorporated into the
> script.   The published Rain script is the script
> taken off the screen after all our changes before
> and even during the production ... not the script
> Betty and Adolph gave us.   Adolph's forward in the
> book is incorrect.

The script possesses an astute knowledge and an intense affection for what it ribs--Hollywood and the movies--
and is brilliant in its use of film's thematic and technical
vocabulary as its own raw material.   And since the collaborators' memory of this naively giddy time and its equally giddy
artifacts are happy ones, it is idealized and tinged with the
yearning to return, relive, and be a part of it--thus the pathos
so characteristic of Comden and Green's writing.

The movies' archetypical romantic motif is deliciously
spoofed: boy meets girl, boy loses girl, boy finds girl.   Also

parodied is the on-screen fire but off-screen ice of star teams;
the industry's collaborative friendships, where recognition
and appreciation vary directly with one's proximity to the
front of the lens (the Lockwood-Brown combo has much in
common with the Kelly-Donen one); and the stars' egotism,
gall, and insecurity.

These motifs are set against the farcical turmoil that resulted when the hoydenish movies learned to talk and act like a
lady: the weird sound demo pics, the excruciating diction lessons for the players, the thorny business of recording sound,
the previewing of those embarrassing 100-percent squawkies,
the insertion of numbers in dramatic films solely to exploit the
soundtrack, the haphazard birth of the musical film, and the de-
mise of the star who could not speak. The film's first three
shots deftly set the scene with their emphasis on the so-called
miracle of sound: the tinny voice of the woman at the micro-
phone heard even as far back as the last rows of the audience
watching the première, the three children straddling a huge
amplifier in the treetops that makes the sound possible, and
the portly commentator dwarfed by the mike.

Embroidering this rich tapestry are a thousand and one
loving lampoons. Honky tonks are seen to be the training
ground of a screen god. The movies' thrilling feats are performed by stuntmen, the screen's real heroes. Classic slapstick routines, such as the kick in the pants, the tux caught
in the jalopy door, the pie in the kisser (even acknowledged
by Kathy as she takes the object in hand, "Here's one thing
I've learned from the movies!"), and the cop at the end, are
winked at. Also razzed are the silent swashbuckler; the studios' assembly-line production of college pics, westerns, jungle adventures; the MacDonald-Eddy operetta; the use of title
cards to provide narrative continuity; and the Hollywood montage, always visually arresting and enlivening a movie's pace.
But the roast does not stop here. The razzle-dazzle pre-
mières at which the new royalty tread a scarlet carpet to the
picture palace, the rainy (good luck) preview at the nabe
where the stars hide behind dark glasses and slouch hats worn
very low, and filmdom's fabulous parties also come in for
their fair share of knocks.

Yet the creators, no matter how clinical the dissection
of Hollywood, never dispel the enchantment. As a matter of
fact, the magic of movies and movieland is so pervasive--the
premiere's beautiful people, the flickering silent images, a
jalopy catching a falling star, a pull of a few switches turning

an empty sound stage into a rose trellised bower, Kathy's
voice coming from Lina's mouth--that it emerges as a definite motif.   Of course, Rain's homage to the most popular of
all the arts was practically lost in the pre-Bogdanovich days
of the film's release.

The characters, as written, bear just a trace of caricature so as not to eclipse their humanity, which the performers in their enactment, never lose sight of either.   We connect with these people.   Dora Bailey (Madge Blake) is the
gushing Louella Parsonsish gossip columnist who watches like
a mother hen over her brood of stars.   These include the
flaming flapper of the Clara Bow variety, Zelda Zanders
(Rita Moreno), femme fatale Olga Mara (Judy Landon) in the
Nita Naldi mold, Lina Lamont (Jean Hagen), a Pickford copy,
Don Lockwood (Gene Kelly), Fairbanks through and through,
and eventually Kathy Selden (Debbie Reynolds), Gaynor crossed
with Keeler.

As portrayed by Hagen, who received an Academy
Award nomination for Best Supporting Actress, Lina is at
once childish and shrewdly adult.   The laughter she elicits
never dispels our sympathy for the character, as in her mad
exit-right frame, presumably never to be heard from again.
And her voice, entirely her invention, is a marvelous instrument.   Most surely, Born Yesterday's dumb-smart blonde,
which Hagen essayed on the road, influenced her performance.

As Don, Kelly transposes The Pirate's Serafin from
the nineteenth to the twentieth century, insisting upon the nar-
cissism and insecurity of an actor as well as the prankish-
ness at the heart of every man.   In doing so, he both draws
from and spoofs his own personality.

Donen gives Kelly a marvelous entrance when he has
the camera cut a path through a throng of encircling fans and
then stop to gaze upon him.   The director will continue to
give his leads marvelous debuts and departures (as Hagen's,
above).   Being a lover of movies, he is aware of the power
of entrances and exits, how they linger in the corners of the
mind because of our anticipation of the star at the beginning
and regret at his or her leave-taking at the end.

In her first major role Reynolds is allowed to give the
obliging ingenue a streak of mimicry.   And as for O'Connor,
a Universal-International expatriate, he turns the sidekick
Cosmo into a hilarious clown, full of droll asides, grimaces

<u>Singin' in the Rain</u>: Donen's camera cuts a path through the throng, giving Gene Kelly and Jean Hagen a marvelous entrance. Copyright: Metro-Goldwyn-Mayer.

that occur always behind a person's back, puns, <u>shtick</u> as well as ideas. The directors' insistence on a dancer in the part eventually prevailed over Freed's choice of piano raconteur Oscar Levant.

Director Roscoe Dexter (Douglas Fowley) is a blend of Josef von Sternberg and Charlie Chase. R. F. Simpson (Millard Mitchell), the vastly imposing but easily intimidated head of Monumental Pictures, understands only one thing about movies, box office, as did most of the founding fathers. Rod (King Donovan) is the typical overzealous press agent. And the diction coaches (Kathleen Freeman and Bobby Watson), imported from the New York stage, are a termagent and an epicene, eccentrics really, in keeping with the way Hollywood considered and portrayed New Yorkers at the time.

Art directors Gibbons and Randall Duell relied on production stills and twenty-five-year-old photos of the studio.

Decorators Willis and Jacques Napes recreated old Cooper-
Hewitt stage lights, early recording and dubbing equipment,
even an old glass sound stage.   The actual process of silent
and early sound picture-making in a studio was a unique playing area for the musical in 1952. [2]

   The decor, Walter Plunkett's hideously right costumes,
Sydney Guilaroff's hairstyles, and William Tuttle's makeup
are at once satiric and nostalgic, playing out the film's tone
in another key.   Plunkett, who entered the business at the
height of the flappers' era, was an on-the-spot research library as far as what people looked liked then.

> Freed hated the idea of '20s costumes.   He thought
> it was going to alienate audiences.   He wanted the
> characters to look in '50s vogue.

   Donen, along with Kelly and photographer Rosson, who
replaced the unsympathetic John Alton, here takes his first
bold steps in color experimentation.   The pop of flashbulbs,
the roving spotlight that, when it passes the camera's lens,
momentarily blanches the frame, Don's white polo coat, white
fedora, and mouth full of capped ivories, Lina's silver lamé
cape trimmed in white fox fur, and her platinum hair and
powdered face render the premiere dazzlingly ethereal in the
midst of the drab groundlings.

   The three black-and-white movies within the Technicolor one counterpoint yesterday with today.   The pink, lavender, and apricot rainbow of "You Were Meant for Me" inside the sound stage assails the flat noon light on the tan
wall outside.   The ballet's yellow pinspot, in which the hoofer
stands engulfed by blackness, is suddenly slashed by the garish colors from more than fifty full-size electric Times
Square signs hanging at various angles and heights, which,
in turn, are supplanted by washed-out pastels.   In having
these colors move, along with the actors, camera, and cutting, to the music's beat, Donen and Kelly push their experi-
ment with choreographed film even farther.

   This choreographing of the straight passages, which
makes the transitions between them and the numbers practically seamless, contributes to the film's unfaltering pace
as do the three extended montages, each devilishly satiric,
each illustrative of the magic-of-movies motif.   This vivacious tempo allows us to feel the Jazz Age's frenzy and Tin-
sel Town's tumult in our bones.

The first montage highlights Don's progress from shoeshine boy in a disreputable pool hall to superstar at Grauman's Chinese by matching objects between shots and dissolves. The chronicling of three decades within a few minutes is not the only extraordinary thing going on, for while Don's voice-over insists upon the "dignity" of his background, the images depict the very opposite. This Eisensteinian montage of image contradicting sound, which incidentally happens to summarize the film's central issue, puts us in the godlike position of seeing two sides of the same coin at once.

The second montage is a historical kaleidoscope of musical-picture styles at the advent of sound. Featuring very little, if any, dancing, the montage is achieved by a series of direct cuts climaxing with the intercutting of all the pieces in an accelerated fashion, mirroring the barrage of musicals at the time.

The last montage details the process of dubbing Kathy's voice for Lina's. Its cohesion is ensured by Kathy's singing "Would You?" uninterruptedly in spite of temporal and spatial changes and by slow dissolves, melting one situation into another.

The Musical Sequences

Excepting "Moses," with Comden and Green's words and Edens's music, the tuneful and zingy score was culled from the movie repertoire of lyricist Freed and composer Nacio Herb Brown[3] (Al Goodhart and Al Hoffman contributed "Fiddle's" melody). That zing also derives from the numbers' satirical mounting and their perfect integration with the text.

Don's reprise of "All I Do Is Dream of You" to a bedside photograph of Kathy and her "You Are My Lucky Star" to a billboard of Don were shot but excised before the film's release to make the film play faster.

"Singin' in the Rain" (precredit sequence): In this first of Donen's half dozen precredits, the camera dollies toward yellow-slickered Don, Kathy, and Cosmo singing and tramping in a sea of blue rain: a pleasant irony, since most people grumble and hurry in the rain.

"Fit as a Fiddle": This extended part of the first montage's concert tour finds Don and Cosmo in an antic routine in Kansas City. We are the audience, viewing the act from the other side of the proscenium arch and panning with our eyes as the duo cavorts onstage in the knock-'em-dead but cloying style of novices. Their squeaky violins, which they play in the most preposterous positions, are as spastic as their limbs, even sprouting flowers on the last strike of the bow. Their large-checked emerald suits resemble horse blankets; their inflexible wide grins seem painted on.

"All I Do Is Dream of You": The flapper, with bee-stung lips and frenetic limbs, is joshed at R. F.'s bash, where a double line of pink-and-gold Coconut Grovers, including Kathy, squeal and charleston while hurling confetti everywhere.

"Make 'Em Laugh": Cosmo lightens Don's gloom by proclaiming, illustrating, and especially ribbing the "show must go on" philosophy of entertainers and of the genre as well (every musical dispenses these amphetamines freely). He transforms the adversities he encounters on several dismantled sets into comic gags in spite of a good deal of self-brutalization.

The number works on several levels. It furthers the plot, crystallizes the tone by simultaneously revering and reviling the fabled tradition, and enriches the film's setting by suggesting that it is commonplace for show people to entertain on the set and by featuring a compedium of silent-movie slapstick turns and conflicts. The number delineates character as well, being another instance of the "idea man" slighted, this time by the workers and cleaning help who, despite his humorous entertainment and attendant pain, pay him no mind.

The toned-down color scheme and tight shooting enable us to focus on O'Connor's brilliant but bruising ballet. Unfortunately, the song's close similarity to Porter's "Be a Clown" from The Pirate mars the number's luster.

"Beautiful Girl": The tableau, a type of number Busby Berkeley perfected at Warners,[4] and the fashion show, which inevitably found its gratuitous way into the early musicals, are on the block here.

After crooning among a bevy of ice-blue-chiffoned

cuties, the straw-hatted and caned Dick Powell type individually introduces, by means of doggerel couplets, a dozen showgirls, each exemplifying in a separate panel the attire proper to a month of the year. A Berkeleyesque overhead shot, which reduces the ensemble to two concentric pinwheels revolving around the clean-cut lead, wraps up the sequence.

"You Were Meant for Me": This courtly love pas de deux by Don and Kathy on a transformed sound stage defines a relationship and demonstrates the movies-as-magic motif, while gently kidding the shamelessly romantic passages in movies.

The camerawork and choreography make no false moves. As the romantics' ardor mounts, for example, the camera opens up the space more and more while the movement becomes more tactile and animated: their static stance on opposite sides of a ladder passes on to their descent, with each, still unsure of the other, clinging to the ladder's sides, then her following his nonchalant steps, and finally his taking her in his arms for a spirited whirl. Whereas the space in "The Bandit Chief Ballet" was used to emphasize the rococo and exotic, here it conveys simplicity and purity.

"Moses Supposes": In true Marx Brothers fashion Don and Cosmo pummel the diction coach's pomposity, pedantry, and smugness by throwing his tongue twisters back in his face and by vigorously tapping around him while dismantling his sanctum. At the end the wags seat the startled teacher on the desk and cover him with just about everything that's movable in the room, including the "vowel A" wall sign. The frame suddenly resembles Magritte's "Le Thérapeute. "

In the salad days of sound the studios had to raid theater for playwrights, actors, dialogue directors, and coaches--though somewhat resentfully, for they were aware that the stage fairly contemned the upstart medium. The number sends up this love-hate relationship.

"Good Mornin' ": Don's self-pity over the disastrous preview, the untouched sandwiches on the plate, the gray-and-beige color pattern, and especially the insistent patter of rain outside the dining room window set the melancholy tone.

Cosmo's idea to turn The Dueling Cavalier into a

musical, a swipe at the industry's coping with sound, dis-
perses the gloom in a flash.   Kathy rips off the calendar
page on the kitchen wall--it is 1:30 A. M. --heralding the
celebration that travels all over the star's Spanish-mission-
style home.   The camera even passes through a wall to preserve the dance's energy.   In the movie industry an idea--
good, bad, or indifferent--is regarded as being no less than
the Second Coming.

A collapse onto the sofa, which they tilt back to the
floor with their feet (a variation of the "Open Your Eyes"
finale), and thoughts of Lina plunge them into the dumps once
again.   Thus, the number also teases the genre's mercurial
temperament.

"Singin' in the Rain":   The movie musical's most celebrated sequence is an affecting mood piece that also smiles
at those untrammeled bursts of joy synonymous with the genre.
It is, further, a profound psychological portrait.

The joy of being in love and of saving the movie releases the child that lurks within Don.   Despite the rain, he
discards the trappings of the adult world: his waiting limou-
sine, his umbrella, hat, and the opinion of passersby.   He
begins to sing, dance, and play in and with the rain.   Setting
the expression of joy on a deserted city sidewalk in a black,
soggy night is a highly ironic and dramatically effective conception, turning a musical cliché inside out.

Children are always tilting at gravity: Don jumps onto
the base of a street lamp.   To the child, the animate and in-
animate are inseparable: Don sings to the "bathing belle" advertisement in the pharmacy window.   In a child's imagination
an object or activity can trigger an association with something
else: Don's umbrella becomes his waltzing amour and then a
jolly old stick blithely passed along a grating and twirled in
the air.   Children come up with surprising reversals: Don
places an open umbrella on the ground to catch water.   He
next stands under a broken drainpipe, allowing the torrent to
drench his conservative tweeds.   Only the pure in heart are
capable of such defiance.   He spins around in circles and then
hopscotches along the curb like Chaplin's barber in The Great
Dictator (1940).   No belt on the head from a frying pan in-
duces Don's action, though.   His playfulness is intrinsic and
natural.

In the middle of the street he splashes in puddles,

creating his own little hurricane. He becomes momentarily
self-conscious as he catches the gaze of an incredulous cop.
Despite the appearance of the ultimate parent in black slicker
and cap and brandishing a stick, the child wins out. Don
shakes the water off his feet, shrugs his soaked shoulders,
and matter-of-factly proffers an explanation: "I'm dancin'
and singin' in the rain. " He takes to the sidewalk while
glancing humorously back at the policeman. An umbrella-less
passerby approaches, and Don, with a childlike gesture full
of spontaneous largesse, hands the adult his bumbershoot.

The number's structure is solid. The beginning states
the premise and carefully bridges the transition from talk to
song, walk to dance. On Kathy's stoop Don's last words,
"From where I stand, the sun is shining all over the place,"
give way to humming underlined by soft instrumental music,
then to the famous "doodedoo-doo-doodedoodedoo-doo, " and
finally to the lyrics recalling Don's words. After reposing
in the doorway a moment, he walks down the steps, waves
the chauffeur away, and saunters along the sidewalk.

In the middle section the child's ecstatic mood builds
with the melody. It climaxes with his splashing around in
the street puddles.

The end, marked by the policeman's appearance, contains the falling action, the smooth transitions out: Don's recitativo explanation and return to the pavement and an exquisite final flourish--Don's charity--that flavors the entire sequence.

The artless lyrics and lively melody, the ambling,
jumping, and tapping and their interaction with the environ-
ment, which Kelly's rust-colored shoes never let us lose
sight of, define the state of joyful childhood.

Camera movement and angling enhance meaning: it
stays at rest with Don on the stoop, saunters beside him,
tightens on his transfigured countenance, "Come on with the
rain/I've a smile on my face, " and rises and pulls out to
behold him cutting moving circles all over the place as he
twirls around with outstretched hands grabbing an opened umbrella. The camera skips a beat when the officer enters.

Who could have danced in the rain onstage or captured
it on canvas or on the page? The number's fluidity is the
signature of film itself, resulting in a poetry that can hold

its own beside the graced moments in Renoir, Ford, Bergman, or Fellini. [5]

"Broadway Melody-Broadway Rhythm": This sequence
takes a jab at the Brobdingnagian production number that
Berkeley was so fond of and its hackneyed motifs.   Country
verses city: young-hick hoofer (Don) arrives in Times Square
with his suitcase; after setbacks he auditions at a speakeasy,
where he confronts a curvaceous femme fatale (Cyd Charisse),
who opts for a gangster's diamond bracelet. The rags-to-
riches climb: the kid performs in scratch burlesque on the
Columbia Wheel, in vaudeville at the Palace, and in Ziegfeld's
Follies--the robustness and entertainment level of the same
act vary inversely with the respectability of its surroundings.
The coincidental meeting of the former love: in a swank ca-
sino after his triumph he sees the siren again. The dream:
he fantasizes being with the girl. Unrequited love: the girl
flips a coin in his face and walks away. The work ethic:
he will find happiness in singing and dancing. The phantasm-
agoric finale: a cutout of the tuxedoed star advances toward
us while the throng of Broadwayites recedes in the background.
The gangster film is put on the burner with the coin-tossing
George Raftish leader, his moll in her Louise Brooks hairdo
and makeup, exhaling a plume of smoke from cigarette holder,
and the gambling milieu. Also on the block is the mindless,
and therefore, disruptive, insertion of a number within a
story line: the modern tale is totally incongruous with The
Dancing Cavalier's universe.

Among the amazing things in the dream sequence is
the mellow pas de deux on a pink-and-gray plane, with an
eerie clarity of perspective that counterpoints reality's fero-
cious tap and arm-waving in an expressionistic setting of
hard colors. Also noteworthy is Charisse's Grecian-type
outfit, with its streamer of China silk, about twenty-five feet
long, attached to her shoulders. It undulates in rhythm with
her movements, indicating that even the wind machines were
choreographed.

Donen, Kelly, and musical director Lennie Hayton,
who was nominated for an Oscar for Musical Scoring, com-
bined the thirty-two bars of both songs, "Broadway Melody"
and "Broadway Rhythm" into one piece. The seventeen-
minute ballet took a month to rehearse and was shot in two
weeks.

"You Are My Lucky Star": In this takeoff on the

happy ending every camera move discloses triumph.　After tightening on the embracing lovers' duet onstage at the premiere, we dissolve to Don's Arrow-collar profile vis-à-vis Kathy's marcelled one on a billboard advertisement of their first Monumental Picture and then pull back to the stars themselves hugging on a green hillside bathed in sunshine before their famous profiles.

　　　　Virtually all the critics loved the movie, as did the public. ·

> It's great fun, with an ingenious script and some
> of the most wonderful performances in a musical.
> It was the most expensive film I did at Metro ...
> in the neighborhood of $2.5 million.　But then, we
> only built one wall of Grauman's.　If Vincente di-
> rected, he would have been allowed to build the
> whole damn moviehouse.

　　　　Only in our age of enlightened film consciousness has Singin' in the Rain received the kudos it deserves.　With a successful reopening at Radio City Music Hall in 1975, the film has made the Best Ten List in a startling number of film publications and is studied in schools for its accurate account of the transition from silents to talkies, its technical virtuosity, and its perfection of form.

　　　　Since so much of film is expendable, we cannot help wondering what our descendants will still be viewing in the next hundred years or so:　Chaplin and Keaton, no doubt; Astaire and Kelly's routines; some of Bergman and Fellini. Perhaps Rain will also prove indestructible.

> The danger to each person who happens to be con-
> nected with something which later in life turns into
> something of memorable quality is that you might
> let that inflate you into believing you are some sort
> of historical figure yourself.　Another danger is
> that everybody pays attention to that work alone
> and measures everything else beside it.

FEARLESS FAGAN (1952)

　　　　Kelly left for Europe at the end of 1951, a month after the Rain production closed, to star in the thriller The Devil

Makes Three (Andrew Marton, 1952) and get his ballet film
Invitation to the Dance out of his system.   Freed assigned
Donen, along with Rain alumni Reynolds and O'Connor, to
Jumbo, Joseph Fields's adaptation of a '30s Rodgers and
Hart, Hecht and MacArthur circus musical that Billy Rose
had produced.

> Lenny Spiegelgass started rewriting.   Roger Edens,
> who was Arthur's right-hand man, and I toured
> with a circus to familiarize ourselves with the
> background.   Then we couldn't get Donald. Bobbie
> Fosse was out from New York, and I made a test
> of him as a possible co-star with Debbie.   Then
> the studio decided to scrap the project[1] because
> there were some restrictive clauses in Rose's con-
> tract which prevented tampering with the book and
> score. ...   Producer Eddie Knopf then approached
> me to direct Fearless Fagan, which was essentially
> prepared and ready to shoot.   As with Love Is
> Better Than Ever, I did the film only out of a sense
> of responsibility.

Scenarist Charles Lederer, responsible for some
crackling Hawksian comedies, wrote the script from Frederick
Hazlitt Brennan's adaptation of Eldon W. Griffiths's 1951 Life
report about the true adventures of PFC Floyd C. Humeston.
Humeston raised a pet lion at home and worked up a wrestling
act that toured with the circus.   When drafted, Floyd took the
lion "Fagan" along.

Lederer respects the human-interest aspect by keeping
Floyd's altruism central.   The elliptical construction, which
Donen achieved in his crisp cutting, supplies some pleasant
ironies and keeps things moving.

This cozy comedy was part of the heartwarming,
animal-story tradition that never quite died at MGM, even
with Disney's capture of the field in the '50s.   The film,
meant to cash in on Universal-International's popular Francis,
the Talking Mule series, was different territory for Donen,
whose previous foray in the genre was a romantic comedy.
(Donen has continued to tackle different types of comedy with
each successive work.)

Donen gets a low-key performance from Carleton Carpenter as Floyd that keeps sentiment from lapsing into sentimentality.   The wonderful things Donen has him do with his

Fearless Fagan: Carleton Carpenter in a publicity shot.
Copyright: Metro-Goldwyn-Mayer.

hands (cuffing them behind his back or giving one the support
of his pocket) eloquently captures Floyd's gangling boyishness
and shyness.

Janet Leigh, a Norma Shearer discovery whom the
studio groomed and then showcased in about fifteen films
over a six-year period, is actually playing herself in the
film.   Her stalwart and piquant personality with a who-are-
you-kidding streak is at home here as Abby.

The circus, the bootcamp, and the starlet's home
created by Gibbons and Leonid Vasian and Willis and Fred
MacLean reflect the real world.   The woods, though, resemble a Hollywood sound-stage version of an African jungle
rather than California's north country.   In the black-and-
white rendering of these sets, nowhere does photographer
Harold Lipstein display the virtuosity that will mark his work
on Damn Yankees.

A few ingenious montages also help the film's seventy-
eight minutes fly by.   The search for a home, in particular, with
with five similar segments in which the camera dollies into
photographers clicking away at Fagan and then dollies out to
a captioned newspaper blowup of the action, seems a run-
through for Funny Face's celebrated fashion sequence.

The song "The Loveliest Night of the Year," Irving
Aaronson's adaptation of "Over the Waves" with Paul Francis
Webster's lyrics, handed down from the Lanza vehicle The
Great Caruso (Richard Thorpe, 1951), is used throughout the
film to sooth Fagan.   In one sequence Abby entertains the
boys with the curiously uncredited "What Do You Think I
Am?," taken by Donen from Best Foot Forward.   Catcalls
from an impatient audience and an emcee who calms the
rowdies down--business anticipatory of The Pajama Game's
"Steam Heat"--frame the number, which in its staging and
direction duplicates "You're Gonna' See a Lot of Me."

The inexpensive little picture proved a big charmer
with both the critics and public.   But in Donen's view,

It's a mediocre script and an equally mediocre
movie.

GIVE A GIRL A BREAK (1953)

Jack Cummings, who was Louis B. Mayer's nephew and

who from 1934 on headed one of MGM's musical production units, invited Donen to work on a story he had purchased. (Exchange of stars and technicians among the lot's three musical clans was frequent.) In general, Cummings's material, excepting Kiss Me, Kate (George Sidney, 1953) and Seven Brides for Seven Brothers, was inferior to Freed's but on a par with Pasternak's.

Albert Hackett and Frances Goodrich, MGM's librettists in residence, and Donen tried to offset the conventionality of this backstager. The putting-on-the-show and the getting-the-girl formulas were livened up by the use of six protagonists, who are characterized primarily through dance and triplicate structuring. Each girl is a different type: tyro tapper (Suzy), semiexperienced ballerina (Joanna), and seasoned modern-jazz performer (Madelyn). And each is paired with a respective mate who complements her individuality: fervid stage manager (Bob), temperamental lyricist (Leo), and suave director (Ted). While the dance characterizations follow On the Town's example, the suspenseful structure is obviously a residue from the script's source, a story by Vera Caspary, the romantic crime novelist who shares with Donen a penchant for trios (Laura, Otto Preminger, 1944; A Letter to Three Wives, Joseph Mankiewicz, 1949; Three Husbands, Irving Reis, 1950; and Les Girls, George Cuker, 1957).

The satire on the theater and its folk, though rather skimpy, adds some distinction too.

Marge and Gower Champion, a dancing team from Sid Caesar and Imogene Coca's Your Show of Shows on TV, arrived at MGM in 1950 and appeared on the edges of musicals: Show Boat (George Sidney, 1951) and Lovely to Look At (Mervyn LeRoy, 1952). Here, however, as Madelyn and Ted, they hold center stage. Marge is a dour Vera-Ellen; Gower, a good-looking but spiritless Astaire.[1]

Debbie Reynolds, as Suzy, on the other hand, is a perfect conduit of Donen's exuberance. With a couple of lead roles to her credit since Rain, she is more assured and lively this time around.

Bob Fosse, performed on Broadway and on the road before landing at MGM as a dancer in Kiss Me, Kate and an actor-dancer in The Affairs of Dobie Gillis (Don Weis, 1953). As the stage manager Bob, his reedlike presence, high-pitched voice, and thinning blonde hair do not translate very well to the screen. When in motion, however, these things matter not one iota. This, his third film, initiated an asso-

ciation with Donen that was to include choreography in The
Pajama Game and choreography and performing in Damn
Yankees and The Little Prince. [2]

Helen Wood, in the Cyd Charisse mold, also came
from the New York stage.   As Joanna, her Junoesque figure
bends every which way under Donen's direction.

Completing the sextet is Kurt Kasznar as Leo, one of
MGM's stock and stout supports, who, as usual, makes a
Hungarian-Jewish impression.

Visually, no one makes any great effort in the straight
passages.   Photographer William C. Mellor displays all areas
of his Technicolor frame evenly.   And the Gibbons, Willis,
and Arthur Krams sets seem like allusions to the studio's
past musicals.

The gathering of many people in the frame at once,
the suspenseful crosscutting among three individual destinies--
a technique Donen will refine in Seven Brides, most notably
in the abduction sequence--and the numerous montages make
the picture's eighty-two minutes brisk.

The Musical Sequences

Though Girl's straight passages possess nothing exceptional, its musical sequences are another thing entirely.   Here
Donen's conceptions are merry.   His choreography is vivacious (Gower Champion mapped out his two duets with Marge),
and his executions extremely cinematic.   The dancing from
every cast member, including Kasznar on one occasion, is
bravura.   Composer Burton Lane and lyricist Ira Gershwin's
score, with Andre Previn and Saul Chaplin's interpolation,
"The Challenge Dance," is catchy.   And the designers in
practically every instance display imagination at white heat.

Creating all the "book" numbers save one, Donen further assails the formulaic backstager that relied on the "show"
number, that is, a rehearsal or performance onstage.

"Give a Girl a Break":   An evening conference of the
show's collaborators explodes with a montage of swirling
newspaper headlines, a fast tilt down to a squib announcing
their decision to go with an unknown, a series of bouncy cuts
of ironically hopeless hopefuls singing out the story in the
paper, and a quintuple split screen of these duds.   The high

level of invention that mixes sudden contrasts in movement
and rapid-fire cutting allows us to feel the palpitations in a
prospect's heart.

Donen next introduces the three leads seriatim, each
practicing at home while reading the paper, and then performing at diagonally placed barres in an abstract set of converging gray, pink, and yellow perspectives, bordered by a huge
square outline also placed diagonally. The switch from representational to abstract with its large areas of color and
contrasting lines intoxicates even further. At the finish the
girls pose together while still reading the tabloid, the number's unifying, structuring icon.

"Nothing Is Impossible": Ted, Bob, and Leo dispel
their fear of writing a whole show in three weeks with one
of those irrepressible bursts of hope endemic to the genre
and of camaraderie endemic to Donen's musicals.

Set on a stage bare except for a rehearsal piano, the
dancing is breezy, with jumping and tapping on the piano top
and marching on knees, and comic as well, with fat, inert
Leo constantly resisting the encouragement of his lean, frenetic partners.

Two bits of choreographic magic prove that they are
up to the challenge. In one, the trio join hands to form a
circle, become twisted, and attempt to extricate themselves
from the knotty situation. Ted and Bob succeed; Leo is left
holding his own hands. In the other, Ted and Bob each put
one of their heels together while tapping away with their other
foot. Leo remarks that he doesn't believe what they're doing
while perpetrating his own brand of impossibility, an extrava-
gant keel forward in which his face almost touches the floor.

"In Our United State": Echoing the conceit of trans-
planted New Yorkers as found in "Main Street," Donen laces
this passage with humor that short-circuits the sentiment.
Fosse is made to dance as a hopelessly gaga rustic, all body
swoons and sighs, who nervously mangles his hat every which
way, a structuring gag that weaves through his expansive
dance all over the breakwater. In one incredible move
Fosse completes a somersault with his hat, which had fallen
to the ground, sitting perfectly on his head. The topper has
him lean back too wantonly on the stone bench and topple
backward into the river. The hat, however, remains afloat.

Fosse's dancing is quite different from Kelly's.
It's as though he wants to explode, as though he's
doing his best not to burst. Kelly dances as an
explosion. Fosse tries to keep the lid on--hence
the tension. Kelly, on the other hand, gives you
everything.

"The Challenge Dance": The second romantic interlude, again a night exterior, forsakes humor for emotion.
Ted convinces Madelyn that she is the best of the lot by en-
ticing her from inside her apartment to her garden rooftop.
He sets the steps, she matches them. His rhythmic finger
snapping at the start underscores his teaching position. As
the dance evolves, more touching and interplay make the two
one.

Her white ball gown with a fitted top and a skirt of
beads, his white pants and shoes, their gossamer movements,
the setting at the city's top, the blinking neon sign creating a
slow-motion strobe effect, and the full melody supplanting the
initial spare, suspenseful strains transport them to another
plateau, emblematic of their rekindled relationship.

"Give a Girl a Break" Instrumental and "It Happens
Every Time": The producer, demanding a decision, insti-
gates this psychological probe of Bob, Leo, and Ted's ra-
tionales. A superimposed miniature of Suzy, then a headline,
"Suzy Hailed as a Sensation," spin before Bob's face, which
dissolves to life-size Suzy announcing to a reporter, "I owe
it all to Bob," who gratifyingly joins the "star" in a ticker-
tape parade to celebrate her fame and their mutual love.
The skyscraper-roof setting; the confetti, streamers, balloons,
and clown-doll props; and the yellow, white, scarlet, and
blue parade colors, which the black night makes even more
vibrant, raise the couple to the top of the world, where their
tap and slides are unrestrained.

To add to the gaiety Donen reverses the photography,
creating two sensational moments among so many others:
the confetti's ascent from the floor to the sky and the balloons' deflating everywhere the couple touches.

A balloon bursting before Bob's face returns us to the
reality of the producer's office. The camera moves to Leo,
seated with his back to us in the frame's lower-right corner.
He meditatively swings his baton left to right, wiping out this
image and wiping in the image of himself as a magician whose
flick of the baton/wand makes Joanna appear and himself re-

Give a Girl a Break: Debbie Reynolds and Bob Fosse's "Give a Girl a Break" instrumental. Copyright: Metro-Goldwyn-Mayer.

appear against a gray, white, and yellow abstract set.   A
stately pas de deux later, Donen cuts to another set of
stronger hues, where Joanna executes some hot jazz turns,
suggesting a sexual undertone to Leo's power play.   But the
passage fails to develop this and ends on a confusing note.

The camera then focuses on Ted, standing before a
floor-length mirror in which Madelyn materializes, and mi-
raculously tracks into the mirror, subjectively becoming Ted
as he follows her into a beige abstract set with black poles
and white modernistic oblong lamps.   "It Happens Every
Time," he muses, then chases her.   A dissolve to Ted's
mirror reflection, which we know is a reflection from a pullback to him standing before it, concludes Gower's clichéd
"lost and found and lost again" ballet.   Needless to say, the
last two sections cannot hold a candle to the first.

"Applause, Applause":   Ted and Suzy's razzmatazz
paean to show biz during the opening-night show is all pas-
sable but half-baked.   What is Ted doing dancing the lead?
And why the circus metaphor?

The critical reaction to Give a Girl a Break was lukewarm and audience turnout negligible for this musical made
on a slender budget.   Donen commented,

> The idea for the story is so puny that it's not
> worth spending a year of one's life on it.

SEVEN BRIDES FOR SEVEN BROTHERS (1954)

When theatrical producer-director Joshua Logan re-
linquished his five year option to Stephen Vincent Benét's
short story "The Sobbin' Women," which he planned as a
stage musical, MGM immediately purchased the rights for
$40,000.

> Cummings liked what I did with Give a Girl a
> Break and told me of "Sobbin' Women," which I
> was very eager to do.   MGM said they would allow
> me to direct only if I extended my contract, which
> would run out in a few years....   Howard Dietz,
> head of advertising, renamed the picture.

Benét's twenty-three-page short story is a skeletal
yarn about a rugged pioneer family: Pa, Ma, their seven

sons, and their hired girl settle in the backwoods; the boys grow up and get themselves wives through the machination of the incredibly resourceful Milly, the bonded girl whom the oldest buys and marries. Pregnant Milly now needs help on the farm, so she plants the Plutarchian idea in her kin's heads: "Why don't you marry 'em first and ask them afterwards." This tall tale celebrating the Frontier ethic becomes in Hackett, Goodrich, and Donen's hands essentially a touching romance and secondarily a story of the coming of age.

> Everytime I have an idea for something, I put it
> in the script because it is my way of remembering
> to do it and of informing everyone else of what I'm
> going to do. It's rare I get a script--musical or
> comedy--that I like. In a sense, I have to gener-
> ate the script from myself. For Seven Brides I
> worked for months with Goodrich and Hackett. We
> got Dorothy Kingsley to write one scene that we
> disagreed about. And during the production, I
> added to and subtracted from the script.

Although the script for the most part pasteurizes Benét's details--for example, Milly is now a parson's ward and not a slave whose time Adam buys--it is studded with details that evoke the period and its people, such as Milly adding sorrel to her wedding bouquet because it is good for soup. The dialogue and lyrics, replete with nature imagery, prudish euphemisms, and crude grammar, contribute enormously to this sense of period.

Also, Donen depicts the period, with all its get-up-and-git philosophy, fundamentalism, work ethic, obtuse and sweetness-and-light misses, in his characteristically spoofing and farcical ways, which, while ensuring an intelligent distance, never completely forsake the heart and feeling. Very few are capable of such a high-wire act as this. What especially helps, is Donen's invocation of Horace rather than Juvenal as his model. He derives the slapstick from the situation and character and presents it flat out without indulgence and as being quite the normal course of things.

As written, acted, and directed, Jane Powell's Milly is a strapping pioneer woman, no matter that she reaches-- and only when she raises her head--Adam's shoulders. She is at once adamant and tender, a giddy child and a stern mother, sassy and saintly. Discovering that Adam has six fractious brothers, she hides her surprise and unhappiness: "I guess I should have picked more sorrel," and our hearts break for her.

Under Donen's direction Howard Keel, one of the stiffest presences in musicals, actually appears to be interested in what he is doing, and so portrays Adam's development from an impulsive, proud, and immature tease to a contrite and sentient man quite engagingly. Fortunately, Keel's attempt to replace Donen with his Show Boat director, George Sidney, never succeeded.

The rest of the brothers and brides are realized in varying degrees. Russ Tamblyn comes through as the ham-handed, put-upon, but sensitive Gideon. Jeff Richards' Benjamin appears restless and moody, qualities his rugged handsomeness ameliorates. Tommy Rall's Frank is explosively macho, especially when called "Francis." Nancy Kilgas etches Alice as a repressed romantic who swoons over Milly's wedding vows, while Julie Newmeyer's Dorcas is mildly libidinous.

The ensemble playing contributes to the film's precision and loveliness. And, too, the farce is as beautiful as it is funny because the supports, like the screen's first slapstick clowns, are acrobats and dancers with tip-top physicality and unbeatable timing.

The inconsistency of Gibbons and Urie McCleary's look is the film's only flaw. The overly stylized, almost expressionistic hothouse exteriors of "Wonderful, Wonderful Day," the social, and "Lonesome Polecat," are out of place with the realistic location exteriors of the credits and "Spring, Spring, Spring," while rear projection mars the newlyweds' departure and the brothers' stealing out of town. If ever a musical cried out for the real outdoors--the genre tends to resist the realistic--it is this one.

> I'll give the devil his due. We didn't go on location because it would have taken a year. Obviously, we would've had to be in a place where it was summer, then it gets covered with snow, and then spring comes.... The cost would have been exorbitant. But it would have helped the picture. But I didn't have the wherewithal to get this or to get better sets.

The expense of studio design and ducats for location shooting were allowed first-class citizens, however. Producer-director Mervyn LeRoy did take cast and crew to Canada for Rose Marie (1954), MGM's first Cinemascope musical. And lavish and costly sets were struck on the lot for the Freed unit's Cinemascope venture Brigadoon (Vincente

Minnelli, 1954). Seven Brides, during its production stage and initial release, was hardly the apple of the studio's eye.

The low budget did have some advantages. Never once are the sets, by Willis and Hugh Hunt, or the buckskin suits and quilted skirts, by Walter Plunkett, showily over-done. Rather, they convey a ruggedness and austerity con-sonant with the times, qualities also imparted by George Folsey's cinematography in Ansco Color, a process that favors brown. (With the widespread use of color in the 1950s as an as-sault against the black-and-white tube, Eastman Kodak intro-duced the single-strip system, a filmstock with chemical layers, each layer sensitive to different colors. Despite the colors' lack of staying power, movies could be made more cheaply in this system, of which each studio had its special version.)

Unlike most directors, intimidated by the new screen shape of Cinemascope, which Fox unveiled in the fall of 1953 with the biblical spectacle The Robe (Henry Koster) as another antidote to the home screen, Donen reveled in it. (By 1954 about 25 percent of all Hollywood releases used the giant size.) His deft use of the frame raises the story to mythic proportions at times. Whenever the brothers appear en masse, as during Milly's inspection prior to the social, Do-nen's arrangement makes them look more like a tribe or na-tion. At other times the frame contracts to concentrate upon an intimacy, as during Milly's wedding-night instructions on love. And at practically all times Donen's mise-en-scène and cutting enhance the humor. During Milly's tour, for ex-ample, the brothers' free-for-all transpires along the frame's edges and her honeymoon night is crosscut with her voyeuris-tic in-laws.

> I had to do the film both in Cinemascope and in a
> flat version. Everything was staged and shot twice.
> Metro thought that only so many theaters could play
> Cinemascope so they had to have two different nega-
> tives. [This procedure of dual filming lasted only
> a couple years after wide screen's birth. At the
> end of 1955, in fact, 13,000 houses were equipped
> to handle the new shape.]

One of the most exuberant musicals ever filmed, Seven Brides's pace is pell-mell: a Bible-quoting virgin's courted, proposed to, and married within the film's first five minutes. Because of fourteen speaking, singing, and dancing roles, the frame is frequently filled with at least seven people at a time.

Seven Brides for Seven Brothers: Donen's deft use of the
Cinemascope frame includes intimacies, such as the girls
wondering when spring will arrive (opposite), and expanses,
such as Milly (Jane Powell) turning the table on the brothers
who attack the food without saying grace.   Copyright: Metro-
Goldwyn-Mayer.

Credits are played over Adam's buckboarding into town.
Most scenes, like those in Citizen Kane (Orson Welles, 1941),
open upon an arresting visual-aural detail, immediately bringing us to attention while providing a narrative thrust.   The
dissolve, the mode of transition between scenes, strengthens
continuity and makes the narrative more fluid, as does the
score's technical inlaying.   An unusual amount of cutting
within each scene (unusual for Cinemascope, because the
rule of minimal cutting lessened the exorbitant cost in changing the setup and filling up yet another large frame), characters laboring all the time (after all, frontier folk crystallized
the Protestant ethic), farce that often involves brawls and
mayhem, and the numerous dancing passages fill the screen
with movement and action.   Yet the film knows when to be
quiet and still, affording us needed relief and contrast.

The picture's irrepressibility also has something to
do with its flirtation with the western genre. Whenever the
musical woos or weds the western--and Seven Brides is the
most propitious union of these two forms--the results, more
often than not, are exhilarating. [1] For one thing, the inter-
twining of the Yankee mythologies that the genres have in
common reinforces the narrative drive. Furthermore, the
musical yearns for the western's physical and psychological
expanse. When it attains it, its people kick up their heels
as freely and rowdily as any four-footed critter. And, too,
the expression of fisticuffs, shootouts, and chases through
dance results in a vim and vigor not easy to come by.

The Musical Sequences

> Cummings wanted to use old American country
> songs. How are we going to find songs applicable
> to the things we have to express, I asked. Look
> and you'll find them, he replied. So I spent months
> with all the Americana music. It was impossible,
> so we got composer Gene de Paul and lyricist
> Johnny Mercer.

The felicitous and varied score approximates frontier
diction and rhythms. Even the orchestrations, which favor
banjos, accordions, and harmonicas, stress period. The
casting of such singers as Powell and Keel is an added de-
light--her strong soprano is the voice of civilization; his
rugged baritone suggests the mountain setting--as is the
acrobatic and balletic corps put through the vigorous paces
of choreographer Michael Kidd. Donen set the whole thing
in motion to create another landmark dance musical. Kidd
will team with Donen on two other occasions: It's Always
Fair Weather as one of the leads and Movie Movie as a minor character and choreographer. [2]

> I enjoyed Kidd enormously. His contribution to
> the film was gigantic. He's very good to work
> with, very enthusiastic, hardworking, serious,
> amenable, not filled with any ego.

"Bless Yore Beautiful Hide": Adam's rumination about
finding a wife characterizes him as stubborn, arrogant, and
lusty. The bold, syncopated, clip-clop rhythm accompanying
his stroll up and down the town's boardwalk, alongside which
the camera tracks, makes his manner and gait more deter-

mined.   His occasional respite of leaning his right shoulder
on a post with his left arm akimbo and hand fisted at the
hip to survey the territory also bespeaks of his cocksureness.

Donen's comic bits (as when Adam tips his hat to a
woman retrieving eggs from a hen house, "Mornin' ma'm, "
and a child races up and tugs on the woman's apron, calling,
"Mom") undermine Adam's haughtiness, keeping him sympathe-
tic while investing the song number with a choreographic lilt.

The melody plays over Adam watching Milly at her
chores, after which he struts toward the camera, leans on
a post, folds his arms on his chest, and concedes, "Yes,
she's the girl for me. "   Before a barbershop mirror Adam
sings another stanza.   The melody finally underlines the exchange of vows and furnishes traveling music out of town.
Its technical inlaying and that of "Wonderful, Wonderful Day, "
"The Barnraising Ballet, " "June Bride, " and "Spring, Spring,
Spring" are exceptional in that the music informs an entire
sequence supporting the straight sections and making the
movements therein choreographic.   In Seven Brides Donen
tells more of the story through music and dance than in any
of his previous works.

"Wonderful, Wonderful Day":   While Adam waters the
horses, Milly, whose cup of love overfloweth, bolts the wagon
to gather a wedding bouquet.   The buoyant waltz, the wind
rustling through the birch trees, Milly rushing up and down
the hillocks that are flecked with summer flowers, which the
camera traces in expansive horizontal and vertical arcs, and
the final dolly out to a high-angle overview that finds Adam
on a tree stump, awed by the élan of this stranger before
him, make the passage take off.   The painted backdrop and
papier-mâché props, however, keep it from soaring.   The
melody supports the rest of the journey and evaporates just
as soon as Milly gets the picture.

"When You're in Love":   The film's first pause is a
ballad in which Milly, standing inside the bedroom window
(frame right), instructs Adam, stretched along a tree limb
(diagonally intersecting frame left), about love.   She faces
him while he doggedly looks straight ahead.   Donen's mise-
en-scène both captures and takes a devilish poke at their estrangement.   Adam is literally and figuratively out on a limb
on his wedding night.

During the one-take scene Donen's psychologically

sensitive camera glides slowly toward Milly from chest up as
she becomes more intimate and transported and her surrounding reality is transcended.   The scarlet shawl over her white
undergarment is the film's first splurge of color, giving importance to the entire passage and, within that passage, to
the figure of Milly, encompassed by dark green and brown.
Scarlet is appropriate because of its association with passion
and love.   The camera finally glides back to include the recalcitrant Adam, and the passage ends as it began, with both
locked in their ways.

The song's reprise is part of Adam's advice to love-
sick Gideon.   In an effectively dramatic sequence Donen piles
up poignancies (oldest brother fathering the younger, callow
Adam remembering Milly's words and Milly overhearing) and
then undermines them with Adam's cavalier riposte: "If you
don't get her, you'll get the next; one woman's pretty much
like the rest."   At which point the camera darts to Milly's
tearful face--an uncharacteristic move from a director known
for keeping his distance--and we cannot help averting our
eyes.

"Goin' Co'tin'":   Milly's dance instruction transports
the brothers, who polka with each other and then, stomp,
somersault, and cartwheel all over the parlor.   In the last
part the dance is larded with the force of Gideon trying to
get into the swing of things.   There are seven people: three
couples and Gideon; he, being the youngest, is odd man out.
In the closing moments Donen retards the camera speed so
that the brothers' ecstatic leaps and swirls around Milly,
stalwart in screen center, is rendered even more furious
and gleeful.

"The Barnraising Ballet":   "Goin' Co'tin's" seven
dancing principals set the parlor's walls and rafters shaking.
Fortunately, there are no sides and ceiling in this number,
which features eighteen dancers hoedowning on wooden floor-
boards and eighteen-plus raising a barn.

Besides its sheer magnitude the ballet's dramatic integration is the tightest in a film musical so far.   Neither re-
gurgitating the preceding action nor stopping the plot, this
dance continues the action on a conscious level.   This initia-
tion of the brothers into the courtship ritual also brings the
jealousy of the townfolk to a head and paints, in moving colors,
a frontier social of long ago.

The prelude, "The Hoedown," with the camera rushing with the town boys over to the girls to lead them onto the boards and away from the Pontipees, states the rivalry conceit. The first section, which develops the theme, is all oblique and vertical tension creating lines--the brothers' butting in is the extent of the contest here. A maiden swirling out of line under wistful Pontipee gazes initiates the next section, which is circular. The third section involves the males showing off by means of various acrobatic and athletic contests at the nearby picnic tables. The emphasis changes from breadth to height, from ensemble cavortings to individual turns. Back to the boards, and the initial lineup is reversed for the epilogue, with the demoiselles deserting their beaux and leaping into the brothers' arms.

Throughout, Donen's pans and zooms reinforce the dance's movements. And the more than forty cuts during the eight-minute sequence, while connecting the dance as a whole, help establish the distinct thematic rhythms. At the start the cutting on the stately movements, supported by an andante instrumental version of "Hide," is infrequent. As the antagonism increases, the frisky movements and cutting quicken to the allegretto music. At the climax the feverish intercutting of variously angled and sized shots of the brothers on the plank and swish pan of the ensemble's return to the boards, all to the allegro beat, electrify the dance. Further, dancing styles, colors, and clothes separate and characterize the groups, accentuate movement, and tell the story in another way. The rivals, with mannered steps, are in muted gray-and-green jackets and ties; their hair is black or mousey brown. The redheaded farmers, whose bodies are sources of untapped raw energy, don bright shirts: lavender, yellow with a faint check, aqua, red, orange, and blue. The blonde, brunette, and henna-haired misses, who coyly swirl in circles, wear colorful checked apron skirts over white blouses, linking them with the brothers.

Donen's meticulous preparation of the ballet's second part, "The Barnraising," comprises shots of the unassembled barn, Milly's approval, each competing group, and the prized heifer. It provides the sequence with the needed winding down in order to peak again.

The construction activity clashes with the destructive attacks on the brothers and their forced slowburns, which catch fire only when Adam is rammed in the gut with a plank.

At one uproarious point the barn-owner enters through a door frame to halt the melee, gets bumped around like some pinball, and a second or two later is hurled out of the same opening he came in.

This potpourri of modern jazz ballet, Barnum and Bailey acrobatics, vaudeville slapstick, and western fisticuffs is cut furioso on music beats, howls, hammer blows and thudding punches until an onminous creak freezes the building and donnybrook. The four walls and roof collapse around the Pontipees, all upright in the center, while pinning the townfolk to the ground. The Keatonesque flourish (<u>Steamboat Bill, Jr.</u>, 1928) is right up there with <u>Town</u>'s dinosaur.

"Lonesome Polecat": In a series of languid attempts at work and listless strolls that do not relieve their pent-up sexual energy, which Kidd's movements insist upon, the brothers, against a lento lament, compare themselves to "lonesome polecats, mean hound dogs baying at the moon, hoot owls hooting in the trees," and ululate ("ou-ou-ou-ou") between the comparisons. In grieving for their girls they have never been as lifeless, solemn, frustrated--and funny-- as this.

The spare orchestration, principally a harmonica accented by the natural sounds of a hachet, saw, and ax; the lonely ridge setting blanketed by snow; the blue, white, and beige color scheme; the business of blowing on their fingers and continually pulling their sheepskins tighter against the cold; and their obliviousness to each other even when a chore involves several of them, also make this tableau drolly austere.

"Sobbin' Women": The number's revival-meeting conceit has Adam/preacher on some crates/podium in the barn/tent, urging the example of the Romans on his brothers/flock with a song/harangue that repeats key words in an up-tempo and hand-slapping rhythm.

The players' spatial organization and enactment are thematically effective. At the start each brother is isolated, evenly spaced in an immobile stance about the barn. As conversions pile up, an animated group forms about Adam. The sled's narrow confines, which they jump into after bolting from the barn's doors in a rhythmic cut, unite the group even more.

"June Bride" and "Spring, Spring, Spring": Milly

barges into the attic bedroom to quell the rumpus among the
cooped-up girls with news of her spring baby.   The thought
of possible marriage with their abductors comes into the open
as the bloomered beauties, led by Liza, wistfully pantomine
a wedding and convey the attendant joy with their arms trac-
ing arcs in the air and twirling around the roof-support posts.

        A series of brief calendarlike illustrations hailing the
passing winter months, with appropriate melodic commentary,
provides a neat seasonal transition.

> I wanted to do a stylized production of spring's ar-
> rival, stop-motion photography of fish gestating, a
> little chick being born inside an egg, breaking out,
> and chirping.   One flower would open, then two,
> and suddenly the screen would be filled with flowers.
> Snow would melt.   Water would come down moun-
> tainsides.   Sheep would be born.   Birds would fly.
> The sun would come up....   I'd put all the birth
> images behind, in front of, and beside the dancing
> group.   I told Cummings it would take a year.   He
> said I couldn't delay the movie's release.   What I
> did was a puny approximation done in two days.
> Every time I see the movie it breaks my heart that
> I couldn't realize my idea.   That would have been
> the big number in the movie, the real emotional
> high, even bigger than "The Barnraising Ballet."
> The emotional uplift you get when spring arrives
> is a much better situation for a number than the
> rivalry of the boys.

        What did eventuate was far from puny: a pastel-
painted montage of birth and domestic images celebrating the
new season, budding love, and the arrival of Milly's baby,
thus bringing the sequence full circle.

        With Ephraim rushing onto the hillside with news of
Milly's labor pains, the lyrics stop quite realistically in the
middle of a line.   But the music continues over a dissolve
to the parlor, with the brothers pacing back and forth and
the girls running up and down the stairs with hot water,
towels, basin.   A baby's cry silences all and stops the choreographed horizontals and verticals.   Gideon's "I'm gonna' be
an uncle" and subsequent faint is underlined by an instrumental swelling of the song's last bars, a typical Donen exclama-
tion point.   The instrumental continues, although softer and
slower, over the bringing of gifts to Milly in bed with her
baby.

The critical and popular jubilation that met Seven
Brides pleasantly surprised MGM.   One of the year's biggest
grossers, it made just about everyone's Best Ten list.   Of the
five Academy Award nominations the picture received, in the
Best Picture, Original Screenplay, Color Photography, Editing,
and Scoring categories, it won the last award.   And it has passed
the test of time. [3] Donen thought the movie was "rather good,
except for the painted backdrops and the 'Spring' number. "

Seven Brides was a turning point for Donen at MGM.
The bright kid on the musical block, sans Kelly, delivered a
musical that was even more commercially resounding than On
the Town or Singin' in the Rain and an outstanding example
of the genre as well.   Four out of five big money-making musicals and three out of five "standards" was indeed an impressive track record.

The kid also showed the squares how to use the vast
horizontal.

DEEP IN MY HEART (1954)

Back in 1951 Joseph Fields had completed an original
screenplay for Freed based on the life of operetta king Sigmund Romberg.   The trades carried the squib that Charles
Walters was signed to direct Kurt Kasznar in the title role.
When Romberg died that very year, Freed knew the script
had to be rewritten.

A few years later, when Freed decided it was time
for Roger Edens, his right-hand man and associate producer,
to set out on his own, he handed him The Romberg Story.
To get the production rolling, Edens assigned librettist Leonard Spiegelgass to rewrite the script.

> Had the choice been his, I don't think Roger would
> have selected the life of Romberg.   But he felt that
> as a first-time producer, he should do something
> that would be a success.... It wasn't up my alley
> either.... I would have run from that picture like
> crazy except for Roger, who wanted me to direct.
> I told him I would direct anything he wanted since
> he had been such a great help to me.... I met
> Roger on Best Foot Forward.   He was well into his
> seniority by then.   [Edens became MGM's Pied
> Piper in 1933 at the age of twenty-eight.]   He was
> a knowledgeable and experienced guy.   I think

Arthur held Roger in such awe that he was frightened
by him. Roger somehow terrified Arthur, and knew
it, and he used it to get his way. If Roger was
contemptuous or raised an eyebrow about something
Arthur was doing, it somehow disappeared from the
scene. And Roger would exempt himself from many
of Freed's pictures. He would say: this is a re-
volting picture and I won't have anything to do with
it. And Arthur would come to him and say: would
you do me a favor? Could you bring yourself to
help me on this picture? And Roger would usually
do it. He had really an enormous desire for quality.... Well, Roger was my biggest promoter, not
Arthur. I mean while Arthur let me do On the
Town with Gene, it was Roger who really thought
that I had some talent and who must have been in
Arthur's ear about it. Even back on Take Me Out
to the Ball Game.

Commercial reasons forced Edens, Spiegelgass, and
Donen to stay conservatively within the confines of the musical biography, particularly those established by MGM's popular composer series: Till the Clouds Roll By (Richard Whorf,
1947 [Jerome Kern]), Words and Music (Norman Taurog,
1948 [Rodgers and Hart]), Three Little Words (Richard Thorpe,
1951 [Ruby and Kalmar]). These films each resembled a personality revue, a lavish entertainment of songs, dances, production numbers, and tableaux (the artist's repertoire performed by the studio's musical stable). They were interspersed with comic sketches and dramatic interludes (the
slight narrative line), all linked superficially by the subject
of the homage. We must wait for the second Donen-Edens
collaboration, Funny Face, for a flexing of their artistic mus-
cles.

Based on the life of the Hungarian Sigmund Romberg,
Elliot Arnold's book Deep in My Heart was the starting point
for Spiegelgass's script. Emigrating to America in 1909 at
the age of twenty, Romberg democratized the Viennese operetta and contributed to musical comedy with his seventy-nine
shows comprising two thousand songs.

Arnold's book belonged to a school of historical fiction
far removed from rigorously researched and documented biography. Spiegelgass's libretto is an even more fanciful account.
Borrowing some public-domain facts and a gag or two and
sweeping the historical background (the 1910s through the

1940s) under the carpet, the script shilly-shallies with two
conflicts--Romberg's attempts to sell Shubert his serious music and his efforts to win Lillian's hand--through serviceable
dialogue and stereotypic situations.

Donen gives the material wherever he can an ironic
touch, dusting off the clichés and shaking out the stiffness
that came with the territory.   He counterpoints image with
sound à la Rain.   And he has his cast play against type:
balletist Tamara Toumanova bumping and grinding; diva Helen
Traubel crossing an all-stops-out buck-and-wing with a turkey
trot, and dramatic actor José Ferrer indulging in a pantomine/
juggling act/comic monologue by simultaneously cleaning up
and rearranging the furniture in the messy bungalow, ordering
Beluga caviar on the phone, arguing with his co-writers, and
confronting a distraught producer.

Ferrer plays Romberg as a boundless bundle of energy.
The performance becomes monotonous since the character, as
written, is all effects and, as performed, without modulation.

> Jose was my choice.   He was a luminary at the
> time [Oscar-winner for Cyrano De Bergerac,
> Michael Gordon, 1950 and nominated for Moulin
> Rouge, John Huston, 1953].   He loved doing it.
> He studied singing all his life.

The other players are either serviceable or wasted.
Traubel, America's foremost Wagnerian soprano and Edens's
delightful choice, plays Anna with dignity and sings in rich
full tones.   The equally ample Isobel Elsom supplied some
belly laughs as Lillian's priggish mother.   Toumanova as the
French firebrand Gaby Deslys gives the impression of being
able to chew any man up and spit him out again.   David
Burns is properly loud, crass, and pushy as the agent who
lights his cigars by striking a match on the ostentatious ring
on his left pinkie.   Merle Oberon as lyricist Dorothy Donnolly
and newcomer Doe Avedon as Lillian are called upon only to
be pretty.   And Paul Stewart, Walter Pidgeon, and Paul Hen-
reid have little to do as benign paterfamilias.

As in Give a Girl a Break, we must look for the visual distinctiveness of cinematographer Folsey, who shot in
EastmanColor, another one-strip color process MGM used in
the 1950s; art directors Gibbons and Edward Carfagno and
set directors Willis and Krams; and couturiers Helen Rose
and Walter Plunkett in the musical sections.

The pace of the 132-minute opus is surprisingly brisk. Donen's elimination of interval in narrative continuity, the montages, the succinct and smooth transitional devices, and the inclusion of fifteen musical passages see to that.

The Musical Sequences

Practically all the numbers, chosen by Donen and Edens, occur onstage, making the film more an anomaly in Donen's canon than Royal Wedding. The numbers' arrangement within the text as well as their diverse mounting, however, ingeniously offset each other, rendering the musical catalogue fairly dramatic while giving us some idea of Romberg's range. [2] Donen also invested as much dance and satire in the musical selections as he could. Naturally, these numbers come off better than the straight songs.

> We didn't mind changing the songs' original contexts. We weren't trying to make a documentary. We wouldn't have known how. As Arthur Loew Jr. said back during the '50s: here at Metro, they think a documentary's a picture with only two musical numbers.

Deleted during the previews to shorten the movie's length were Joan Weldon's "One Kiss," which was part of the "New Moon" sequence, and a "Whirl of the World" set comprising a leggy showgirl parade: "Girlie of the Cabaret" and George Murphy's crooning "Nobody Was in Love with Me," which hilariously climaxed with Esther Williams in an American flag that reached into the flies.

Precredit and Credit Sequences: The superimposed dedication, "To all those who love the music of Sigmund Romberg," the medley of his most famous waltzes, and the high-angle overview of the black, white, and gold Carnegie Hall setting, which is the film's framing device, start the film on a typically reverential note.

The timidly experimental credits are supered over the event, frozen and gilt-framed, except for the cameo names that dart at us against bright hues to the spirited beats of "The Riff Song." This foreshadows Donen's significant contribution to the art of title design after his departure from MGM.

Deep in My Heart: Helen Traubel and José Ferrer playing
against type in the number "Leg of Mutton."   Copyright:
Metro-Goldwyn-Mayer.

    "You Will Remember Vienna":   The agent's revulsion
humorously leavens the cafe patrons' lapping up singer Anna
and pianist Romy's old-world waltz.   The number replaced
the originally shot "Dance, My Darlings."

    "Leg of Mutton":   An eye-catching montage climaxes
Romy and Anna's one-step.   A roll of sheet music, couples
executing the new step, a row of tooting trombones, and a
roller piano plunking away are supered against a solid rust
backdrop.   This cubistic touch dissolves to a breathtaking
shot.   From inside a Tin Pan Alley music store we look out
through the display window, decked out in sheet music of the
nation's No. 1 hit, at the agent, the well-heeled Romy, and
Anna peering in.

    "Softly, As in a Morning Sunrise":   Red spangled and
feathered Gaby Deslys slinks down a baroque orange staircase
to join a line of Apache showgirls, syncopatedly chanting ooo-

doo-das while writhing every which way, and then belts out
the romantic ballad in hotsy-totsy fashion.

As a Belascoesque sunburst lifts Gaby to the rafters,
we dissolve to the cafe, where Anna and Romy correctly inter-
pret the piece. This masterful transition keeps the section
taut and creates an ironically humorous juxtaposition as well.
Later in the film the gag is reprised when 1940s be-bop mangles the song.

"Mr. And Mrs.": In this duet of Ferrer and Rosemary Clooney (borrowed from Paramount for the occasion),
the complimentary color schemes of their clothes and the
cottage set, the close harmony, the comfortable soft-shoe
bit in unison, and their actually being husband and wife josh
domestic togetherness.

"I Love to Go Swimmin' with Wimmin': The O'Brien
Brothers (Gene Kelly and his brother Fred), in Gay Nineties
pin-striped suits and straw boaters, frolic in a beach setting
with eight bathing belles.   Their combination strip (down to
bathing suits), unison twisting leaps, acrobatics, and triple-
time tap is rounded off by a dive into background rows of
collapsing cardboard waves, from which their heads emerge
as the camera races toward them to capture not one but two
alligator grins. This act was the sort of thing Gene and Fred
did in vaudeville in the mid-'30s in their native Pittsburgh.

"The Road to Paradise" and "Will You Remember?/
Sweetheart": The camera's opening move, a diagonal glide
from a box seat toward an onstage couple (Vic Damone and
Jane Powell) in a garden arched by blossoming cherry trees
against a gray sky is as smashing as its closing, a swing
back from his bow and her curtsy and swing forth to their
kiss for yet another in-character bow.

"The Bombo Audition": "Girls Goodbye," "The Very
Next Girl I See," "Fat, Fat Fatima," and "Zazza-Zazza-
Doo-Doo": To impress his sweetheart and her mother and
get the producer off his back, Romy runs through the entire
show he is composing in a matter of minutes. He plays six
roles, including Jolson out of character, while offering critical
commentary. Edens's funniest and most amazing musical collage, inimitably rendered by Ferrer, takes to task the daft
enthusiasm and egomania of footlight folk as well as the inan-
ity of librettos. Donen's camera, as if awe-struck, merely
stands back and records.

"It": Donen's camera is on the rove again, missing not one detail: flaming youth party against a giant cubist mural by '20s cartoonist-chronicler John Held Jr., studded by the sparkles from a revolving crystal ball. Ann Miller's sensational dance is at once a robust buck and wing, sexy shimmy, red-hot black bottom, lively charleston, and machine-gun tap that keeps her shoulders, chest, and hips perpetually in motion, the 50,000 bugle beads on her dress quaking like aspen leaves. She is the epitome of the All-American Girl: bright eyed, vivacious, imbued with a power that rivals General Electric, naughty but nice. "It's" the film's best stage number.

"Serenade": To mark Romberg's first collaboration with Dorothy, Donen begins the haunting serenade of the student prince (William Olvis) to the barmaid with Romberg conducting in the pit and ends with a pullback to the audience. Olvis is extremely hard on the eyes. With head thrown back, arms extended, and a pronounced waddle, he is somewhere between a crucified Christ and a capon.

"One Alone": A camera winds its way through a moonlit desert and a Moorish archway with bronze grillwork gates. The sinuous Cyd Charisse twirls her black velvet cape on the marble floor and cascades in a white lace, skintight wrap-around over James Mitchell's graceful yet brutal body, which the camera describes in expansive arcs. This hypnotically sensuous study in arabesques runs a close second to "It."

"Your Land and My Land": This mechanical tableau features a waxworks Howard Keel chanting the robust march at the tip of a converging perspective of Union and Confederate soldiers against a plantation. The blues and grays finally mix in an elemental march toward us.

"Auf Wiedersehen": Donen's camera pans from Dorothy propped up on the sofa (her unruffled physical and emotional appearance belie her expiring state) to the other side of the crystal-and-brocade living room, where at the keyboard Romy and Anna bid farewell while Lillian looks on. No one handled death as prettily and tidily as MGM.

"Lover Come Back to Me": A fisherman (Tony Martin), drawing in the net on an inky beach, laments for his love (Joan Weldon), who appears in time to harmonize the ballad's reprise.

<u>Deep in My Heart</u>:   Ann Miller's got "It."   Copyright: Metro-
Goldwyn-Mayer.

"Stouthearted Men" and "When I Grow Too Old to
Dream":   To the stately march "Stouthearted Men" we travel
from Anna's cafe solo to Carnegie Hall, where she finishes
the song against an orchestra under Romy's baton.   Romy
then dedicates the simple waltz "When I Grow Too Old to
Dream" to his wife.   The business Donen gives his players--
Romy bringing out the reluctant Lillian from the wings, their
sitting on the edge of the conductor's stand, her head resting
on his shoulder--adds up to a touching finale.

The reviews of <u>Deep in My Heart</u> were fair to good.
Despite the Legion of Decency's "Morally Objectionable in
Part for All" rating, due to the suggestive costuming and danc-
ing (an unheard of classification for a musical), the picture
was one of the most popular Christmas gifts that year.   In
Donen's view,

It's a banal biography with a string of musical

numbers that aren't very imaginative in general....
It was extremely cheap to make.

That Deep in My Heart turned out to be the most ap-
pealing of MGM's musical-biographies was important for Donen: it got him Funny Face.

IT'S ALWAYS FAIR WEATHER (1955)

Having returned from Europe to star in Brigadoon,
Kelly was gung ho to direct again with Donen. Comden and
Green, after their Band Wagon stint, had in progress a rough
outline for a Broadway show that dealt with On the Town's
sailors ten years later. Kelly liked the idea and commis-
sioned it for his next movie.

> There was no particular reason for the navy-to-
> army switch.... Metro only halfheartedly wanted
> to make the film. We weren't given the same kind
> of freedom as we had had. Then, during production,
> Gene and I were at swords' point. What happened?
> I don't know. I would have quit in the middle, ex-
> cept that I said I would do it. [The last months of
> 1954, when Weather began production, were particu-
> larly rough for Kelly. The Devil Makes Three and
> Crest of the Wave/Seagulls over Sorrento (John and
> Ray Boutling, 1954), another war melodrama he had
> made in Europe, went down the tubes. His Briga-
> doon was not performing very well. And the studio
> did not know what it was going to do with his high-
> brow Invitation to the Dance. On the personal side,
> his twelve-year-old marriage to actress Betsy Blair
> was on the rocks--they would divorce three years
> later, when Kelly would marry Donen's first wife.
> And, as far as Donen went, Seven Brides had mas-
> saged his ego considerably.]

As in their other Donen-Kelly collaborations, Comden
and Green give male camaraderie the treatment, only this
time it occupies stage center and takes on a peculiarly dark
cast.

Sharing this center is the put-down, also not-so-
friendly, of television and Madison Avenue: the cloyingly
cute "Little Miss Moppett" commercial, the bathetic Midnight
with Madeline show, a lampoon of Ralph Edwards's then-

popular This Is Your Life series, the porcine producer who
accepts even insults to make a buck, the career woman, and
so on.   The film completes Comden and Green's satiric tril-
ogy on the image professions, having put Hollywood on the
block in Rain and Broadway in The Band Wagon.

     Throughout that burlesque, as well as through the farce
of Ted's masquerade as a skating-rink manager, Doug's turning
the penthouse inside out, and the TV studio fracas, is the theme
of the transitoriness of all things.   Middle-aged Tim, the bar-
tender, sternly reprimands the boys on their return from the
war: "Aren't you people going to grow up?"   A decade later
they do, but the child in them is gone forever.   The montage
of their civilian life achingly expresses the diminishment of
the ideal.   They fail to remember "Bootsie, " the Southerner
from their outfit who unwittingly saved their lives at Dunkirk
and the former subject of their every toast.   And Ted's sad
awareness of friendship's fragility has no effect on Jackie
(Cyd Charisse), who prosaically states that it is part of the
human condition by quoting Shakespeare: "Most friendship is
faining, most loving mere folly. "[1]

     The cyclic structure, which is repeated in the film,
also connotes pathos, movement but not progress.   In the
film's initial movement the buddies arrive at Tim's tavern
at noon.   For the next twelve hours Doug (Dan Dailey) and
Angie (Michael Kidd) console Ted (Kelly), who has just received a "Dear John" letter, by carousing around town.   They
return at midnight to Tim's, where they take leave of each
other.   The film's elaborate second movement, which takes
place ten years later, also ends where it begins: the arrival
at Tim's, a half-day's escapade around town to console themselves, and the return to Tim's.   This replication of incidents
heightens the sense of stasis, of sadness.

     The ending, however, does suggest some growth.   In
looking for the other two each has begun to find himself.   And
too, the men, sadder but wiser, make no plans to meet again.

     A deep-down sadness also infiltrates the characteriza-
tions of the males; even Madeline, the TV show hostess, has
a pathetic quality about her.   And the title itself is ironically
disheartening: "fair weather, " after all, means loyalty only
during a time of success.

     The actual souring of Donen and Kelly's sweet partner-
ship must have given the film's poignancy its cynical edge.

As a result the film is primarily dispiriting--a strange effect
for a musical at this time, though a similar noir overlay was
infecting quite a few musicals over at the gritty Warner Brothers:
The Jazz Singer (Michael Curtiz, 1952), She's Back on Broadway (Gordon Douglas, 1953), Young at Heart (Gordon Douglas,
1954), A Star Is Born (George Cukor, 1954), Serenade (Anthony Mann, 1956). Actually, It's Always Fair Weather and
these Warners films anticipated, by some twenty years, the
unpleasant but sobering aftertaste of the Hal Prince-Stephen
Sondheim works: Company (1970), Follies (1971), A Little
Night Music (1973), Pacific Overtures (1976), Sweeney Todd
(1979), and Merrily We Roll Along (1981).

     The vehicle was originally expected to unite Town's
male triumvirate, but Sinatra nixed the role and Munshin was
unavailable. Kelly insisted upon another male dancing lead.
He ended up with two: Dan Dailey from the Fox musicals--
actor, clown, dancer, and singer, all wrapped into one--
who, as Doug, delivers the film's best performance, and
Michael Kidd as Angie, Donen's choice, who throughout looks
as though he is in a good deal of pain. Kelly's own fireless
performance as Ted is not much better. Undoubtedly, his
offscreen situation with Donen affected his onscreen presence.

     The women, on the other hand, are both winners.
Cyd Charisse's aggressively liberated woman, Jackie, brings
to mind a Sturges wench, especially during her exchange with
Ted in the cab, where she finally KO's his masculinity by
towering over him in a long kiss while pressing him against
the upholstery to end the boredom of his seduction. And
Dolores Gray, a young blonde Merman in her film debut as
the mercurial and hungry hostess, Madeline, whose desires
are as overwhelming (she wants 40 million people to love
her) as her bouffant and gowns, actually defines camp a decade and a half before Sontag. Though the film lacks Freed's
customary expensive lacquer (people were just not turning out
for musicals as they used to, and studio head Dore Schary
had instituted budgetary restraints), the film's look is distinc-
tive. The sets, by Gibbons, his assistant, Arthur Lonergan,
Willis, and his assistant Hugh Hunt, shot in Eastmancolor by
Robert Bronner, depicted places that had rarely if ever cropped up in musicals before: the infantry on the battlefields of
France, the underbelly of the Third Avenue El, Stillman's
Gym, a roller-skating rink, and a TV studio's control booth.
Donen recalls,

          Of course, I wanted to go on location but the studio
          said no.

Donen and Kelly's savvy Cinemascope sense also abets the film's special look: the triple screens of the civilian montage and "Once I Had a Friend" (just about every Donen movie hereafter will contain a split-screen sequence); the masking of "I Shouldn't Have Come"; the melee seen through windows of the control booth and then picked up on three different monitors with each TV screen occupying a third of the frame, which augments the brawl's rabidness while jabbing at the exploitational instincts of the media people; and the horizontally convulsed black-and-white cartoon commercial.

Naturally, the trio of protagonists helps the deployment of Cinemascope space as the cast of fourteen helped that of Brides. In this film, though, Donen makes a further advance in his use of the wide screen not only by enhancing the humor of the script but also by creating more humor through the new shape.

The film curiously tends to falter at the tails of numbers. The finale flourishes are frequently poses held much too long. This time Donen could not control Kelly's penchant for designing material for applause.

The Musical Sequences

Though Comden and Green's lyrics and neophyte Andre Previn's music are clever due to the parodic level of most of the numbers, they are not very rich. (Edens dashed off lyrics for "Music Is Better Than Words.") "March, March," "Once I Had a Friend," and "Situation-Wise" are mere snatches, repetitive choruses without bridges.

A romantic duet between Ted and Jackie is sorely missed. "Love Is Nothing but a Racket," an andante beguine, had been written for the romantic principals. Kelly insisted upon an allegretto rendition. Consequently, the song and dance, set at the Grove Costume Company with him and Charisse donning various hats from the racks and jumping on and off a circular platform, turned out to be a frenzied farce rather than a romantic mood piece. And the passage ended up on the cutting-room floor.

Though Ted and Doug each have a self-confrontation number, Angie goes without, making the piece wobbly. "Jack and the Space Giants," a ten-minute ballet of Angie preparing a meal for his kids, had been shot, but it was deleted before

It's Always Fair Weather: The GIs' binge (Gene Kelly, Michael
Kidd, and Dan Dailey).   Copyright: Metro-Goldwyn-Mayer.

the film's release.   Donen felt the sequence was good enough
to remain in the picture, but Kelly wanted it out.

"March, March":   This spoof of military marches,
sung by an off-screen male chorus, is a war montage.   All
dissolves and superimpositions of infantry lines, flags,
trenches, PT boats, explosions, VJ Day celebrations, it
takes the protagonists from a ravaged French village to a
serene Third Avenue bar.

The melody later accompanies a montage of bars that
the buddies visit, in which a succession of garishly colored
neon bar signs, supered over the trio, builds to a riot of
color against a black background, connotative of the men's
blotto condition.   Later that night, on a deserted street under
the El, the inebriates frolic.   In a startling cut, a cab, with
the camera behind the driver's front seat, comes to a screeching halt to prevent running over the soldiers, who are seen
through the windshield.   The taxi becomes their plaything.
The novelty wearing off, the revelers lace their left feet with

garbage-can lids and rhythmically tap out a god-awful racket. The climax has them wildly scampering down a sidewalk in expansive jetés. The camera races in front as well as along each side of them (the crosscutting of three distinct sides increases the exhilaration) and finally rests with them, out of breath, atop Tim's bar.

The melody also underlines the brilliant civilian montage--depicting the passage of ten years--of clocks, calendars, newsreels, and the trio's upwardly mobile lifestyles in a triple-split frame.

"Time for Parting": The pals' leavetaking lament is mockingly plaintive, with the number parroting "The Whiffenpoof Song," and the extravagantly forlorn dolly out to a severely high-angle overview of each walking his separate way from the tavern. (The number's reprise, architecture and all, closes the film.)

It's Always Fair Weather: Dolores Gray introducing Dan Dailey, Michael Kidd, and Gene Kelly to her TV audience. Copyright: Metro-Goldwyn-Mayer.

"I Shouldn't Have Come":   Lunching at the elegant
Turquoise Restaurant, the reunited "chums" mentally remon-
strate with themselves.   Their acerbic ruminations are accompanied by blank stares into space and gauche gestures.
Ted bangs his silver teaspoon against a crystal waterglass;
Angie munches celery; and Doug belches--all set to the dul-
cet strains of "The Blue Danube Waltz" cascading from a
string quartet in the background.

As each delivers his soliloquy sound-over, the camera
floats in for a tight shot, while masking out the other two,
recalling Olivier's masking of the soliloquies in Hamlet (1948).
The end, with a belligerent allegretto supplanting the soft andante and the trio's snipes falling pell-mell, is rendered in
snappy, tension-inducing cuts from one to another.   Their
applause, the number's capper, is meant more for themselves
in facing the reality of "eternal friendship" than for the orchestra.

"Music Is Better Than Words" and "Thanks but No
Thanks":   In the TV studio Madeline rehearses "Music," a
travesty of all those vacuously gushy TV intros by a musical
hostess, particularly Dinah Shore's Chevrolet Hour.

Wit distinguishes "Thanks," a rose, black, and white
production number in which Madeline vociferously rejects, in
her enormously hefty contralto, a male line of suitors offering her diamonds, furs, "a cruise ... oil wells that ooze--
and that pair of Fred Astaire shoes," by gunning them down,
blowing them up, and finally dispatching them, with the pull
of a lever, through the collapsing floor.

"Stillman's Gym" and "Baby, You Knocked Me Out":
This sly spoof of alma mater songs is a paean croaked by
the Runyonesque managers and pugs to describe the landmark
of the boxing world to visiting Jackie.   Impressed by her
knowledge of boxing trivia and her visionary quality (in a
lime jersey outfit, she sits cross-legged on the ring's ledge,
a lush oasis in the tawny surrounding), the denizens go into
a spin: "Baby, you knocked me out...." The punchy dance
--equal parts ballet, modern jazz, and gymnastics--comprises
accurate boxing characterizations.   Donen's swish pans to
various training exercises and his thumping cuts on sound effects cause the heart to pump faster just as exercise is intended to do, thus reinforcing the dance's meaning and effect.

"Once I Had a Friend":   While Ted waits for Jackie at

the Grove Costume Company, the gray-curtain background
and wisp of smoke from his cigarette enhance the nostalgia
of his wartime friendship.   The screen once again divides
into three panels, but this time with a different result.

Doug in his hotel suite (left) and Angie in the corridor
outside the TV studio (right) share Ted's thoughts.   Their
voices, their identical gestures, and their casual tap glissades,
all in perfect unison, unite them despite the different locales
and self-absorption.

> The three cameras had to move at the same speeds
> so the figures in the frame would be in sync with
> each other.   We had to count the music beats ac-
> curately since the pace of the music dictated the
> camera.

"Situation-Wise":   At a penthouse cocktail party Doug
berates the Madison Avenue crowd, including himself, for its
pomposity and bathos.   In vino veritas, he appends "wise,"
a business suffix, to every word, as he unnerves the guests
with various ethnic and farcical shticks that used to be part
of his outrageous yet winsome personality.   He has not been
this alive since the war.   For his pièce de résistance he
chooses his famous trick of pulling the tablecloth out from
under--a disaster since the table in question flaunts a silver
and crystal setting for twenty-four.

The number is Donen's only strained slapstick bit (due
to length) and falls well below its exemplar, "Make 'Em
Laugh. "

"I Like Myself":   Ted's flight from the gangsters
through alleys, down a fire escape and scaffolding alongside
a building, and into a roller-skating rink, where he fuses
with the skaters, is a lyrical introduction to his self-
confrontation.

Leaving the rink, he exchanges his clothes but forgets
about his skates.   But he has a lot on his mind: the fixed
fight, the tailgaters, and especially Jackie.   Shrugging his
shoulders and whistling, he gently floats down a street and
glides in arabesque around its corner.   The street, pavement, hydrant, mailbox, and curious passersby, who eventually bring him to the realization that he is wearing skates by
moving when he moves and stopping when he stops, are part
of the choreography built from skating figures, ballet, and

tap.   Skating is a nifty metaphor for being in love since it
enables Ted/Kelly--as it did Chaplin in Modern Times (1936),
Astaire and Rogers in "Let's Call the Whole Thing Off" from
Shall We Dance (Mark Sandrich, 1937), and Donald O'Connor
in "Life Has Its Funny Little Ups and Downs" from I Love
Melvin (Don Weis, 1953)--to sail, glide, and stamp even
more loudly because of the ball bearings, all of which are
near correlatives of this felicitous state.   Only Kelly's mas-
turbatory pose, framed by applauding passersby no less, de-
stroys this moment's magic, which comes near to the perfection of "Singin' in the Rain. "

       Mixed reviews, although more yeas than nays, greeted
Fair Weather.   Most critics congratulated the directors on
their use of Cinemascope.   The Academy applauded its scoring with a nomination.   Public response was lukewarm.

            It's a wonderful idea for a musical and it has some
            really good numbers in it.   Yet there's something
            about the movie that's odd, it doesn't quite come
            smashing through.

       Fair Weather was Donen's last picture at MGM (though
he was still under contract to them) and with Kelly.   (To this
day, their fifteen-year friendship that involved two shows,
seven films, and a million intangibles, has not been renewed.)
Donen was now about to enter another phase of his career,
one in which he would have more control.

3. ON LOANOUT: 1956-1957

FUNNY FACE (1957)

Leonard Gersche's libretto Wedding Bells was loosely based on some incidents from the life of the famous high-fashion photographer Richard Avedon, who trained a model and then married her. It was outfitted with a score by composer Vernon Duke and lyricist Ogden Nash and planned for the 1951 Broadway season. At producer Clinton Wilder's suggestion Gersche flew to MGM to ask Robert Alton if he would direct. Alton would go along only if Kay Thompson would play the role of the fashion coordinator. Thompson could not be budged. The producer lost interest and eventually his option ran out.

Alton gave the script to Edens, at whose request MGM acquired the rights. After a time-consuming round of memos between an excited Edens and a skeptical Schary, Wedding Bells was finally given a green light. Gersche started the rewrite, and Donen, who liked the material, was asked to direct.

Edens felt that the original score was too theatrical. Besides, it was always difficult to sell a completely new score to a movie audience. The bulk of the score had to be made up of standards, Gershwin it was hoped.

> Warners would sell Metro the use of the Gershwin score if Metro would loan me to them for The Pajama Game, which was slated for production at the end of 1956. Roger and I then went through

the entire Gershwin repertoire. While we were
preparing the film, Freed asked me to shoot an
additional scene with Howard Keel and Vic Damone
for Kismet [1955].   It involved about a week's
work.   Minnelli, Kismet's director, had already
gone abroad to do Lust for Life [1956].

Astaire, who was to play the male lead, wanted to
co-star with Audrey Hepburn, a Paramount contractee, who
in turn wanted very much to dance with Astaire.   (At the
project's gestation stage Edens saw Carol Haney and then
Cyd Charisse in the role.)   But Paramount would not hear
of loaning out their plum.   Also, the studio had recently
signed Astaire to a two-picture deal, and producer Robert
Emmett Dolan was even then on the lot preparing Papa's
Delicate Condition[1] for him.   After months of negotiations
the Edens subunit moved to Paramount and rechristened the
piece Funny Face after one of Gershwin's songs. [2]

Gersche's script, imbued with Donen touches, crosses
the stories of Cinderella and Galatea, setting them against
the milieux of high fashion, photography, and the countercul-
ture.   The foreground romance and transformation provide
sentiment; the backgrounds provide the fun.   (The only major
change from libretto to script was the relegation of the wedding from first-act finaletto to finale.)

Jo's ambivalent reaction to Dick's kiss, her timorous
confession of love, and their reunion are sweet moments indeed.   And her emergence from the gray curtains in a pink-
and-ivory sheath, after wearing funereal smocks for two-
thirds of the film, on the mellifluous strains of " 'S Wonderful, " is one of the most rapturous transformation scenes in
the movies.

Fashioned after Harper's Bazaar's Carmel Snow, the
character of Maggie gleefully caricatures the career woman
and the la di da whirl of haute couture.   This steamroller
lets nothing stand in the way of her pursuit of "be-zazz, "
the epitome of chic.   The film also tickles fashion photography, an image profession wherein appearance belies reality.

Empathicalism twits Existentialism in particular and
the whole countercultural movement that coalesced in the 1950s.
For Flostre, read Sartre, the leading exponent of the philosophy that enshrined an individual's freedom.   Flostre's
stringy-haired and blue-jeaned adherents, the decade's beat-

niks, gather in a gloomy cellar, a send-up of the Café de
Floré, Sartre's well-publicized haunt, where everyone does
his or her thing.

Not only are these two spheres new to the film mu-
sical but so is Hepburn (Jo) who in 1957 was still a rara
avis. After bits in English comedies and melodramas she
bewitched New York as Colette's Gigi on stage in 1951 and
Los Angeles as the runaway princess in Roman Holiday
(William Wyler, 1953), which won her an Oscar as Best
Actress. Only Sabrina (Billy Wilder, 1954), War and Peace
(King Vidor, 1956), and another Broadway show, Giraudoux's
Ondine (1954), intervened between her auspicious American
film debut and Donen's musical. Hepburn was also one of
the extinct species of normal-chested screen women in the
1950s.

> Audrey, as Fred, makes my soul fly. She opens
> me up to beautiful feelings.

As we would expect, Donen gives Hepburn a sensational entrance. As the fashion horde invades the bookshop,
Dick forcefully pushes the wheeled ladder away, oblivious to
Jo huddled on one of its top rungs. Her scream slashes
through the pandemonium as the ladder sails clear across
the bookshelf toward us and crashes against the far wall.
And throughout the film Donen's camera seizes upon her
coltish movements, doelike eyes, and sudden grin.

Hepburn's childlike yet trained voice contributes a
great deal to the film's sentiment, and her patter has a
throaty charm and intelligence to it. Here is someone who
is actually paying attention to the words. And she dances
assuredly and gracefully.

Astaire's words and movements are entirely at Hepburn's disposal. As Dick he wants to show her off, and as
himself, he is quite clearly taken with her. They both seem
to be having such a good time that their "empatico" transcends the slight book and the May/December romance, a
formula that becomes an irritating factor in Hepburn's next
film, Love in the Afternoon (Billy Wilder, 1957), in which
she played opposite a fifty-six-year-old Gary Cooper.

In addition to the bewitching Hepburn and the debonair
Astaire, there's the vivacious Kay Thompson as Maggie, a
handywoman on MGM musicals, towering nightclub performer,

and author of <u>Eloise</u> (1955). From her ominous entrance to
her razzing exit, she is outrageous, incorrigible, nonstop, but
thoroughly captivating, and lets go with the best lines in the
show.

The high jinks of slick haute-couture still photography,
rendered even more brilliant by VistaVision, a Paramount
process that affords enormous high-contrast clarity, are the
film's vocabulary, appropriately so. <u>Funny Face</u>'s look is
ravishing and unique. Photographer Ray June, art directors
Hal Pereira and George W. Davis, visual consultant Richard
Avedon, special-effects man John P. Fulton, and photography-
enthusiast Donen had a field day.

For example, in the ingeniously thematic and engaging
credit sequence--to become a Donen trademark--the director
sets Avedon's designs, resembling typographic and art lay-
outs of fashion glossies, dancing to Astaire's flawless phrasing of the title tune.

> Yes, I think titles should be thematic. I also look
> for something entertaining. I also want my titles
> to be separate. I want them to be able to stand
> on their own. I don't much like titles that are in-
> volved in the plot of the picture--superimposed
> over an action or going on during dialogue.

Photographing the collection results in another ravishing musical montage cast in the idiom of photography. Shots
of Jo, moving against Parisian landmarks in clothes by
Givenchy, are frozen, matted, negatively printed, or flashed
in the four separations of still color photography. It is Donen's most famous montage, and, besides making us privy
to a photographic session, forces Jo and Dick's relationship
to a critical point while winking at both it and the image professions.

> To get around the obvious loss in photographic qual-
> ity of the freezes, I put a two-way mirror over the
> camera lens. The camera photographed through
> the mirror while Avedon had his still camera fo-
> cused on the mirror. On signal, he clicked his
> shutter. The lab matched Avedon's still photograph
> with the frame of the film.... Avedon's methods
> and effects inspired the sequence--the way he builds
> a scene and sets a mood for a model, the move-
> ment he insists upon in his pictures. His subjects

aren't posed; they're caught in the middle of a
movement. [3]

Maggie's pop-art offices and the impressionistic French
locations continue this look of haute-couture photography.
Breaking the Hollywood law that demands photographing on
sunny days in sharp focus, many scenes were shot under
gray, drizzly skies and with diffused lighting.

Color is fundamental to fashion photography, and
therefore to Funny Face, where, besides being both the chief
carrier of movement within and between shots and a cutting
principle, it is choreographed as well. Color travels on
music, as in the first sequence, when a black door, occupying full frame, is pushed open and a gray figure moves toward an ivory wall against a roll of drums, and pink soon
invades the premises on a relentless rhythm. This choreography of colors, which fulfills the promise of Rain, makes
the film look pretty and flow gracefully.

The Musical Sequences

Composer Edens and lyricist Gershe's "Think Pink!,"
"Bonjour, Paree!," and "On How to be Lovely" and Edens's
"Marche Funebre," with French lyrics by Lela Simone, al-
loyed the score of Gershwin gold. With Ira Gershwin's per-
mission Edens and Gershe also rewrote the introduction and
tampered with the second refrain of "How Long Has This
Been Going On?," modified the intros to "Funny Face" and
"Let's Kiss and Make Up," and inserted "Clap Yo' Hands"
patter to strengthen the integration of the songs from previous
Gershwin shows and update the lyrics. [4]

"Think Pink!": Maggie's literal and metaphorical light
from a pink matchbox, her alliterative ultimatum, "banish the
black, burn the blue, bury the beige," and her flinging a bolt
of pink cloth, like Zeus his thunderbolt, toward an advancing
camera; the splash of pastel in a basic gray, white, and
black office; and the contrasting prop and camera movements
--all are like a rush.

The subsequent montage of photos in the revamped
Quality magazine of models wearing pink clothes or using
pink products lambasts the fashion industry's absolutizing in-
stinct. Back in the offices seven painters put the final pink
touches to the semicircle of office doors from which six pink-

suited secretaries emerge just before the high priestess of
style--in charcoal gray!--bolts the center door and stalks up
to a timidly retreating camera while still tossing off impera-
tives.

"How Long Has This Been Going On?": During this
revelation of Jo's embryonic state and crystallization of the
film's conflict, Donen's psychologically accurate construction
and mise-en-scène, built around a single prop, are exquisite.

Thousands of books are scattered everywhere. A
straw hat draped in seductive lemon, orange, and lime chiffon, a prop accidentally left behind, contrasts sharply with
her somber salt-and-pepper smock; the hat's full horizontal
shape, with her skinny vertical figure. And, too, the photographer has just kissed her. The invasion of her fortifications
--the thematically titled "Embryo Concepts" shop, her clothes,
and her heart--has just been completed. Donen's ever-
tightening camera imprisons Jo, behind the ladder's rungs,
even more. The camera, by staying close to her every
move, whether holding a pole for support or peering in an
oval mirror (a self-confrontation emblem), seem to be pinning her down. Donen's cut to an extreme high-angle overview expands the room. The values are higher. And Jo
runs with the hat as if it were a kite. Then, with feet
planted solidly apart, she waves the hat, puts it on again,
and whirlingly pirouettes around and around in a moment of
discreet abandon, accentuated by the hat's streamers. The
space's enlargement, the brightening of the hues, and the
dance movements are correlatives of her expanding soul.
Donen's slow diagonal dolly down closes the space as she
discards the hat and, quite realistically, the lyric. The
camera then dollies up and out as the forlorn figure tosses
the hat on the sofa, illuminated by a pool of light, and climbs
the ladder to replace the books--arriving back where she
started but knowing the place for the first time. Throughout,
Hepburn's delivery, ever looking above and to the right of
the camera, is a stance indicative of awakening, fear, and
beseeching.

"Funny Face":

> He was a photographer. Why not have him develop
> a picture of her face, which he's trying to promote
> for the magazine, during this lovely song? There
> are only two possibilities in the darkroom--a red
> or yellow light. Every photographer knows that at

Funny Face: The imaginative conceit of developing a picture.
Copyright: Paramount.

that time it would have been a yellow one.   But
yellow didn't look very attractive, so we made it
red.

Similarly, Eugene Loring's dance arises ever so naturally from the situation.   With three hand taps on the de-
veloper bins and a tug on the exposing light string, delight

spreads to Dick's limbs.   He goes to the back shelf in search
of more solution, but really to keep his cool.   Jo follows too
close for comfort.   When he turns around, they almost bump
into each other.   To hell with coolness, and his arms slip
around her waist and they are off fox-trotting and jitterbugging in the ironically confined space.

At the encore's finish Donen pins Jo's real face in a
tight closeup against white photography paper, highlighted by
the bright beam of the enlarging camera that Dick throws
upon her.   White, black, and flesh clash with the previous
crimson.

"Bonjour, Paree!":   This sweet and comic montage is
a valentine to Paris and collaborative friendship and a poke
at the pseudosophistication of the three principals.   It also
joshes both the Cinerama triple-screen travelogs and the
travelog sequences that invariably cropped up in wide-screen
dramatic features, which were a way to fill the frame.

The allegretto first movement, against a steady, anticipatory tomptarrah of drums segueing into a rousing march,
takes the trio from TWA-ing over La Guardia to shooing the
ciceroni away at Orly and hurrying into separate cabs that
will take them to their respective hotels.

The andante second section describes their separate
but similar paths, one at a time and then together in a triple
split screen.   Exiting a cab on the Champs Elysées, Dick
slowly turns around, all eyes, against a silent track.   A musical phrase starts up and stops three times.   The orchestration here is remarkable.   With a straw hat cocked over his
right eye Chevalier-like, he takes a half-step backward,
jumps slightly forward, and struts down the boulevard on the
blaring, forthright tune.   It is one of Astaire's most exhilarating moments.   Meanwhile Maggie points an umbrella, an
extension of her pontifical index finger, at the shops on the
Rue de la Paix.   The extraneous presence of French tour
guides, with American accents no less, who back Maggie at
the Place de Vendôme, momentarily breaks the spell.   Here,
even more than the "Think Pink!" painters, the male line
seems a nod to Thompson's club act.   Finally, there's Jo,
scrutinizing the beatnik-strewn Montmartre alley.

The allegretto third part shuffles the three principals
within a postcard collage of famous sites.

Funny Face: The arm-in-arm strutting of Kay Thompson,
Fred Astaire, and Audrey Hepburn in "Bonjour, Paree!"
Copyright: Paramount.

The largo fourth movement comprises a series of
languid ninety-degree panoramic pans of the city atop the
Arc de Triômphe, the Grand Palais, and Notre Dame, as
the trio wistfully harmonize, "There's something missing I
know. " In a triple split screen they conclude, "There's
still one place I've gotta go. "

The final allegro gets the adrenalin going as we tilt
up the Eiffel Tower, where the trio bump into each other in
the elevator.   Here Dick brings their overlapping recrimina-
tions, accompanied by rhythmic circling around each other,
to a halt: "Let's all let our hair down. " Strutting arm-in-
arm off the elevator, they admit "We're strictly tourists. "

"Cellar Dance/Basal Metabolism": La belle intellec-
tuelle and a pair of basement beatniks engage in an "inter-
pretive" dance full of weird, arhythmic, and angular contor-
tions and extensions, approximating basal metabolism: "The
turnover of energy in a fasting and resting organism using
energy solely to maintain vital cellular activity, respiration

and circulation as measured by the basal metabolic rate."[5]
Against a slow, syncopated, atonal instrumental, "How Long
Has This Been Going On?" they segue into a cacophonous
but briskly paced "Funny Face," reminiscent of the belabored
style of Varèse.   It is a dig at the <u>danse modèrne</u> associated
with the intellectual avant-garde.   The figures are barely
visible at times in the murky milieu where garish blues,
limes, and reds provide color rather than illumination.

The scene, eons apart from "the stone age" in which
Dick lives, assails the kind of dance, ambience, and clothes
associated with Astaire.   Donen here plays on audience expectation.   This new mode of expression puzzles and threatens
Dick, even makes him feel older, as the cutaways to him
register.   He will counter the challenge in his solo "Let's
Kiss and Make Up," the next musical passage, and transcend
it in the pas de deux "He Loves and She Loves."

"Let's Kiss and Make Up":   This example of the art
of courtship from a bygone era is set in a lamplighted court-
yard before Jo's second-story balcony.   In a variation of
"When You're in Love"'s mise-en-scène, Dick, proper in a
tie and gray suit, perches on a tree's limb across from Jo.
After delivering verses and violets, he jumps below, where
a Citroën hauling a cow in a cartback inspires his bullfight
metaphor.   The camera's horizontal arcs accentuate Dick's
wide movements; its low angle picks up his high leaps.   The
metaphor, however, is abruptly abandoned when the umbrella
becomes such items of sports equipment as a baseball bat or
golf club, and Dick various sportsmen.   Its tenuous link with
the dance's premise and its lack of shape keep the number
from five stars.

"He Loves and She Loves":   The soft focus and the
early morning's foggy light; the country-churchyard setting
in Chantilly; Jo's short bridal gown, net veil, and lily-of-the-
valley bouquet; and Dick's cardigan, which perfectly matches
the azure heavens, add up to a Corot-inspired fairy tale.

Their pirouettes on a buttercup-flecked sward and onto
a raft that gently floats across the rivulet to the other side
is just as fantastic.   A dolly out to a high-angle overview of
the couple walking away from us under a row of arching trees
with doves that glide into frame and swans that swim out of
frame is the finishing touch.

"On How to Be Lovely":   In mock fashion Maggie ad-

Funny Face: Audrey Hepburn at the Opera House in Donen's famous fashion montage.   Copyright: Paramount.

vises Jo on handling interviews.   The tablecloth-aprons and napkin-babushkas, the scat puncturing the round in which Jo repeats Maggie's words and apes her caricatured poses, and their gloating bows turn them into a pair of cleaning women unable to resist the lure of the constructed set in Duval's showroom.

"Clap Yo' Hands": As the Barkers, spiritual singers
from Tallahassee, Dick and Maggie are asked to perform.
Their rendition is Bible-belt fundamental: thick southern
drawls, hallelujahs galore, and hand jiving. In a rousing
moment Maggie dauntlessly shuffles up to the camera while
vandyked Dick kicks the back of his guitar with his right
heel and burlesques the earlier "metabolism" dance by hurling himself on the floor and cutting endless circles.

" 'S Wonderful": The finale mise-en-scène reprises
that of "He Loves and She Loves, " though now the raft floats
away under a leafy canopy on lines that summarize the plot:
"You've made my life so glamorous/You can't blame me for
feeling amorous. " Hepburn's exit, just as her entrance, " 's
marvelous. "

Save for some East Coast critics who rapped the book,
Funny Face was warmly received. Vogue, by the way, gave
the movie a rave. The Academy nominated the film in four
categories: Best Original Screenplay, Photography, Art
Direction-Set Decoration, and Costume Design. It was chosen as one of the four official American entries at Cannes.

Audience response was good, though not overwhelming.
The film's charm has proved ageless, and the admiration for
its technical originality has deepened.

> I was critized harshly for Funny Face by Sight and
> Sound. 6 They told me I was an anti-intellectual.
> Why shouldn't intellectuals be teased as much as
> anybody else?.... I think the picture is a little
> sticky at times, but quite touching. It has wonder-
> ful Gershwin music. It has no overextended num-
> bers ... It wasn't expensive to make [about $3-
> million].

A good deal of development marked Donen's first assignment away from the womb and, as a matter of fact, this
entire loanout stage. First and foremost, he had found Hepburn, a woman who elicited warm and loving feelings from
him, which he conveyed in his direction of her. The film's
romantic sentiment, consequently, was deeper than that in
Seven Brides, yet not so deep as to preclude a spoofing edge.
The film's look and design came even closer than Rain's in
expressing thematic values. The bravura use of credits design, locations, color photography, and optical effects helped

particularly in this regard.   The conception, staging, and
transcription of all the numbers were intoxicatingly fresh.
And throughout the film color danced to tell a story.

THE PAJAMA GAME (1957)

Since pajamas had become the most fashionable attire
along the Rialto in May 1954, and continued to be so for the
next two and a half years, Warner Brothers bought the line.

> While preparing Funny Face, I received a letter
> saying: Dear Stanley, we want to make a film of
> The Pajama Game.   Would you like to direct it?
> Yours sincerely, George Abbott....   The question
> of adaptation bothered me.   I don't particularly en-
> joy taking a hit show and making it into a film be-
> cause I'm locked into things that are good and into
> trying to figure out how to put that on screen with-
> out changing it drastically from what is already
> successful.   But then, the Gershwin score was at
> stake.

So the Culver City loanout, on a twenty-six-week service guarantee, trekked to Burbank to work on his first adaptation and renew his acquaintance with Broadway's silver fox,
George Abbott, who would allow him to put into practice the
concept of one leader in a collaboration.

> During rehearsals I asked George, who had directed
> the show on Broadway, to come by and tell me and
> the cast how this or that was staged.   I said it
> would save time.   He asked if I would just work it
> out and let him look at it.   Since I felt he was em-
> barrassed, I suggested he put his name on the mo-
> vie as co-director.   He really didn't think it right
> because he was doing only a little bit of direction.
> What was really happening, he said, was that I was
> producing the picture almost entirely on my own.
> So if I wanted to put his name on as co-director,
> then he would insist that my name appear as co-
> producer.   As a result we filmed it in less than
> six weeks.

Abbott helped Richard Bissell chisel the libretto from
the latter's autobiographical novel $7\frac{1}{2}$¢.[1]   (Bissell had at one
time been a factory super in Dubuque.)   Both men worked

with Donen on the screen adaptation, which respects the distinct qualities of the film medium.

The adaptation plays faster than the footlight version. It must, since a script's running time is an hour less than a play's. The precredit sequence of Sid's leap from a boxcar inching its way through town, followed by his entrance into the factory, replaced the play's initial scene of Hinesie in stagey master-of-ceremonies style introducing the factory workers and the conflict of labor versus management. This cinematic maneuver establishes the springtly pace while shedding the corny self-consciousness of the play's opener, which would have appeared even more so on the screen. The film text shrewdly excludes all Hinesie's emcee bits. All three picnic scenes (a wooden path on the way to the picnic, the grounds themselves, and the same path on the way back from the picnic) are collapsed into one. This eliminates the need for Prez's seductions of Gladys at the start and Mae at the end, which were there more to provide the necessary time for set changes than for characterization. Censorship considerations, which also had something to do with the deletion of Prez's horniness, homogenizes and naturally abbreviates the sexy kitchen scene in which Babe takes off her twenty-dollar dress to avoid grease spots. The factory gossip between the lovers' two romantic duets is also excised--the players need no breather in film. And throughout Donen overlaps dialogue, a new time-saving device for him. As a matter of fact, the movie's breakneck pace, from the studio logo supered on the boxcar to the cutting on Hasler's figure while he continues his rally palaver at the pajama party--a technique that Donen will refine in Two for the Road and Movie Movie--leaves us somewhat dazed.

The adaptation contains a considerable amount of realism not found in the original, since theatrical stylization and convention would have looked phony. As mentioned previously, gone are Hinesie's common-man routines. A convertible and Babe's front porch replace the factory's exterior as the setting for "There Once Was a Man"--an up-in-two necessitated by a set change. Besides, this employer-employee relationship and the concomitant ugly gossip would make any sentiment on the factory grounds verboten. Poopsie yelling, "Hey, where'd 'ya get that hat?" to the onstage entertainers, and Mae popping out of the audience to scream her down-ground "Steam Heat," dispel the aura of a solid second-act opener. Babe reprises "Hey There" concretely planted in her bedroom and not through curtains of a window

frame at stage left, while the rest of the playing area is
darkened in preparation for the next set.   "$7\frac{1}{2}\cancel{c}$" abandons
the vague street near the park for an impromptu platform
in the factory's lot.   Additionally, the film retains more of
the novel's social significance than the play.

The charming evocation of a small Midwest factory
town and its citizenry through dialogue, manners, and lyrics
was the libretto's strong suit.   It is the scenario's, too.

Subject matter, yes--but also the ensemble playing
makes this one of the most democratic of all musicals.   Despite a humorous distance from them, we come to know and
care about nine characters.   The group within a frame is
surely another reason for Donen's blissful adaptation.

> I wanted the original cast to do it.   Doris Day,
> however, played the Janis Paige role.   Doris was
> wonderful: energetic and lovable.   It's the best
> thing she ever did.   I also liked Janis, who was
> something quite different.   She was made of iron
> in that part.   Had you been able to see her in a
> movie up close, she would have been so tough that
> you wouldn't have been able to love her, to think
> she was vulnerable....   I know nothing about Patti
> Page ever being considered for the lead or the
> Janis Paige-Frank Sinatra combination.

Day's portrayal is unfalteringly complex.   Her Babe
is robust and peppy, as her initial appearance indicates:
she takes determined, hurried steps, legs apart and arms
folded across her chest, with her smock's rolled-up sleeves,
her overly done lips, her peroxided duck's tail, and her talking over Sid and Mae.   But Babe was born "Catherine."
Day knows this well, displaying an insecure and susceptible
underside as she trembles with the apple on her head or re-
sponds with a soft, confused "I am?" when fired.   Donen's
sleight of hand reveals the quintessential Day.   This had
rarely dawned before: in Calamity Jane (David Butler, 1953)
and The Man Who Knew Too Much (Alfred Hitchcock, 1956),
perhaps, and parts of I'll See You in My Dreams (Michael
Curtiz, 1952), Young at Heart (Gordon Douglas, 1954), and
Love Me or Leave Me (Charles Vidor, 1955).   It was to be
even more rare afterward, when her enormous talent was
usually merchandised rather than directed.

John Raitt's Sid, on the other hand, does not translate

that well to celluloid.   To be sure, his perfectly pitched
baritone voice and strong good looks work, but not his dialogue delivery and movement, except in the one instance of
the character-capsule intro that Donen created for him.
Donen wrongly presumed that what Raitt did onstage would
work on screen.

As Hinesie, the pathologically jealous ex-vaudevillian
turned time-study man, Eddie Foy Jr.'s farcical pantomines,
such as gnashing his teeth at Gladys or getting his shirt cuff
stuck in his trousers' zipper, are worthy of a psychological
case study as well as a comedy textbook.   As the oversexed
Gladys, Carol Haney's croaky voice makes her lines even
more wry.   All her gestures, as when she plasters down
her close-cropped pixie with spit before entering the boss's
office or napping on a tabletop, are wonderfully droll.   Besides being a brilliant comic, MGM's former assistant dance
director is also one of the premier jazz dancers of all time.
Freed had encouraged her to accept the part in the show and
even arranged for a contract release.

Reta Shaw as the ever-proper Mabel--she always
wears a hat--is the factory's motherly matron.   Thelma
Pelish's fat, no-nonsense Mae foils Jack Straw's wiry, full-
of-beans Prez (Stanley Praeger created the role onstage).
The Breen Office suggested Prez be an amiable gay blade;
Donen insisted that his married status be retained.   A com-
promise was reached by making him a married man but also
an unsuccessful Don Juan.   WB contractee Barbara Nichols,
in place of Broadway's Rae Allen, is hot to trot as Poopsie.
And Ralph Dunn fulminates as old man Hasler; his purposeful
strides give only himself a sense of importance.

Donen's collaboration with the masterful photographer
Harry Stradling, art directors Malcolm Bert and Frank
Thompson, set decorator William Kuehl, and costumers
William and Jean Eckart results in yet another musical with
a striking countenance that enhances the piece's realism.

The teaser is the Dubuque location.   The browns, in-
digos, and grays of the factory walls and machinery are offset by naked light bulbs that dangle over the workers' heads,
fluorescent lighting, and bright neon signs deliberately dis-
torted to give off more light, and over 1,000 pairs of polka-
dot, striped, plaid, and solid pajamas of every hue in various
stages of manufacture.   (Lubin Weeker, manufacturers of
Weldon pajamas, supplied the equipment and the garments

for the set, which needed a total of 40,000 amperes to be
lighted.) The sun-bleached windows give a feeling of day-
time, summery heat and the oppressiveness of factory work.
Sid's 1910 office, with its golden-oak desk, hat rack, and
striped awnings outside the two back windows, suggests middle America's conservative ways. The annual Independence
Day picnic, shot at Los Angeles's Hollenbeck Park, is a
carnival of blue skies, vest-pocket lake and jeans, green
grass and trees, rainbow pennants, white shirts, and yellow
sunshine. Babe's kitchen and bedroom, which sport every
style of furnishings, are made green or red by the railroad
semaphore outside the windows. Eagle Hall, with its gray
curtains and smoke-filled air, its black-and-white blowups
of two officials of the Associated Garment Workers and its
tritely decorative American flag bunting, is as monotonous as
such a place would be. Hernando's, a low riverfront dive
with Chinese Gothic booths and lanterns, paper flowers, neon
beer signs, and a bar far back in the gloom, is rendered
bleary and boozy by the use of filters. Donen thus neatly
satirizes those intimate bistros that are dimlit to the point
of darkness. Strings of naked electric bulbs, about 800 of
1,500 watts each, outline the rally platform provided by the
flatbed of a truck. And not a single studio set contains a
painted flat.

The street clothes for the players and the repetition
of them--no star wardrobes here--the garish haircolors and
hairdos, the harshly made-up faces and less-than-Greek figures, all in keeping with the characters' blue-collar status,
are also responsible for the musical's unusual and realistic
look.

The Musical Sequences

Richard Adler and Jerry Ross together wrote the exceptional lyrics and music. Were it not for Ross's untimely
death in 1955 at the age of twenty-nine, shortly after their
other major collaboration, Damn Yankees, opened, they perhaps would have inherited the Kern-Bolton-Wodehouse, Cole
Porter, Rodgers and Hart, and Frank Loesser mantles.
(Loesser, in fact, was originally asked to write the score,
but he recommended his protégés Adler and Ross instead.)
Each number arises from an everyday situation, each is a
different kind of song, which makes for a down-to-earth,
contextual, and richly versatile score. Adler penned a slow
ballad for the movie that went unused: "The Man Who In-
vented Love. "

Five numbers and three reprises were snipped from the original show. "A New Town Is a Blue Town," Sid's moody ballad about his nostalgia for Chicago's State Street and the difficulty of being accepted in his new job, was sung after his run-in with the help and reprised after a reprimand by the boss. Prez was given the mambo "Her Is" to seduce Gladys and Mae at the picnic. "Think of the Time I Save" was Hinesie's recitative description of his job before Max discloses the sabotage. The points of these three character songs were covered by dialogue and/or action, thereby making their inclusion extraneous. There was enough picnic detail, cinematically handled at that, also to do without "Sleeptite," Babe and her co-workers' praise for the factory during the holiday. "I'll Never Be Jealous Again Ballet" was sotted Hinesie's nightmare of married life with Gladys that occurred after he finds her with Sid at the nitery. In their bedroom Gladys scampers with an assortment of lovers while Hinesie renews his "I would trust her" theme. Hinesie then reneges and chases Gladys with a large knife while guardian angel Mabel vainly tries to dissuade him. Donen, objecting to the extended ballet that interrupted the action, replaced it with a frisson sequence. Since no first act curtain was needed, Sid's reprise of "Hey There" after he fires Babe was deleted. And the lovers' reprise of "There Once Was a Man" at the rally's end was also cut, since the film medium made the interval needed to change sets, which was the reprise's function, unnecessary.

> We all talked about what numbers should be cut. There were George, Hal Prince, Bob Griffith [two of the show's producers], and Dick Adler around.

Besides being an occasion for renewing acquaintances, the film cemented the friendship between Donen and Bob Fosse, who, along with his assistant Zoya Leporska, turns in a top-notch job. Jerome Robbins, unable to choreograph, had suggested Fosse for the show, which launched his choreographic career.

> Fosse's choreography is as physical as Kelly's but not filled with as much athletics or gymnastics. [It is also abstract, with its isolation and exaggeration of dance and corresponding body movements, as well as its sectional splintering of the ensemble.]

"The Pajama Game": Hinesie's brief announcement of

the story's setting is garnished by an eccentric rubber-leg
step suggesting his official position as foot-counting-out-time-
study man.   His report strings together a color-and-beat-cut
montage of the manufacturing process, over which credits
are supered.   This is the next entry in Donen's list of inventive titles design.   The song's finale reprise features the
cast in a Sleeptite Pajama parade at Hernando's to celebrate
the raise.

"Racing with the Clock": Gladys has just accompanied
the new super into his office, and Hinesie must compensate
for his insecurity by turning tyrant.   (Back at the Majestic
knives were an outlet.) His stamping foot inaugurates the
novelty song with repetitive lyrics and melody and a staccato
rhythm approximating the tedium, tension, and perpetual motion of the sewing machines and the workers stuck to them.
The rapid cutting to individual seamstresses, shipping clerks
on a forklift truck, workers washing up in the lavatory, and
the camera's audacious horizontal scurry across vertical rows
of machines with apprentices running up and down the aisles,
underscore the feverish atmosphere.

In a later reprise Donen's undercranked camera de-
personalizes the laborers by reducing them to automatons.
Where they leave off and the machines begin is indistinguishable.

"I'm Not at All in Love": The blue aprons' taunting
Babe about her infatuation with Sid is a fine way to release
some steam during a lunch break.   Babe's retaliation begins
with a nifty conversational put-down of her co-workers, which
turns into a waltz whose romantic melody ironically ratifies
their insinuations even while the lyrics deny them.   Delicious
bits of business flavor the quandary: Babe munches an apple
or rests on a garment truck, which the girls wheel from time
to time; when they do, Babe is startled as the cart moves--
a remarkably naturalistic detail--or holds on for dear life
with the apple in her mouth as the cart sails away from the
girls.   Just as the vehicle reaches the elevator, which opens
to emit Sid, Babe is propelled off the cart and into his arms.
Her apology mixes with a piece of fruit.   The business was
lifted from the stage version, but Donen's smart camerawork
and cutting enhance the incident's danger and humor and,
above all, strengthen our identification.

"I'll Never Be Jealous Again": At workday's end
Mabel entices Hinesie into a therapy session to cure his

The Pajama Game: Doris Day's "I'm Not At All in Love."
Copyright: Warner Bros.

jealousy.   This round, with the doctor concocting various
examples of Gladys in indelicate situations (the lyrics were
whitewashed) and the patient responding to them, swipes at
the then-burgeoning, but still suspect, field of psychiatry.

The number builds to a soft-shoe, befitting their age
and Hinesie's two-a-day heritage, which the camera follows
by crossing or going up and down the aisles.

Toward the film's close Hinesie's stalking of Gladys
with a knife in the chiaroscuro-lit stockroom eerily punc-
tuated with dummies and hanging pajamas, is ironically choreographed to an instrumental version.   This is a cinematic
replacement for the show's ballet and a rehearsal for the
comic thrillers Charade and Arabesque.

"Hey There": Sid's various positions during the ballad,
his replays of the memo to himself on the dictaphone, which
he talks back to, sings counter to, and finally harmonizes

with, eloquently express his agitation over striking out with
Babe.

As in "When You're in Love" and "Once I Had a
Friend," Donen fashions the entire sequence in a fluid one-
shot take with the camera attentive on the other side of the
desk, then moving around to get closer as if in sympathy.
When Sid decides that he is "just too far gone to hear," the
camera resumes its original position and finally leaves him
by slowly dollying up and away and fading.   The fade turns
the lights out, which renders his state lonelier and sadder.

Babe's nighttime reprise occurs before her bedroom
mirror, which is on a bureau containing her personal history
(a cupie doll, an athletic cup, photos of her high school grad-
uation and her bowling pals, etc.).   These visual reflectors,
replacing the audial one in Sid's rendition, continue the conceit.

A pale green light from the train signal infiltrates the
room's blue cast, reinforcing her melancholy and echoing her
coolness to Sid in the previous scene.   Her throbbing fist,
which pounds the bed's brass footboard as she flails herself,
"You're acting cold to him," sends chills through us, as
does the tomato-red light from the signal, which slashes the
room, accentuating the sequence's tension and Babe's fire
underneath the ice.   And then, our hearts go out to her as
she moves to the side of the bed and lies down--a bit too
stiffly perhaps--and the lyrics are lost in sobs.   To preserve
the intricate combination of singing, recitative, and crying,
the number was shot as performed, that is, without a playback.   Day's sensitivity to lyric phrasing and ability to act
through song is truly extraordinary.

"Once a Year Day":

> Fosse and I talked about the number for what it
> was: outdoors, full of sunlight and good times, a
> contrast to the factory dross.   During the restag-
> ing, he invited me to make any suggestions that I
> might have.   Then we took the eighty boys and
> girls, in addition to the leads, to the park, where
> we rehearsed and made changes that were helpful
> regarding the location and camera.   We spent a
> full week there.

The starting point of Fosse's dance is the situation of

workers enjoying themselves at a picnic.   The inspiration of
the movements comes from what such people would do in the
situation, such as running up and down hillocks or playing
games like leapfrog.   These movements are then culled,
stylized and placed in a continuity.   In such ensemble dances,
Fosse invariably divides the group into small units.

Donen assembles the number from innumerable transpatial cuts of these units on the polka's slaphappy beats.
Donen's favorite romantic icon, Sid and Babe under a lake-
side tree, ignites the blast, which, after nods to every cast
member, focuses on Gladys.   Buzz Miller from the show and
Kenneth LeRoy, who replaced Broadway's Peter Gennaro, ac-
company the great Haney in her terpsichorean revel.   Fosse,
like Donen, loves movement replication.

"Small Talk":   In a conversational romantic duet Sid's
smooth melodic line about making love is thwarted by Babe's
syncopated chatter about the newspaper headlines.   The black,
white, and gray kitchen scheme, warmed by the gold ersatz
Tiffany lamp above the table and a lighted match, the rain
softly falling on the background panes, and Donen's tight
camera ensure the intimate mood.   The movement is all
parry and thrust until Sid wraps her in his arms to cuddle
in a Morris chair.

"There Once Was a Man":   Caribbean calypso weds
western hillbilly for Sid and Babe's explosion of love.   The
one-upmanship conceit, the grotesque pantomimes of history's
torrid romances and humankind's insatiable desires, which
each precipitately race through since each loves the other
more, and the tracking and dollying camera gives the passage
an apocalyptic edge.

"Steam Heat":   This amateur entertainment by Gladys
and a couple of the cutting-room boys at the meeting is a
symbol of the workers' anger.   The slogan's sound effects,
the grating melody, and the angular movements of the skimpy
tuxes and Fossesque derbies reduce the trio to pipes full of
red-hot energy.

"Hernando's Hideaway":   As befitting the situation's
secrecy (in the file room Gladys describes in tangoese the
local hangout to Sid), Donen's camera closes down the space
by remaining tight on his players, thereby catching Gladys's
look over her shoulders for the omnipresent Hinesie before
beginning.   In an ingenious transition, the frame goes black

and silent and is eventually pierced by a series of matches'
nimbi and sounds detailing the Hideaway.   Then the track
comes up, the lights turn on, and the space is opened by
Donen's loose camera, all of which plant us smack in the
middle of a seedy joint throbbing with good times.   The
stagey facing-front arrangement of the chorus line when the
frame comes to life, the only time that there exists a sense
of the proscenium arch in Donen's musical and comedy adaptations, should have been rethought for the screen.

"$7\frac{1}{2}$ ¢": To inaugurate the strike the workers huddle
around speakers Prez and Babe, raise them on high and
carry them on their shoulders, flash placards, and march
in place and around the platform while litanizing the effects
of the raise.   The march's lyrics jab at American consum-
erism.

         The film received excellent notices.   Most critics
felt that the screen version enhanced the original--an excep-
tion to the stage-to-screen rule.   On the basis of this film
Godard proclaimed Donen the master of the movie musical.[2]
The film, however, was only a moderate financial success.
Musicals were just not turning people on in the late '50s.

         I think it's full of energy, fun, and good dancing.
         Even though George allowed me the control, I still
         didn't get a great sense of personal accomplishment
         since I didn't feel as though I was making a film.
         I felt I was remaking or transferring something.

         Nevertheless, with The Pajama Game and his next
musical, Damn Yankees, Donen gave the industry a model
of stage musical-to-screen adaptation that included utilizing
practically the entire original cast, substituting, when necessary, a musical player, deleting a good forty-five minutes
of the playing time, cinematically rethinking the piece, and
exploiting the genre's lyricism, energy, and magic.

         That The Pajama Game and Damn Yankees did not go
through the financial roof was probably why the prophet went
unhonored in his own country.   Instead, the music men, who
by the mid-'50s had turned almost exclusively to the presold
Broadway hit as source material to insure their investment,
took a sacrosanct attitude that made the musical into an event.
Box-office stars were cast rather than singers and dancers.
"Significant" directors who did not really understand or

The Pajama Game: Doris Day's "7½¢." Copyright: Warner Bros.

appreciate the form's expressionism were assigned. The two-and-a-half-hour running time of the original was preserved, as were the theatrical procedures of nine shows a week, reserved seats, and souvenir booklets.

The adaptation syndrome was, of course, a nail in the coffin of the musical. The originals, remember, were largely responsible for the genre's period of grace, quite

simply because the film medium was there at the very moment of the piece's conception.   The breakup of the studio
system also played a large part in the musical's decline.
(Due to its myriad elements that are not so much used as
paraded, the musical, more than any other genre, needs the
community of talents that the studios fostered.)   Worldwide
film distribution following World War II, which required either
lip-sync dubbing or subtitles, both approaches inimicable to
musical sequences, also contributed to the musical slump in
the mid-'50s, as did the TV variety show and the prolifera-
tion of supper clubs.   The country's demythological bent, the
change in popular music, rock concerts, and filmed documents
of these "happenings," only aggravated the situation in the
next decade.

KISS THEM FOR ME (1957)

When distinguished Warner Bros. producer Jerry Wald
sought rights to Frederic Wakeman's best-selling first novel,
Shore Leave (1944), he discovered that Luther Davis was busy
adapting the work to the stage under the title Kiss Them for
Me.   More than a decade later Wald, now headquartered at
Fox, still thought it would make a fine movie and suggested
it to Cary Grant, who was working for him on An Affair to
Remember (Leo McCarey, 1957).   Rising Fox contractee
Jayne Mansfield was eager to work with Grant, and there was
a part for her.

> Grant requested me as director.   I have no idea
> why.   I never met him.   I was very flattered.
> [Had the work's similarity of situation to Donen's
> service musicals--a trio on leave--influenced Grant's
> choice?]   Then I read the script, which I detested.
> Wald asked me to fix it up.   I consented to do it
> only if he would pay Metro for the rest of my time.
> I still had a year and a half or two left on my
> Metro contract.   I worked on the film for a year.
> I feel the same way about adapting a stage comedy
> as I do a stage musical.

John Moses and Mark Hanna produced the comedy-
drama, which opened on Broadway in March 1945.   Herman
Shumlin directed Richard Widmark as Crew, Jayne Cotter
(later Meadows) as Gwynneth, and Judy Holliday as Alice.
New York Times critic Lewis Nichols thought that the play's
potential was never realized.   In particular, he found the

last act anticlimactic.[1] The play folded in June after 111
performances. The war had ended and war stories became
unpopular with the public. As a matter of fact, the play's
very opening was untimely since, with Guadalcanal, the Coral
Sea, and Midway already in their pockets, the Allies' future
looked bright.

To remount the piece in 1957 was not too swift either.
But then Kiss Them for Me had an undertow. And this type
of comedy--dark comedy as it came to be called from the
works of Howard Hawks, Joseph Mankiewicz, Billy Wilder,
and, to a certain extent, George Cukor--was chichi in the
'50s. Considered realistic and therefore adult, dark comedy
proved to be the only oasis in the decade's comedy desert.
Too, Kiss Them for Me had lineage, having been both a novel
and a play. Lineage was particularly revered in the '50s in
all genres, since it endowed the property with a presold aura.

Though Julius Epstein, of Casablanca fame (Michael
Curtiz, 1943), and Donen considerably open up the play's
space, which comprised the suite's living room in Acts I and
III and the hospital solarium in Act II, the problem of setting
--and situation--replication, which causes a visual dreariness
and sluggish pace, had not been licked. The Fairmont's two
interminable parties occupy most of the film's running time,
while most of the interim, spent carousing at two bars, is
pretty much a case of out of the pan and into the fire.

But the script's in hotter water than that. Donen's
romantic, farcical, and musketeerish graftings only somewhat
alleviate Davis-Epstein's brooding cynicism. Crew, less
nasty though as moody and disgusted as ever, and Gwynn,
whose role is expanded, spend much more time together. To
the already large cast of supports, who are practically all
retained along with their stagey entrances, are added a few
more comics such as the two drunken Marine entertainers at
the Onyx Bar, who incidentally provide Donen with an excuse
for a number. And with camaraderie seeping through where-
ever possible, our servicemen emerge as a cross between
Town's frolicsome gobs and Weather's disillusioned ex-GIs.
Even the upbeat wrapup--previously, hospital tests had
grounded the emotionally unstable Crew and they had Mississip'
for an oversized spleen--smacks of Weather, where another
enemy attack on one of their own, albeit on a much smaller
scale, rejuvenates and reunites the men. Diluted, too, is
the snipe at the paper navy's bureaucracy and ineffectiveness
as well as war's sting, especially due to the abbreviation of

Mississip's part.   Yet the acrid satire of war profiteering
(Mac's character is revamped from a law student awaiting his
wife to a policito) and of civilian idolatry of military heroics
(honed by the night-on-the-town sequence) remains intact.
Countering Donen's lightly comic sensibility with Davis-
Epstein's much darker one results in an inconsistent tone.

And the dialogue, of which there is plenty, is only
ho-hum amusing and often spills over into rhetoric.   This is
unusual in the work of Donen, who is essentially a social observer rather than evaluator.

For Donen, Grant is Astaire in the comedic key (and
another reason he took the job).   His dash, for example, into
the barracks to pack his gear all the while rapidly and mellif-
luously informing his pals about the leave, is visual and verbal choreography.

> He's funny, charming, nice to see, and never offen-
> sive.   He doesn't want to let out what's inside,   so
> you get this polished veneer.

Would that their curtain raiser--they will make four
films together--were memorable.   Besides the script's identity crisis, fifty-ish Grant, as the dashing war pilot Crew,
is a bit too gray.   (And surrounding him mostly with middle-
aged men does not minimize this incongruity.)   His performance, nonetheless, has breadth.   His introduction is also notable.   By the use of war footage he is shown being lifted from
a raft onto a sub's deck.   His demeanor is pained and unut-
terably weary--he has just eluded several Japanese Zeros.
Yet his parched lips, at great personal suffering, form the
query: "Are there any women aboard?"

Mansfield was in 1957 one of the top ten stars of
tomorrow.   Even if an untimely auto accident had not cut
short this promise, it would not have been kept.   Her fourth
screen appearance (as Alice) is padded to her specifications:
the albino hair, a mouth full of capped teeth, and the fabled
41-18-35 contour--she even gets to close a door with her
butt and to disclose her bust size.   At best she comes off
as a cut-rate Monroe--she was groomed by Marilyn's studio
to keep the superstar in line--with breathy dumbisms prefixed
and suffixed by irritating squeals and underlined by equally irritating wiggles.   Donen's broad, vulgar, at times even contemptuous direction of her out-Tashlins Tashlin, eventuating
as it does in a shrill self-caricature.

She made fun of herself. Certainly I was aware of
Cary making fun of her in the movie. He gave her
those withering glances which she was not supposed
to see. How could you not? She was catastrophic
to the movie because in the play, the character had
a sort of gentle, sweet quality about her in spite of
her stupid side. Jayne was a stupid, unlikeable
person in the movie. But that's all she was capable of doing.

In the part of the deceptively distant model-mistress
Gwynn, Suzy Parker, one of Paris's top models, makes her
film debut in a major role. Fox hoped that this slim, tall
redhead with a perfect face would fit the glass slipper left
behind by Grace Kelly, but, alas, acting was beyond her.
Her reading is so monotoned, except for adjectival and ad-
verbial stresses, that it makes you repeat her every line in
your head the way it should sound. Her "excuse me for
speaking" toward the film's end, however, does draw the biggest laugh. But Donen and Grant are on to her from the very
beginning, when the camera holds on the actor's ardent advice
to her: "Don't say much, just be decorative." Much to no
one's surprise, Suzy's movie career was short-lived. Acting
can begin, but also end, with bone structure.

As Ray Walston plays the Waspy politico Mac, we can
see the wheels always spinning in his head. And Larry Blyden as Mississip' pulls off some bizarre gestures that hint at
war's traumatization.

Aside from the credits and some vintage songs ("Chat-
tanooga Choo-Choo," "You'll Never Know," "Pennies from
Heaven") on the track, the film, which commanded an expensive budget, does not attempt period recreation, and that goes
for the dialogue as well. The stingers and taxi driver are
as negligible in this regard as Alice's triangular butt ruffle.
But back in 1957 the early '40s would not have been considered period. Even the '20s of Love Me or Leave Me (Charles
Vidor, 1955) and Man of a Thousand Faces (Joseph Pevney,
1956) had a hard time applying for period status. Rain's period look, remember, was way ahead of nostalgia time.

The skillful credits consist of black-and-white photos
of soldiers kissing their loved ones upon leaving or returning
that form panels against a gray background, cut to the McGuire
Sisters warbling the rousing title tune of composer Lionel
Newman and lyricist Carroll Coates. The song and its rendi-

<u>Kiss Them for Me</u>: Donen's humourous mise-en-scêne of Cary Grant and Suzy Parker's first encounter: on the ground in a forest of legs. Copyright: Twentieth Century-Fox.

tion recall "Beer Barrel Polka" by those popular '40s choristers, the Andrews Sisters.

> I went through <u>Life</u> magazine, which had some incredible pictures of soldiers saying good-bye and hello. <u>Life</u> said I could use them but Fox was afraid to because they were real and we had to get clearance from the people pictured but we didn't know their names. So I staged an imitation of the <u>Life</u> photos. I also shot those stills.

Interspersed with the '50s sets of Walter M. Scott and Stuart A. Reiss from the designs of Lyle R. Wheeler and Maurice Ransford are some location scenes. As in <u>On the Town</u>, Donen could only whet his appetite. Only four days of location shooting were permitted him.

Yet, whether in the studio or on the streets, Donen's Cinemascope mise-en-scêne is arresting and humorous enough to warrant a look. Of course, he had <u>Seven Brides</u> and

Weather to his credit, but there the genre and stories worked
to his advantage. A landlocked service comedy is hardly the
stuff for the vast horizontal frame except when the imaginative
Donen is around. The opening film-within-a-film scene, in
which silhouetted Wallec speaks before a black-and-white documentary and a reverse image of the war footage tatoos the
audience's faces and uniforms, is a parody of Citizen Kane's
projection sequence. The Onyx Bar, with its tripartite stage
and dancing and table areas, lighted by a series of white baby
ceiling spots, is made romantically misty by smoke and Milton Krasna's filters. The jeep flagging down the plane during
takeoff, besides distributing space beautifully, is an inventive
visual joke, as is Crew and Gwynn's sitting on the floor before a jukebox, a clearing in a jungle of standing and dancing
calves. In a hilarious telephone triptych, two hospital opera-
tors (center frame) get their lines crossed and Crew (far left),
though in-and-out calls are verboten to him, actually reaches
his party (Gwynn in far right) and she reaches hers (Crew)
but without ever realizing it. And by playing a love scene
on a bed horizontally in a tight medium shot with Crew and
Gwynn's heads occupying left frame and their torsos right
frame, Donen ribs the unwieldly screen shape. What's more,
Donen's mise-en-scène is never static, his editing never a
series of cuts between setups.

The critical response was as tepid as the audience's.

It never escaped its theatrical beginnings. It
doesn't smell of the life of the guys on a weekend
in San Francisco. I think Cary, Ray, and Larry
are good in it.

This strikeout stretched Donen as much as the two
hits (Funny Face and The Pajama Game) during this inning.
Grant, of course, entered the scene and in a sense, took
over from Astaire and Kelly as the crystallizer of Donen's
sense of grace, lightness, control, and energy. Furthermore,
the subject matter brought Donen for the first time into dark
waters, even though he resisted them. Thus Kiss emerges
as Donen's first comedy reflecting the decade's transition to
more realistic fare, unlike Love or Fagan, both throwbacks
to the family programmers that every major grinded out during its golden age. Too, Kiss Them for Me saw the start
of Donen's playing with the relationship of songs and background scoring with dialogue, visuals and cutting in comedy.
This also was derived from his experience with the musicals.

Third, the picture enabled him to fly the MGM coop--happily,
it might be added.   For at MGM Donen disliked being treated,
despite his attainments, as a second-class citizen.   During
the three reigns of his stay, which included that of the des-
potic Mayer, then Mayer-Schary's armed neutrality in 1948,
and finally that of Schary in 1951, when a hard-edged realism
was more welcomed than decorous escape, Donen rankled
under the bureaucratic setup in which the director answered
to the producer, who in turn answered to the head of production or head of the studio.   Donen also felt the rumblings of
the studio system's collapse.   By the mid-'50s, in fact, the
heavens once again had more stars than MGM; in 1956, when
Kiss was in production, MGM was operating at a $3-million
deficit.   There was a new way of making pictures; most of
Leo's other directors seemed or preferred not to know of it
and so eventually fell victims to the debacle.   But Donen, a
shrewd man, knew and got out.

4. PRODUCER-DIRECTOR, PHASE I: 1958-1960

INDISCREET (1958)

With the umbilical cord severed, the thirty-three year-old independent hustled as never before. He was now part of a changing Hollywood, which, in response to the antitrust decrees, the new income-tax laws, TV's threat, and the new audience, set up various production companies, sometimes a different one for each picture. Though the units used the studios for technical resources, financial backing, and/or distribution, the pictures they turned out veered from the outmoded studio formulae and styles, or at least tried to. These pictures generally were more individual, thematically bolder, and technically more virtuoso than formerly, since there were fewer hands in the stew (and that went for the censor's as well) and since the initiator of the project, whether star, director, writer, or producer, exercised the control. This type of filmmaking promised more money for the creator(s) through profit participation.

> I was an aspiring young film director trying to get on and having a terrible struggle. Norman Krasna was a friend of mine and had sent me a screenplay he had written, which I didn't like very much--The Billionaire. [1] I turned it down. I guess it's the seat of my pants that tells me what to accept or disregard. So he said: You know I wrote a flop play called Kind Sir. I thought it was a wonderful plot about an artful dodger who, in courting a woman, tells her that he is a married man, unable to get a divorce. If you like, he said, you can have it

for nothing because nobody else is going to buy it.
If you make it, pay me. So he and I got together
and wrote a screenplay, which I submitted to Cary
on the set of Kiss Them for Me. Cary thought it
was a good idea. He would do it only if I could
get Ingrid Bergman, whom I also wanted. Ingrid
was engaged in a Paris theater and had a commitment for a film to be made in Taiwan and England
[The Inn of the Sixth Happiness (Mark Robson,
1958)]. I sent her the script. She said yes. We
switched the location to London. We made the film
before she left for the Far East. Cary and I
formed "Grandon [Gran(t)-Don(en)] Productions. "
A deal was struck with Warner Brothers, who had
an interest in the Associated British Elstree Group
where we filmed, to distribute. . . . I turned producer because I wanted to make a picture and feel
I was doing it myself. It might be ego. I had an
impulse to do more, to contribute more to a film
than I ever had. I guess it comes down to wanting
to control the idea. . . . I never handle the advertising of my pictures. I try to handle the logog-
raphy, however, but I don't always succeed. . . . I
used the little filled-in square inside a circle as
the trademark of my company. It seemed a very
symmetrical and pleasing image. Everything is
right, balanced. The square is a perfect symbol;
so is the circle. They are perfection. And the
circle is contained. The world is contained.
Everything we know is contained. . . . The "associate" producer on this film and my others worked
on the physical side of the production. They were
the foreman on my pictures.

Joshua Logan directed Mary Martin and Charles Boyer
in Kind Sir five years earlier. "Superbly cast and directed,
with opulent settings, including a gold-plated piano by Jo
Mielziner ... fashionable and trivial theatre that is spas-
modically entertaining, "[2] was New York Times critic Brooks
Atkinson's verdict.

Donen, refusing to be locked interminably in the living
room of the actress's Manhattan hotel suite of the play, as
in the comedy-of-manners tradition, mounts the action against
Anna's entire flat in the Buckingham Palace gate area and
other fashionable London environs. He also shakes out the
tedious digressions by trimming the sister and brother-in-

law's roles and scrapping the servants' function as chorus to
their master's private life, along with the show-biz satire attendant upon their backgrounds as wardrobe man and actress.
Deleted, too, is the swipe at American politics: both Philip
and Alfred were Yankee diplomats in the play.   Now there's
more time for the characterization of the principals and the
delineation of their relationship, thereby making the piece
more resolute, touching, and credible and the most romantically felt of all of Donen's works so far.

        Love's tension and tenderness unfold before our eyes
and also, as we would expect from Donen's restrained sensibility and the characters' respectable status, through innuendo.   The new title is itself an innuendo.   An indiscretion is
"an act at variance with the accepted morality of a society."[3]
It is also a polite term for adultery.   Though the protagonists' relations are discreet and proper, they are so calcu-
lating that they effect the very opposite of their intention.
They actually attract rather than divert attention, since such
extreme artifice, as with all extreme behavior, can only be
a subterfuge for the exact opposite.   Consequently, the pair's
démarches also elicit our gentle laughter.   Even when it is
largely a matter of a finely textured romantic sentiment,
Donen never omits the needling.   And this sportiveness exists
in such a perfect degree that instead of diminishing feeling it
sharpens it.

        Also marbling the romance are bits of farce, tame
rather than robust this time, in deference to the movie's
tone, such as Philip's Scottish reel gone loose.

        While visiting the Painted Hall in the Palace of
        Greenwich, where I wanted to shoot a sequence,
        the Naval College performed a Scottish eight in
        axe reel.   I thought it was hilarious and would
        be great for Cary to do. [4]

        Besides the humor, the dance is more original, con-
textual (again the use of local color and detail), animated,
and cinematic than conventional ballroom dancing.

        Krasna's dialogue is mildly pleasant and well oiled.
As delivered by Grant and Bergman it sounds much better
than it really is.   There is much less of it in the movie,
of course, due to Donen's paring of the subordinate parts
and his eloquent mise-en-scène, which Krasna himself praised
in an interview. [5]   All in all, Donen, Krasna, and the two

stars transform a mild, relaxing hot toddy into a glass of piquant champagne.

For Grant Indiscreet is a film of many renewals and one farewell. His second outing with Donen, and second also with Bergman--Notorious (Alfred Hitchcock, 1946) was the first--recalls the great romances in his past, such as Penny Serenade (George Stevens, 1941) or An Affair to Remember (Leo McCarey, 1957), and his dandy clowns as in The Awful Truth (Leo McCarey, 1937), or I Was a Male War Bride (Howard Hawks, 1949). Though there will be more Touchstones--North by Northwest (Alfred Hitchcock, 1959), Charade, and Walk, Don't Run (Charles Walters, 1966), Indiscreet is his final Romeo.

Indiscreet marks a renewal for Bergman as well. The picture is her second American feature since her exile after the Rossellini affair in the late '40s. By the time Fox's Spyros Skouras okayed Anatole Litvak's choice of her for Anastasia (1956) she was no longer the perverted perpetrator but the injured party. Also, the picture taps the light-comedy vein that McCarey discovered in The Bells of St. Mary's (1945).

As exquisitely played by Bergman, Anna emerges as a complete woman, insecure yet resourceful, vulnerable though staunch. She fiddles with her feathered hat when she asks Philip to the ballet, terribly conscious of having made a definite lead. When Philip declares that he is married, she looks at him for a second, hides her disappointment, and emits a laugh to rescue herself. It is another memorable moment when, by love possessed, she asks him to obtain a divorce; then, self-sacrificing and penitent, she kneels before him, begging him to forget her request. Reentering the living room after smashing the perfume bottle, an indiscretion only heard not seen, she puts on her sixteen-button gloves for the ball, like Achilles donning armor for the fray. And Bergman is lovely throughout, glamorously attired by Dior, Balmain, and Lanvin-Castillo.

The supports are also in top form. Cecil Parker's Alfred is courteous, underwrought, and rational even when those around seem to lose their heads. His query and subsequent remarks to Philip are curious, never censorious, matter-of-fact, never exclamatory. Phyllis Calvert, one of England's popular actresses, who replaced Margaret Johnson, allows the right amount of pushiness and prying, endemic to

Indiscreet: The dance begins with an unsuspecting Cary
Grant and a scheming Ingrid Bergman in the Painted Hall
in the Palace of Greenwich.   Copyright: Warner Bros.

the matchmaking profession, to filter through Margaret's
class and breeding.   And the timidity and gaucherie of David
Kossoff's Carl humorously offset Anna's direction of him as
her bold and suave midnight caller.

Location shooting made me feel freer to do what I wanted to do.   [Most of the interiors were real too: the stairway of the Garrick Club dotted with Zoffanys, Covent Gardens's Royal Opera House, the Scala theater, and Leichester Art Galleries, where Searle's drawings formed the backdrop.]   It made the picture handsomer, too.   I preferred not to use Cinemascope because of the enormous number of closeups.

Reproduced, however, was Anna's flat, which art director Don Ashton and Donen filled with original Picasso drawings, Dufys, Rouaults, and Pipers.   These paintings, along with the vividly hued lampshades and pillows and the soft Regency-blue walls, provide a good deal of color in her suite.

Also reproduced was the club's dining room (the real one was too dingy) and Sir Christopher Wren's Painted Hall. The Lords of Admiralty would have given permission for shooting on the spot but the Hall's upper reaches were a maze of scaffolding for restoration work.

The locations and sets are lighted with a feeling for time of day, weather conditions, and seasonal change by Britain's eminent photographer Frederick A. Young, who, in an interview, acknowledged that Donen took more interest in lighting and color than the average director. 6

Such visual texture and handsomeness as this had not been seen in American film comedy since the heyday of Leisen in the '30s.   Despite its opulent look, however, the film was inexpensive.

In keeping with the film's subject and tone Donen's mise-en-scène, which sports some expert horizontal staging, is also a series of innuendos, discreet gestures that imply exactly their opposite, as when Anna invites Philip in for a nightcap and we dolly into the door that closes in our face and then fades out, a transition indicating rest, closing eyes, bed, and that this is none of our business.   Of course, during the midnight Paris-to-London call, we can hop in bed with them in a tight medium shot and stay around for a long time, since they are countries apart.   That sequence, by the way, is Donen's most adroit and sauciest split-screen affair: Philip on the phone in Paris (left panel) appears to be in the

same bed with Anna on the phone in London (right panel).
The synchronization is so perfect that at one point, when
she turns over with her back to him and he adjusts the
blanket, it can be mistaken as a pat on her derrière.   As
a matter of fact she immediately turns over as if in embar-
rassment.

> I filmed the action simultaneously with two cameras
> on two separate sets built very close together so
> that Cary and Ingrid could hear each other's voices
> and react accordingly.   Two microphones were
> used to pick up the dialogue, one for each player.
> The business I gave them also had to be synchro-
> nized.   In the editing the lengthy shots were then
> broken up and appropriately placed side by side.

Part of Donen's mise-en-scène throughout is the insertion of Big Ben, a continuity device and sly gag.   Sometimes the landmark is insouciant, as in the first establishing
shot; sometimes, a stern moralist, as when it chimes 2 A. M.
during Philip's nightcap and sends him on his way; now and
then, a herald of pleasantries, as in its 6 P. M.   stance introducing Philip's arrival or its midnight one signaling his
call; and at other times, an agent of unpleasantries remind-
ing the couple of his forthcoming absence on her birthday,
or setting Anna's avenging scheme in motion.

In his first Donen collaboration titles-designer Maurice
Binder introduces the film's motifs and attitudes in animated
fashion.

> I came upon Binder when he did an advertisement
> for me in California for a movie.   We worked to-
> gether up to and including The Little Prince.   If I
> have an idea what I want, I tell him.   If I don't,
> then we talk.

The multicontexts, the elimination of interval, and the
montages are most responsible for the allegretto playing.   In
addition to his customary allegro-cut mosaics, Donen also
constructed an andante dissolve montage, very Stevensesque,
of the night stroll along the Thames.

Sammy Cahn and James Van Heusen's title song is
given an unobtrusive classy piano arrangement over the credits and during key romantic moments.   The spare scoring,
which Donen insisted upon, keeps things intimate and politely
restrained.

Indiscreet was a critical and box-office success. Donen's control had paid off.   In his fourth comic outing he
beautifully blended romance with manners in a way that in-
voked both McCarey's heart and Lubitsch's intelligence but
yet was characteristically his own.   Through his sophisticated
touches Donen also averted the censor's ink.   (By this time,
the Production Code and the Legion of Decency had been considerably weakened.   The Supreme Court had approved The
Miracle [Roberto Rossellini, 1948].   Otto Preminger had released The Moon Is Blue [1953] and Elia Kazan, Baby Doll
[1956], minus the seal.   And the Supreme Court had ruled
in 1957 that "explicit sex was not necessarily obscene."
Nevertheless, Mrs. Grundy was still on the watch for the
very type of situations that Indiscreet espoused.)   Furthermore, Donen served the whole thing up not only slyly but
sumptuously.   Lastly, he gifted the '50s with a comic gem
and future decades with a paradigm of stage comedy-to-
screen adaptation.   Needless to say, the film remains as
charming now as then.

> The script's amusing and touching.   I thought it
> was different to make a love story about people in
> their middle years.

DAMN YANKEES (1958)

> While we were in the midst of production on The
> Pajama Game, Warners had bought another Abbott
> show, Damn Yankees.   George asked me if I would
> like to do Yankees the same way as Pajama Game....
> Yes, it was an adaptation but I liked the material
> very much.

So Game's sextet--Abbott, Adler, Fosse (this time as-
sisted by Patty Ferrier), the Eckarts and Donen--reunited at
Burbank one year and three months later to film the sockeroo
musical that had slid into Broadway in May of 1955 and played
to standees for two and a half seasons.   This baseball-cum-
Beelzebub yarn, Donen's second musical adaptation and second
time out with a baseball background, was his first crack at
Faust.   Bedazzled and The Little Prince, a decade later,
would be his second and third.

> We prepared for three weeks, rehearsed for two,
> prerecorded in one and planned a ten-week shoot,
> eight at the studio and Wrigley Field, two on loca-
> tion in D.C., which we boiled down to about six.

Abbott and Donen adapted the scenario from the libretto, which Abbott co-authored with Douglas Wallop from the latter's best seller <u>The Day the Yankees Lost the Pennant</u>. Their adaptation came down to rearranging scenes and numbers, so as to strengthen motivation and tighten continuity, and paring dialogue, extraneous business, and scenes so that the movie would whiz by.

The script has fun with just about everything in its ken, the way a Comden and Green script does. The infidel and the game are razzed. Suburbia gets its comeuppance, as do limelight heroes.

Relieving the satiric thrust from time to time are the tender moments of Joe's leavetaking, the couple's memories, Lola and Joe's reciprocity, and Joe's return, moments that are never allowed by Donen the luxuries taken in the stage show. In fact Donen scraps entirely the park-bench meeting with Meg and Joe.

Besides its satiric bite, the text boasts a luminous characterization of the devil. We all know that it is easier to portray evil than good, but it is not evil that is incarnate here but plain old orneriness, spite, defensiveness, derision, bombast, and duplicity--the very qualities all of us live by. As such, Applegate is immediately recognizable. Even his name, though it has a biblical Garden of Eden ring to it (Satan gave Eve the apple to eat and she and Adam were expelled from the garden, which they left by passing through a gate), is small-town ordinary. [1] That much of Applegate's diction is couched in biblical imagery makes for additional pleasant ironies.

Theater critics cheered Stephen Douglass's singing but not his emoting as the rookie Joe. Replacing him was Warners' contract Adonis Tab Hunter. Hunter had amassed a teenaged following after a spate of action and romantic melodramas and, it was argued, would sell tickets. In this career switch Hunter brings presence to the part, and his playing is a right blend of ingenuousness and confusion, nervous earnestness and energy.

> He was inadequate musically. He was partially
> dubbed. We used to do that a lot--some of the
> high or low notes, the harmonies, things like that.

There are no ands, ifs or buts about Ray Walston's friendly fiend. In his nuanced portrayal of all the facets of nastiness he brings along a vast bog of nifty tricks (magical feats he mastered on stage) and a fine assortment of human emotions.

The show made a star of Gwen Verdon as the _femme fatale_ Lola; a season or so earlier she had danced a sexy siren in "The Garden of Eden" sequence in Can-Can. Her carrot hair, large eyes, raspy, childlike voice, and fabulous figure translate beautifully to the screen. Verdon also has the ability to be funny without losing her attractiveness and tender without losing her impish side. (Kay Kendall, whom Verdon physically calls to mind and who is to be Donen's very next leading lady, had this rare quality too.) And finally, Verdon happens to be especially kissed by Terpsichore. Despite her successful stint, which she enjoys as much as Ralston, she never became a film star. [2]

The rest of the cast is right on the mark, too. Jean Stapleton and Elizabeth Howell as the Miller sisters, only a few years away from Capra's pixillated duo, accurately and uproariously epitomize spinsters, holding hands as they scurry home from ballet class while yammering about the ballpark hotdogs, which aren't what they used to be. Rae Allen's Gloria comes across as a tough, taunting professional with a fierce competitive manner. Russ Brown's Benny is a wiry, stern father to his club. Robert Shafer's Joe is callous with his wife but scared without her. And Shannon Bolin's Meg is a boring and bored housewife whose fire is banked by Joe's disappearance.

Wittily authentic are the frames of Donen, art director Stanley Fleischer, set decorator John P. Austin, photographer Harold Lipstein, and costumers William and Jean Eckart, creating one of the most distinctive-looking musicals ever.

The Boyds's Chevy Chase white frame house is lived in, brightly lighted in hot colors with a TV enshrined in the living room's center. In contrast is the devil's baroque rooftop suite overlooking the Capitol, with a cherub-adorned bed illuminated in subtle blues and lavenders--the subterranean serpent has not shaken off his heavenly aspirations. The gray locker room has just the right amount of duffle bags atop lockers, pinups inside them and Spaulding equipment scattered everywhere. (Donen held out for real brand names.) Joe and Lola rendezvous on a bench, embowered by weeping willows, along the Potomac in a misty night--even nature is melodramatically in tune. The club they proceed to is a netherworld, with the only light coming from the pink, red, lavender, and amber bulbs carefully blended in arrangement and intensity.   With everything here diffused through gauze, the light and other bright objects are blurry, thereby conveying Joe and Lola's alcoholic stupor.

L. A. 's Wrigley Field substituted for D. C. 's Griffith Stadium, the Senators' homefield.   Canvas backdrops, painted to resemble an infinity of sky, hid the telltale palm trees and building fronts of Southern California.   The game sequences, imagined onstage, are filled in on screen.   Seven cameras were used to photograph three actual Yankees-Senators games so that there would be available footage of every possible play between the two teams to fit into the story line.

Both Applegate and Lola are made to look terrestrial, a ploy to help us into the fantasy.   Brooks Brothers suits, wingtips, and a crewcut limn him as a Madison Avenue exec, a type of '50s idol and so another instance of the piece's swipe at limelight heroes.   Besides the tricks, he is given several Faustian characteristics: a V-shaped hairline resembling a flat horn, a sartorial dash of red, and an index- and middle-finger pitchfork zap, and an on-all-fours crawl. With one exception she wears either black or white or a combination to outline her in the colorful frames and to remind us, through the absence of color, of her immaterial status.

Besides its story's multifarious strands, Yankees's driving tempo is a matter of the accelerating power of ellipsis, transtemporal montages, the construction of scenes based on action and reaction, as well as crosscutting, adept transitions, the framing of simultaneous actions, smart scenic valedictions, and a rip-roaring opener.   For this one Donen pulled out practically all his corner-cutting devices.   For example, in that precredit opener, Donen's fourth and thus far most dextrous, we cut from an actual night game to a black-and-white TV broadcasting it in the Boyd home.   Sound and image are soon drowned out by Joe's explosion "Those damn Yankees" and a rage-connoting red square over which the film's title flashes.   The other credits are then worked in with Binder's animated and metamorphosing thematic figures.

The Musical Sequences

Some tampering with the cunningly satiric Adler and

Ross score, though motivated, is regrettable.   Excised is
the lilting ballad "A Man Doesn't Know," young Joe's bout
with conscience in Welch's office about leaving his spouse,
which motivated his renting the room.   The number's reprise
later on by young Joe and Meg marked them as kindred forlorn spirits while twisting the ironic knife in deeper.   And
its reprise at the end by the old couple staunchly counter-
pointed Applegate's enticement-turned-harassment.   Alder
gave Meg the rather dismal ballad "An Empty Chair" to ru-
minate and clean house by.   And as a finale reprise, the
song is not as haunting or as appropriate as "A Man Doesn't
Know" and comes off second-best to Screwtape's snares.
Another wispy ballad, "Near to You," eventuating in some
waltz turns, was dropped.   This sadly ironic duet of young
Joe and Meg on a park bench just prior to his hearing gives
her hope that her husband will return.   Casting a nonsinger
in the romantic lead, as well as Donen's preference for humor
over pathos, militated these changes.

Also axed was "The Game," a rousing hymn to ath-
letes' abstinence sung by the team in the locker room to re-
animate them as they face the Cleveland Indians without Joe,
who is trying to clear his name at the Commissioner's.   Movie censors would have had a hard time letting the Rabelais-
ian incidents narrated in this rib-tickling novelty number under
the rope.   "The Game"'s snappy beat supports the credits,
however.

"Six Months Out of Every Year": This study in cross-
purposes features Meg mulling over Joe's whirlwind courtship
and marriage in November and December, and the horror that
arrived in April, while Joe watches the game on TV.   Her
color sphere of yellow curtains, floral wallpaper and print
dress assails the gray monotone of his slacks, tie, chair,
and TV image; and her soaring melodic anger, "Six months
out of every year when I'm with him/I'm alone," counterpoints his staccato patter, "Strike three, ball four, walk a
run'll tie the score/Yer blind, ump...."

Donen closes on a brilliant six-part mosaic.   Though
the couples who fill each piece are of various ages and races,
their situation is identical with that of Meg and Joe, who occupy the center piece.   This filmic ploy, which shows how
widespread the disease is while raising the counterpoint to
the sixth power, is an amusing and detailed advance over the
stage show's male and female chorus lines dressed the same
as the principals, who enter from the wings and kneel down-
stage.

"Goodbye Old Girl":   The opening is an inchoate ballet,
a halting, pianissimo waltz, of Joe slowly tiptoeing through
the bedroom, where he retrieves glove, spikes, and jacket
and pecks his sleeping wife.   (This choreographic staging is,
of course, Donen's doing.) Ambling from the kitchen with
pad and pencil, he sits on the second-from-bottom staircase
step, emblematic of his crossroads position between Meg upstairs and Applegate on the sidewalk with the scales tilted in
the latter's favor, and whispers his farewell in the direction
of the top of the stairs.

In an astounding mood switch, exuberance eclipses
pathos as Donen juggles the central action with Old Goose-
berry's instructions to a curbside cabbie and zap through the
screen door, uses shorter intervals, kids the transformation
as Joe rises young, wiry, energetic, but, alas, pulling on
pants that don't fit, and has the track gather up the tinkly
melodic notes into a gigantic swell as Joe takes a batting
stance and swings at an imaginary ball.   Joe's histrionic
arm-flinging farewell at each regret point (porch steps, pick-
et fence, and cab's door) piles up the humor.

"You've Got to Have Heart":   Donen's cuts on each
new development of this excessively glib and schmaltzy, and
hence satiric, ode to courage, which Benny passes on to
Rocky, Smokey, and Vernon, who reiterate in god-awful but
hilarious Chinese harmony.   His frame contractions of essentially long shots to emphasize words, his easygoing pans of
the strutting quartet, and the smooth transitions from the
locker room to the corridor to the playing field via the song
are masterful.

Sister Miller and four "Youth of America Club" kids,
all in Senators uniforms, deliver an equally off-key reprise
onstage during the Hardy tribute.

"Shoeless Joe from Hannibal, Mo":   On the infield
during morning practice while trashmen pick the stands clean
and a machine sweeps the turf--crisply authentic details--
enterprising Gloria, egged on by the team, uses Joe's under-
sized spikes and unheard-of birthplace as the starting points
of the Hardy mythology.

Donen serves up this hoedown, a dance associated
with backwoods America, in a thirty-shot montage of ever-
decreasing intervals cut on contrasting screen directions,
image sizes, and angles, reinforced by the music's lively

Damn Yankees: The finale reprise of "An Empty Chair" with Ray Walston enraged over the reunited Robert Shafer and Shannon Brolin. Copyright: Warner Bros.

beat. Especially dynamic are the contrapuntal diagonal movements of the low-angle camera in the lower-right-frame corner and the players in the opposite corner, and the alternation of ensemble long shots and choker closeups of an individual ballplayer's head.

This lampoon of the press, hero-worship, and the game (with the exaggerated baseball signals and plays during the dance's second part) is endowed with an electricity unmatched even by the theater's live performance. And real dust from the players' audacious movements on a real mound never rose onstage.

"An Empty Chair": Even this number's dispatch cannot conceal its bland melody, trite (lyrics about a female being completed only by a man), equally trite business, and lack of satiric bite.

To dilute the sentiment Donen ruefully cuts away to Joe, in sunglasses, passing a small fry scraping a bat along the fence while chanting he wants to be "Joe Hardy."

The song's mediocre quality, the stage-regurgitated mise-en-scène (the embracing couple on the right and Applegate jumping up and down on the left), and the hasty pace make for a disappointing finale-reprise.

"A Little Brains--A Little Talent": Lola bestirs the chief's confidence in her by a recitation of past glories, embellished by a demonstration of present ones around his bedroom, that include a sultry stretch on his luxurious bed, exquisitely framed by a high-angle overview.

During her mini-<u>Canterbury Tales</u> with clever internal and end rhymes, the camera, as if enslaved, keeps her in frame and indulges in some advances of its own to better. catch some of that talent: the isolated undulating shoulder, the swiveling hips, the turned-in body line, the long legs that break at the knees, and insouciant head flip--all characteristically Fosse.

"Whatever Lola Wants, Lola Gets": Donen's prudent camerawork captures Lola's passion and Joe's pain while moving in to highlight her every indelicate gesture, as in her over-the-shoulder fling of a glove unleashing her right index finger, which, like her right foot, never ceases to beckon, command, or berate.   Each of the seven intelligent cuts stresses a new line of her attack, as when her derrière advances on the floor toward her victim while wiggling out of the toreadors to rise, like some Phoenix, in French tights.

Role reversal, costuming (she is the apotheosis of Puerto Rican tacky while he, in shades of white, is the American virgin), the double entendres and Verdon's mocking prance through the textbook of seduction from Cleopatra to Betty Boop make this one of the screen's great satirical seductions.

"Those Were the Good Old Days": Donen zanily visualizes Applegate's nostalgic withdrawal, while resting on a thronelike chair in his suite, in comic-strip balloons materializing in various parts of the frame.   Two of the best involve double ironies: in one, unable to plunge a knife into a sleeping maiden's bosom, Jack the Ripper must use his hand for a hammer; in the other, an executive jumps from his office window, then his partner, but a third is prevented from jumping by a body tumbling from the story above--heavy Depression traffic.   In an ironic Donen finish the fiend closes the door before him and walks through it.

Damn Yankees: Gwen Verdon explains to Tab Hunter that "Whatever Lola Wants, Lola Gets." Copyright: Warner Bros.

"Who's Got the Pain?" Although part of the Hardy fête, this mambo is basically a vehicle for Verdon, who choreographed with Fosse. Fosse himself stepped into Eddie Phillips's shoes for the film.

Their West Indies getup, as well as the inane lyrics, palpitating rhythms, and wry body formations, intoxicate while joshing the '50s dance craze. A cut from Joe's shoulder in the wings to the pair in the background is so rhythmically right that it does not disturb the dance's construction and energy.

"Two Lost Souls": The business of plastered Joe trying to keep the equally tanked Lola off the dance floor smartens their wail in a nitery's booth. Of course, there's no keeping Verdon down. Along with the patrons, she engages in a torrid and rowdy bacchanal, while chanting the title in hushed tones as if she were a shade.

With very few exceptions, the critics loved the adaptation. The Academy nominated the film in the "Best Scoring of a Musical" category. The public was indifferent.

> It's lively and fun. It didn't lose money. It came in under schedule. We had very little money to make it because Warners spent a fortune in buying the rights and was nervous about their investment-- the same as Pajama Game. [Warners bought the rights for each at $750,000 and 50 percent of the profits. Game came in around $2.5 million; Yankees at $3 million.]

AN ASSESSMENT OF THE DONEN MUSICAL

Yankees turned out to be the close to Donen's musical career. The '60s will see only comedies. And The Little Prince, a musical fantasy some sixteen years later, will be more a postscript than anything else.

By the ripe old age of thirty-four, he and his collaborators had created a distinct type of musical that set the genre on its heels, making it leap and bound as never before, and bringing about its next stage of development.

Implicit in the genre's archetypical motifs (romance, production, and name, fame and fortune) is the sense of togetherness from a shared effort. In a musical, people come together to get it together. This is the genre's elemental thrust and meaning. Donen so enthuses over and exploits this dimension that it becomes the most pronounced strain in his work.

This collaborative camaraderie, except for that between two sibling hoofers and among seven farmers and their gals, invariably takes the form of a trio. (In The Little Prince an alien reaches out in friendship to a Pilot only after being schooled in its ways by a Fox.) As in Weather, The Little Prince explores the nature of friendship. People strutting arm-in-arm encapsulate Donen's central concern.

This celebration of, and at times sporting with, collaborative camaraderie undoubtedly was nourished by Donen's initial experience of putting on a show and making a picture.

> Nothing is more fun than finding someone who stimulates you, and who can be stimulated by you. You find yourself doing much better things.

The featuring of several or more principals in a common effort, moreover, had aesthetic advantages: more plot action and energy within the frame (energy varies directly with mass), quicker pace through character contrast, more humor by making one of the leads carry the comedy, as well as the elimination of the chorus, which appeared even more artificial on the screen than onstage.

This main motif and the characters' work status (most often, the collaboration involves their work) evince a proletarian quality. Down with Lubitsch's royalty and Minnelli's patricians! Aside from Royal Wedding's Lord John Brindale, Donen's people--principals and supports--are workers seen at their trades, most often unglamorous ones, and this includes the extraterrestrial devils who come in all occupations and the Prince who keeps his planet in shape by sweeping out volcanos and watering a Rose. If glamour is involved, Donen is at pains to take us behind the scenes. Besides there is more humor in doing so.

Donen's landscapes also evoke this proletarian feeling. Our few glimpses of wealth are shaded: Brindale's manse is sheet-shrouded; Simpson's soirée is as studded with sycophantic nobodies as stars; the Manhattan penthouse and Parisian salon are reduced to shambles; and in The Little Prince the estate elicits great anxiety in the Pilot. The street, which Donen's people continually take to for talk, romance, or celebration, solidifies his egalitarian sense. And the street is not exclusively theirs but shared by passersby and sometimes crowds. The desert, of course, substitutes for the street in The Little Prince, except in "It's a Hat," where the street speaks for itself. Most of the numbers, in fact, are street numbers, which provide more expanse for the players, more movement for the camera, as well as uptempos and snappy rhythms. Of course, Kelly's athletic dancing style helped to force Donen out in the open.

Save for The Little Prince, the sexes share equal time. No star vehicles here. Donen's men are charmingly wide-eyed, boyish, idealistic, and vulnerable. (The Pilot and the ex-GIs are endistancing at the start, for they have lost the child within. Both films are concerned with the search for this state of innocence.) As essentially childish and childlike, they are confident, active, and extroverted. The Pilot, however, is a contemplative in action. (Kelly's personality, which stamped his characters, heightened Gabey's self-conscious idealizations, Don's second thoughts, and Ted's brooding, which make all three distant cousins of the Pilot.)

They make the moves, whether private (romance) or public
(work).   And, in making these moves, they are often glib,
self-serving, and aggressive.   Gabey, Tom, John, Ted Sturgis, Leo, Dick, and the Little Prince, for instance, are
sweet-talkers, Don and old Joe braggarts, while Adam, Romy,
Ted Riley, Sid, and Applegate are hustlers.   Chip's, young
Joe's, and the Fox's initial shyness is eventually overcome.
Although Chip learns to palaver with the best of them, young
Joe and the Fox remain defensive.

        The men's naivete also gives rise to some sort of
excess on their parts.   In the course of each film a male,
struck by a mild case of hubris (the tug of the dark side is
resisted), overreaches in the private and/or public spheres:
Gabey's apotheosis of Ivy; Tom's insistence that career come
before marriage; Don's image of himself as star; Ted's,
Bob's, and Leo's desire to give a girl a break for private
rather than professional reasons; Adam's proposal to Milly
and his incitement to steal the maidens; Romy's bucking public taste and courtship of a society girl; the GIs' plan to
meet, their showing up, and their defenses with each other;
Dick's reaction to Flostre; Sid's belief that labor and management can mix; old Joe's sale and Applegate's suburban temptation; and the Pilot's expectation of the adult world and his
antisocial stance and the Prince's reaction to the Rose.

        Consequently, these men make fools of themselves
and twinge with self-consciousness and disillusion, which
easily spill over into self-pity (the child again), but they
quickly shake it off.   To avoid the bathetic, these self-
remonstrating passages are made as discreet as possible by
an ironic sabotage or a dolly away.   This inner moment in
the outer moment of collaborative camaraderie usually results
in some development on their part.

        Though there is a touch of the clown (the kid again)
in all of them, one of the leads is essentially a witticist and/
or prankster and/or fall guy, as are Ozzie, Cosmo, Bob,
Doug, Angie, Applegate, and the Fox.   When this does not
occur, there are people on the sidelines, such as the brothers
Klinger, Jamie, the six brothers, Flostre, Hinesie, and the
Snake, to take his place.

        Donen's women are matter-of-fact, savvy, on the
move, determined, and robust.   Some, like Claire, Jackie,
Babe, and Lola, are downright tough, but never to the extent of losing their appeal.   Once again, the light side of a

personality's moon is preferred.   Their strength tends to
cloak a susceptibility and softness.   The disclosure of this
underside, elicited by love, which is the full blossoming of
camaraderie, educes some very tender passages in Donen's
oeuvre, which he invariably situates in a night, tree, and
water setting.

It is the female who provides the male with a direction for his energy, points out his faux pas, forgives his silliness, and helps him through his momentary insecurity.   She
is the occasion of his growth.   The Rose's influence on the
Prince ultimately effects his ministrations to the Pilot.   This
is, of course, a lyrical reworking of the eternal Innocence-
Experience dialectic.   (Funny Face, with its variation of two
females and one male lead, shifts the scene somewhat by
having Jo function essentially as the male does in the other
films.)

All the women are teasing and playful (the touch of
the child in them) and wily.   Brunhilde, Lina, Suzy, Madeline, Maggie, and Gladys, as well as Dilyovsky, Lucy, the
brides, Mrs. Harris, Mabel, Mae, Meg, Gloria, and the
Miller sisters are yin versions of the ironists, jokers and
pincushions.

The males' cockiness and the females' craftiness cause
deceptions along the way, still another inner moment in Donen's musicals: Ivy's sustaining illusion, which Hildy and
Claire abet; Ellen keeping her love for John from her brother, as well as brother Tom keeping his love for Anne from
his sister; Kathy pretending not to recognize Don, Don and
Lina's duping the fans, Don basking in the glory of Cosmo's
ideas; Joanna's marriage, Madelyn auditioning only to win
Ted back; Adam keeping the whole story from Milly; Romy
writing commercially in order to write personally, Dorothy
tricking Ziegfeld into backing Romberg; Jackie hoodwinking
the ex-GIs into doing the show, Madeline's hype with her
public; Maggie's pretext in getting Jo to her office, Jo taking
the job only to meet Flostre, which is, to a certain extent,
a self-deception, Flostre's interest in Jo; Sid's bluff and manipu-
lation of Gladys, the workers' sabotage; old Joe and the devils' masquerades; and the Rose and Snake's fancy footwork.
The males' excesses involve a self-deception.   In all these
instances Donen almost immediately discloses the reality behind the appearance and eventually brings villain, victim, and
situation down to earth, which confirms the proletarian feeling.   If the professional sphere involves deceptions, such as

Monumental Pictures, a Broadway show, a TV program, the boxing arena, high-fashion photography, and the factory do, Donen is quick to strip the mask away.

These potshots by Donen at pretence, hypocrisy, and deception in both private and public cases are fundamentally nonreformist.   They make us laugh at our foibles--the only way to deal with them, Donen would contend.

Finally, Donen's people can be recognized as a most sanguine and resilient lot, life's livers and enjoyers rather than its beholders and survivors.   These very character types make for more action, movement, and energy in the frame.

Unlike Minnelli's characters, they don't have to re- treat into memory, dream, or hallucination to repair, sta- bilize, or enhance their reality.   Only one memory, three daydreams, and one vision occur within Donen's work.   (The twinkling stars at the finale hold out for The Little Prince's reality.) Donen's creatures live on a conscious level.   In fact reality is a source of wonderful, incredible, magical things in their lives: New York City, Ivy at the turnstiles, Tom's infatuation turning up as an audition for his show, Kathy's voice coming out of Lina's mouth, an unknown chosen to headline a Broadway show, dancin' for the brothers, mu- sic that fuses the old world with the new, buddies coming to the rescue after ten years, the City of Light, a toadstool turning out to be a truffle, a $7\frac{1}{2}$¢ raise, the Senators snap- ping up the pennant, and the recovery of the child within. No wonder these people are continually, and iconically, thrust- ing themselves forward in the frame, almost touching the camera lens at times and taking to heights.   Whereas Hitch- cock played the extraordinary-in-the-ordinary theme in a sin- ister key, Donen uses a buoyant one.

The librettos are written in bold strokes, making es- sential points with dispatch--the Abbott influence--and elimi- nating intervals in narrative continuity, which, no matter how great the jump, never confuses but rather delights and flat- ters us by presuming a sophistication on our parts.   In help- ing to fashion the script and in tightening the shot film, Donen displays an uncanny ability to select and order scenes that move the story along briskly and suspensefully while cutting a scene just as it reaches its intensity point.   Thus he es- chews the elbow-in-the-rib emphasis so characteristic of classical Hollywood editing and prefers a level of action that takes precedence over our subjective involvement with character.

Irony, which renders things more dramatic as well as funny or sad and so enlivens the proceedings and makes them play faster, is Donen's favorite literary tool, as it was Lubitsch's. He is always careful to note the slightest discrepancy, to rein in the romantic and sad moments with contrasting but never contradictory, bits so as to prevent them from toppling over into sentimentality, to turn one of the trio into a witticist, prankster, or fall guy, to employ the principle of alternation in scene chronology, and to close a scene on an ironic flourish. His second favorite is parody, a brand of satire that implies esteem, even love, for what it mimics. Donen spoofingly etches his characters' manners and life styles, their spheres' conventions, the musical genre, and even the film medium itself, which makes his work self-reflexive and one of the first instances of modernism in the Hollywood cinema.

To achieve this, of course, the creator had to distance himself from his people and their situations, both spatially and temporally, for nothing subverts humor more than closeness and longevity. In so doing, the works emerge on the whole as being more intelligent than passionate, lean and aggressive rather than bloated and sweet. This trait was uncharacteristic of a genre often associated with mushiness and indulgence, and it is, above all else, what enables Donen's musicals to hold up today. Though as a brilliant ironist and parodist Donen (and we through him) assumes an objective stance, he still manages to create our identification with a character, our sharing a character's experience of the film's world.

Besides, the skylarking characters, the debunking, the ironic glints and spoofs, and the generous doses of farce make for more fun and humor in his musical universe than in any other. Five of the ten works, in fact, are recognized as being the merriest movie musicals ever: On the Town, Singin' in the Rain, Seven Brides for Seven Brothers, The Pajama Game, and Damn Yankees.

Donen also introduces local detail and color to a script, thus suffusing the frames with an authenticity that also contributes to the proletarian feeling. He makes a number commensurate with the story's idea, rendering only the important moments in song and dance, which are elevated talk and walk. Donen's sensitivity to a number's dramatic

motivation and function is reminiscent of Minnelli's. Moreover, he gives a number a psychologically accurate shape
and progression. (Aesthetics, for Donen, is based on human
psychology.) And this shape and progression are more often
than not strikingly original, inventive, and cinematic. Finally, a number's technical inlaying is, in a Donen film,
even smoother than in a Minnelli musical.

> It's hard to come up with a beginning or end of a
> number. The harder thing is to get it started un-
> less it occurs on a stage, where it's realistic in
> a sense. It's hard to get into a number without
> having people sneer, particularly if it's just singing,
> so you have to struggle [another reason for the
> prevalence of dance in his work].

These musicals are made with musical players and
show Sinatra, Garrett, Miller, Munshin, Pearce, O'Connor,
Powell, Keel, Tamblyn, Charisse, Gray, Hepburn, Thompp-
son, Day, Haney, Foy, Walston, Verdon, and The Little
Prince's Kiley, Fosse, and Wilder at their musical best,
and Dailey at their second best. [1]

> You can't make musicals without a musical talent.
> I don't like to tell actors how to play their parts.
> Most like to find everything for themselves. Most
> actors are extremely sensitive of the director's re-
> action to the way they're acting and if you show
> some doubt, they'll come to you and say: is there
> something you don't like. ... There's very little
> improvisation in my films, if any. ... I like re-
> hearsals because they take away a lot of pressures
> on the set. I usually rehearse the numbers that
> have to do with all the artists first, then the num-
> bers involving only the star. At this stage, the
> dialogue in and out of the number is worked out.
> I shoot the number where it comes into the schedule
> with the scene and set but it would have already
> been rehearsed. I might have an extra rehearsal
> a day before the shoot.

And in between their snazzy entrances and exits Donen
gives his players ironic business and eye-catching movements.
Yet he never abandons the ensemble nature of the playing.
He sails smoothly between a number's thematic grounding and
a performer's talent.

Give a Girl a Break: Miniature Debbie Reynolds pirouettes
before Bob Fosse.   Copyright: Metro-Goldwyn-Mayer.

The staging of the action within the frame is always
varied: vertical through the use of multi-planes, horizontal
across one plane and diagonal from corner to corner.   These
types of architecture encouraged ironies and led to Donen's
frolicking with film-within-film and the split screen.

These musicals always have a look, a right but never
precious one.   They never give the impression, as Minnelli's
works often do, of being set in an antique store or flower
shop.   And the looks differ, one from another, while quite a
few of them are new to musicals, thanks to Donen's pioneer-
ing use of location shooting, color, and titles design.

The visual structuring of the straight and musical passages partakes of both composition in depth and découpage.
In addition Donen employs another structuring device, the so-
called Hollywood montage: a collage of rapidly dissolving
and superimposed images and cutouts to indicate a passage
of time, an expanse of space, a mood, a process, which he
makes entirely his own, elongating it through narrative and
pointing up the incidents with ironies.   (In fact Donen's mon-

tages have become as distinctly recognizable as say those of
Vorkapitch at MGM in the '30s or Siegel at Warners in the
'40s.) The effect of all this variety is exhilarating.

Donen's transition devices range from the silent-movie
technique of transitional title cards (in the form of marquees,
lobby cards, souvenir programs, posters, banners, headlines,
names on door, invitations) to rhyme cuts on formal values,
especially color, and razor-sharp direct cuts. The devices
cement the scenes, provide narrative continuity and thrust,
and, in the case of the rhyme cuts, imbue the passages with
a poetic intensity.

The shot's structure is also inventively varied. No
other musical director comes in striking distance of Donen's
bracing range of technical choices.

> The feeling I'm trying to express is my criterion.
> Take, for example, the shot in The Little Prince's
> "I'm on Your Side" where Kiley is running across
> a very flat desert from background to foreground
> in left frame and at the same time, the camera
> is going forward at about seventy miles per hour
> from foreground to background in right frame.
> The shot's over in a few seconds, but it works
> in the context of his being in a vast desert looking
> for something he has lost and being frantic. I
> could have equally put the camera still and had
> him run around it, as I did in other parts of that
> number, but here I felt this was the most expres-
> sive way to convey the emotion. Why was it never
> done like that in any other movie? Because that
> series of events had never come up before. There's
> no point in having that image in your head before
> the fact because you could go for fifty lifetimes
> with it and never have the opportunity to use it.
> So, you see, I have no preconceived rule about
> how to photograph something. My technique as-
> sembles itself in a sense from a series of givens--
> the situation, the type of character, the setting,
> the time of day, the weather condition, etc. All
> these givens get assembled and you are left to con-
> trol them and put them together in the most ex-
> pressive way possible.

In addition to the pleasure that such diversity and in-
novation afford, the staging, the look, and the scene and shot

structuring and cutting display a command of the expressive
value of film's spatial and temporal dimensions. These musicals appear and feel comfortable on the screen.

Essentially dance musicals, they realize, more than
Astaire's art-deco mosaic did, dance's dramatic possibilities
and film's capacity to preserve the dance's continuity, energy,
danger, and poetry. They perfected a new combination, "cine-
dance."2 Donen pushes dance out of its cozy home (the stage)
onto the street, where it assumes much more responsibility
and grows up. Not only does he understand dance, he understands decor, lighting, and costumes and their contribution
to spatial depth, breadth, and height. He understands the
camera that unerringly frames the most expressive part of
the dancer's body, moves and stops on the right beat, and
appropriately contracts and expands space. He understands
cutting, whether on a dancer's movement, at a new development in the dance, or even away from the dance, but always
on a beat and always to link and enhance movement. And he
knows how to interrelate dance, spectacle, camera, cutting,
and music.

> When photographed, a dance movement--and all
> that this movement contains--is considerably les-
> sened for a number of reasons. Because it's on
> film, it doesn't have the same physical thrill to
> it as it has when you watch it live. You can't
> see around objects and around dancers. When a
> person dances toward the camera, considerable
> amounts of movement are not nearly as powerful
> as when he dances toward you in reality, because
> you can't adjust to the depth of a flat photograph
> the way you can in life. To show the size of the
> space a dancer travels or the difficulty he may
> have if it's an athletic trick, like the brothers
> dancing on the width of a plank, is not the easiest
> thing in the world. You can't compensate for
> these things, but you can approximate them in
> terms of camera positioning, angling, and cutting.

The persistence of choreographed scenes in these musicals, by adding and heightening movement, gives lilt to the
song numbers and lyricizes the straight passages, thus rendering the fabric seamless. The prevalence of choreographed
scenes, along with dance, makes these musicals essentially
moving pictures, stories told through movement.

> The boring part of movies is talking. When
> talkies became a reality, movies lost much of
> those stylized, operatic gestures that were a type
> of movement and a very mesmerizing type. These
> gestures were necessary because it was a way of
> expressing ideas. When sound happened, the first
> thing that occurred to everyone was let's have not
> only talking pics but singing and dancing pics be-
> cause singing and dancing are the best parts of
> sound. But dancing went with films more than
> singing. Singing is the least interesting part of
> music to put on screen because the character is,
> in fact, talking. And photographing people talking
> isn't very interesting. Photographing people mov-
> ing is incredible. The interest in movies is bas-
> ically movement. If the story somehow can be
> told through movement rather than through charac-
> ters talking, whether that be in dialogue or song,
> we must seek it out.

Donen's preference for the light over the dark, the ingenious over the ingenuous, and the robust over the tender;
the group protagonist; the ironic and parodic strokes; the
dense and busy frame; the participating camera; color movement, rhythmic cutting, and scene-structuring montages; and
dance and choreographed passages results in an ingratiating
vivaciousness. No musicals before or since take our breath
away as Donen's do. This trait, even more than their proletarian feeling and their predilection for dance over song,
makes possible the suspension of disbelief that is a sine qua
non whenever that most realistic of art forms, the cinema,
comes to grips with that most fantastic and festive of genres,
the musical.

Special effects, part of the movies' appeal since the
very beginning, are so constant in these works that they give
rise to yet another motif, the magic of movies. As in Méliès,
Clair, and Welles, the pyrotechnics are rampant enough to
make us wonder at both the movies' potential and at the ac-
tualization of that potential. The many film allusions that
Donen sprinkles throughout his work hones this theme of the
magic of movies. As Donen so well knows, the reference to
other films, whether in dialogue or mise-en-scène, implicitly
says that the original sequence has had a special appeal. And
this is, in itself, a kind of magic.

Although the Donen style is unmistakable, making the

works all of a piece, there is an astonishing diversity within
the unity.   And this diversity cannot be claimed by any other
musical auteur, nor can any of the others claim the number
of consummate works therein.

ONCE MORE, WITH FEELING (1960)

> I signed a four-picture, nonexclusive deal with
> Columbia in the late '50s to produce and direct.
> I had gone to the Coast to see about casting a
> film I'd been working on all summer.   I had just
> arrived, in fact, when I got a call from Yul Bryn-
> ner who insisted I come over immediately to read
> a play.   Yul said: I'll play in it on the condition
> you direct.   Next stop was a trip to New York
> that same night, bidding on it, and then suddenly
> it was ours.   Kay Kendall agreed right away to
> co-star and almost as quickly we got Gregory
> Ratoff, whom Harry Kurnitz, the author, wanted
> for the play.   I've never had a film shape up so
> fast and smooth.

Dramatist Kurnitz, side by side with Donen, transmog-
rifies the play, first presented on the New York boards in
October 1958 under George Axelrod's direction.   New York
Times critic Brooks Atkinson found "Kurnitz' taste for charla-
tans in the world of art, his facility with comic lines, his
easy manners in the company of swindlers and the humorous
performances the actors have given him ... smooth and
amusing."[1]

Following Indiscreet's penny-pinching example, the setting was switched to London, a town Donen found more con-
genial to work in than Hollywood and where his production
company was set up.   Besides, London was more picturesque
and classier than the play's Sioux City and Chicago.   The
text's other changes are the result of temporal, spatial, and
comedic visualizations.

The play opened with Victor, a symphony conductor,
at the end of a two-year tailspin due to Dolly's departure.
The film, however, starts two years earlier, with examples
of Dolly's involvement in Victor's world, her devotion to him,
and the cause of her abrupt egress.   A montage of Victor's
inability to perform charts his descent.   The university visit
shows us what Dolly has been up to and further motivates her
return.

Once More, with Feeling: Notice the satiric tone of the art
direction in this shot of Kay Kendall appraising Maxwell Shaw's
complaint against Yul Brynner as Gregory Ratoff looks on.
Copyright: Columbia.

        The play never steps from Victor's dressing room and
living room.   In the film we see Victor conduct, rehearse,
and manhandle his musicians.   We are witnesses at the wedding, which in the theater occurred offstage between Act II's
first and second scenes.   We see Dolly's fiancé at his work.
(The research-lab scene also allows for some gentle mockery
of modern technology--a new area for Donen.)   And we see
Mrs. Wilbur, a cast addition.   Furthermore, the introduction
of the supports, first in their respective settings and only
later in Victor's flat, rids the film of the play's synthetic
entrances--an advance over Kiss Them for Me in this regard.
Also, a TV interview replaces the original radio version, allowing Donen to play with one of his favorite toys, film-
within-film.   Finally, the film replaces the play's satire and
background of the classical-music profession with a hefty
amount of farce.

        Despite all these imaginative visualizations, the script
is not much better than the play, which was essentially a star
vehicle for the innocuous Arlene Francis, that idol of the

Manhattan (mostly Jewish) theater in the Eisenhower era, who
was paired with Joseph Cotten and clothed in Scaasi by her
co-producing husband, Martin Gabel.   Neither version has a
theme, and without theme comedy has no soul; it is "tinkling
brass, a clanging cymbal. " Even the conceit (Victor and
Dolly have been live-togethers; so when she wants to marry
another, she must marry Victor first in order to divorce
him) is not as consequential, then and now, as the play would
have us believe and as a result is too weak to energize and
coalesce the humdrum incidents.   Repartee, one of the things
we expect and enjoy most in a comedy of manners, is nonexist-
ent.   And the farce that Donen pumps into the piece is unfortunately beyond the range of the male lead.

Brynner's despotism in The King and I (Walter Lang,
1955) and in all his subsequent features is here transposed
into a comic key, but his comedic touch proves as light as
a stone crusher's.   In Brynner's recalcitrant and one-note
way Victor emerges less as a screwball Svengali in the Barry-
more Twentieth Century (Howard Hawks, 1934) tradition than
as a certifiable psychopath with manic overtones.   His obdur-
acy pays off only once, when Dolly, extremely piqued, slaps
his shoulder again and again and he budges not one micron.

British Kay Kendall, the film's other half, is something else, possessing as she does Bea Lillie's berserk precision of gesture and Carole Lombard's zany elegance and
forthrightness.   This Trilby enters howling in an unzipped
sheath and exits blowing her runny nose in the wings.   And
in between her farcical bits sparkle more than her Cartier
jewelry.   The way she hurls books and records out of a window, kicks shins, pitches a jar of cold cream at a bedroom
intruder while brandishing a pistol to protect her honor, and
hurls a bust at a TV tube without losing an ounce of cool and
grace raises mayhem to a fine art.

Kendall is a gorgeous fox, made even more so by
Givenchy's black or white ensembles.   This absence of color
in the midst of George Perinal's crisp Technicolors makes
her stand out all the more.   Her contribution to film comedy
would have been vast had not leukemia ended her life at thirty-
three, two months after Donen motion-painted her luminosity
for the last time.

The supporting cast's turns, which border on caricature, are diverting when we first meet them.   Geoffrey Toone's
Dr. Hilliard is discombobulated and a beat or two behind
everyone else, as we have been made to expect from an in-

habitant of the placid and patterned pinnacle of academe.
Gregory Ratoff as Maxwell Archer wears the marks of his
trade, huffing and puffing his way down a road of inveterate
and backup lies in Yiddishese. Grace Newcombe's Mrs. Wilbur is an exacting militarist who commands the porter to an-
nounce the time as "1400 hours" and marches to a Sousa
beat that must continually play in her head. As her son,
who hates music (the orchestra came with the pickle business),
Mervyn Jones is a sixty-year-old elf who comes up only to
his mother's shoulders and who, under Donen's direction, always stands behind her. Martin Benson is a prima-donnish
impressario. And Maxwell Shaw's face as violinist Grisha
Gendel matches his long overcoat and floor-length muffler.

With Paris's Théâtres des Champs Elysées doubling
for London's Festival Hall and interiors built on Studio de
Boulogne's huge lots in the Parisian suburbs, the local color
and detail that have distinguished Donen's comedies thus far
are absent.

> Kay wouldn't work in London because of taxes.
> So all my location plans fell through. Of course,
> it would have been cheaper to film in London and
> the film would have had less of a false look. It
> was moderately expensive to make.

Donen's plans to give the decor a satiric slant, however, was carried out to perfection by Alex Trauner: Victor's
posh townhouse, for example, is nothing less than a shrine to
himself, with flowers before innumerable portraits, several
prominently displayed busts, and even a mural.

Donen's camera is unusually static throughout, opting
to stand back and observe rather than participate slyly in the
proceedings. Four extended montages, however, provide some
visual flair. So too, Binder's credits, which open on a pair
of animated lovebirds flying against an aqua sky and which reform themselves into the leads' profile silhouettes, which
come together from the frame's edges to kiss. These dissolve to various lines reforming themselves into the outlines
of thematic figures. As the closing credits end, the silhouettes advance to kiss "once more, with feeling," referring,
of course, not only to the repatched relationship but the per-
fectionist's grueling, "stop and take it from the top" rehearsals.

If Kay Kendall is something worth looking at, the
film's score, brilliantly conducted by Muir Mathieson and

hilariously mounted by Donen, is something worth listen-
ing to.   The collage of Liszt, Wagner, Beethoven, Sousa,
Rimsky-Korsakov, Chopin, Strauss, Tschaikovsky, Schubert,
and Borodin, besides being source music at various rehearsals and concerts, accompanies scenes to wry and
piquant effect while endowing them with a choreographic lilt.
This, along with the abundance of farce, makes the film unfold faster than the play.

There were only a few exceptions to the favorable
critical reaction.   The public, though, never warmed to the
piece.

> It's not very good.   It should have been romantic.
> I thought Yul was good in it though.

SURPRISE PACKAGE (1960)

> I desperately needed money for personal reasons.
> [In 1959 Donen's second marriage, of seven years,
> to actress Marion Marshall ended in divorce.   He
> had met the recently divorced Lady Adelle Beatty
> during Christmas of 1958.]   So I gave Art Buch-
> wald's A Gift from the Boys, which I owned, to
> Yul, who said, OK, let's go, but discovered he
> could fit it into his schedule only during the last
> months of 1959 or else he had to shelve the proj-
> ect for a while.   Harry Kurnitz did me a favor
> by writing a script.   Five weeks later we were
> shooting.   Harry continued to write the screenplay
> when we started to shoot.   It was my second for
> Columbia.   I threw it together.   It was one of the
> few times I've made a movie for money.

Mixed reviews greeted humorist Art Buchwald's first
excursion into novel-writing, A Gift from the Boys, when it
bowed in 1958.   From this dull narrative, recounted in un-
funny journalese by a crime reporter, Kurnitz and Donen bor-
row only the central Napoleon-to-Elba situation and a few
characteristics of Frank Bartelini (Nico in the film), a middle-
aged Mafioso exiled to Sicily, and his "gift from the boys,"
Karen Withers (Gabby in the film), for their leads.   All the
rest, incidents and characters, are Kurnitz-Donen's flirtations
with Garson Kanin, Damon Runyon, Noel Coward, and Frank
Tashlin.

> What attracted me to the book was its topicality.
> Also, I thought the situation of a guy being de-
> ported to a place and then running it funny.   It
> wasn't much of a book.   So Harry and I made up
> what we thought was more of a reasonable, coher-
> ent, and funny story than Buchwald's.   Buchwald
> was very angry we didn't use his story.

This package is indeed surprising, not so much for
its shady characters--who bring to mind Ball Game, "Broadway Melody-Broadway Rhythm," and Weather's hoods and
anticipate the realms of Charade, Arabesque, Lucky Lady
and Movie Movie's "Dynamite Hands"--or the element of adventure, which Fagan adumbrated and later works will revel
in, as for its sloppiness, a quality we do not associate with
Donen's narratives.   Only the schizoid Kiss Them for Me
had let us down.   Here the plotting is so fragmented by unmotivated scenes (the introduction of the divinity student so
late in the tale that he is easily recognizable as a deus ex
machina), underdeveloped ones (all the romantic interludes),
and a violent tone change (Tibor's death) that the point of the
enterprise is left up in the air.   This choppiness and confusion slow things down after a well-paced beginning that includes the license-plate montage, pinpointing the geography
of the criminal network, and Nico's journey montage, reminiscent of Funny Face's TWA flight.

> There was much cut out in the editing because it
> didn't play well.

Brynner's delivery and Donen's listless direction of
many conversations (at rest, usually across tables) sabotage
the actually amusing lines.   Repartee, which requires two
intelligent people, is absent.   In fact there is very little
interchange between the leads.   His insults thrown her way
are never contested, while her remarks are never listened
to.   Consequently, an unintentional but disturbing misogyny
hangs over the piece.

Some ethnic and political satire does shine through
from time to time.   The gags, though, are hoary (Donen
even steals from himself when the cronies encircle Nico's
cigar with lighters in the fashion of the gigolos attending to
Lina's cigarette) and unpleasantly vulgar, like Pavel's turning
his pretties into house pets, further enforcing the film's
misogyny.

<u>Surprise Package</u>:   Adventure, in Donen's satirical and far-
cical way, shows the baser instincts of people, as here with
Noel Coward nibbling at the bait (Mitzi Gaynor) cast by Yul
Brynner.   Copyright: Columbia.

       A vulgar, even prurient, strain infiltrated many Amer-
ican comedies at this time.   Hollywood just did not know how
to handle with sophistication the more controversial topics
and liberal body exposure permitted by the relaxation of the
Code.   Donen's comedies do escape this bug except here (and
the Mansfield scenes in <u>Kiss</u>), where, with taste taking a
back seat, he set out to make a buck.   This, too, is another
reason that the picture surprises.

                Yul certainly was the ideal.   Mitzi and Noel were
first choices, too.

       Brynner is as despotic and despicable as when we last
saw him.   As Nico his pell-mell declamation of every line
forsakes nuance, tempo, even clarity.   (How can he or Donen
forget that softness quickens pace?) Accompanying these out-
bursts is the distasteful business of attacking everything in
sight from punching bag to mistress.   Also left over from
the previous comedy are his black ensembles, here topped

with an omnipresent chapeau, which make him the spitting
image of Mr. Harvey (Herbert Lom) in The Ladykillers
(Alexander MacKendrick, 1955).

> Black made him more gangsterish. Besides, Yul
> has a black fetish. Everything he owns is black--
> clothes, car, luggage, apartment.

No matter the movie, Gaynor perennially played the
bubbly showgirl--even "Honey Bun" Forbush had a streak of
the entertainer in her (South Pacific, Joshua Logan, 1958).
Here, as Gabby, with her effervescence short-circuited, she
delivers everything in hushed tones. Though muting her personality, Donen's direction emblazons her Junoesque endowments. The emphasis on her physiognomy is downright ex-
ploitative, crass, and misogynistic. Mattli's tackily chic
clothes add to the vulgarity. Had her wardrobe been as garish as the character warrants, there would have been some
wit to them.

Coward plays himself--well, almost--and no one plays
Coward better than Coward. He, as Pavel, with his '30s
pomaded slick hair, double-breasted blazer, ascot, and stain-
lapeled dinner jacket and dressing gown, is an anachronism
and also a great raconteur, brightening elliptical anecdotes
with dry monotone asides. Only Coward's out-of-the-closet
epicenism contradicts the character's satyr status.

Some of the supports, as written and played, are inter-
estingly multifaceted. Eric Pohlmann's steely chief lords it
over the island until the Commies arrive, when he shows that
he is strictly plaster of Paris. The polite but hardnosed
Commie duo of George Coulouris and Alf Dean, in three-
piece business suits and bowler hats, hint at the capitalist
influence in their Marxist homeland. And Guy Degby's porcine,
rumpled, half-wit Hungarian is a perpetual eating, scheming,
and perspiring machine that wins our hearts.

The small town of Lindos on the Greek island of Rhodes
about 250 miles southeast of Athens, with its tortuous cobbled
streets dotted with ancient acacias and cypresses, Acropolis,
and sandy harbor form an arresting backdrop, which Donen
and art director Don Ashton (Indiscreet) make the most of.
After a month of location shooting the company moved to Shepperton Studios outside London for interiors and a few exteriors.

The locale was switched from Italy to Greece be-

cause we had to make the picture in winter so we
had to go farther south to get a sunny island.

Photographer Christopher Challis, inaugurating the
first of five collaborations with Donen, keeps his black-
and-white frames multiplaned with every section, no matter
the distance between, in sharp focus.

> I had stumbled upon Challis in England.   He was
> a very knowledgeable and able camerman.   He
> grew up in the laboratory and photographed a good
> many British features for Powell and Pressburger.
> I found him extremely helpful in trying to achieve
> my aims.   He's also a gentleman.   The reason he
> didn't do Charade, Lucky Lady, or Movie Movie is
> because they were filmed outside of England; he was
> unavailable for Bedazzled. ...   It just seemed that
> the picture should be in black-and-white.   It would
> have been more beautiful in color but not as funny. ...
> It was a very modestly budgeted production.

Binder's credits, a metaphor of the forthcoming events,
with its sudden appearance and disappearance of guns, gun-
shot, players, and a box that collects coins and diamonds,
jive to Van Heusen and Cahn's peppy "(Love Is a) Surprise
Package," a bargain-basement imitation of their own composition "(Love Is) The Tender Trap" for the Charles Walters's
1955 comedy of the same name.   Toward the film's close
Coward, at the piano, and jitterbugging Gaynor showcase the
number, staged and executed in a most ordinary way.

> The critics sat on their hands.   The audience
> stayed home.   The film's very poor because it's
> a bad script.   It does have a lot of wonderful
> jokes by Harry, though, and Noel's terrific in
> it. ...   Noel accompanied me to the preview,
> which went miserably except for his scenes.   As
> we were walking out of the theater, a lady came
> right up to him and said: Mr. Coward, you were
> absolutely wonderful; you stole the movie.   He
> turned to her and very dryly replied: My dear,
> believe me, it was petty larceny.

THE GRASS IS GREENER (1960)

While making Indiscreet, I saw The Grass Is

Greener onstage in London and I thought there
was a good part in it for Cary.   I took him to
see it and he thought so too.   We bought the
rights.   Once again, we flew Indiscreet's Grandon
banner.   At this time Cary was making pictures
for Universal, so they financed and released the
movie.   It was a moderately expensive production.

The Grass Is Greener premiered onstage December
1956 and played to a packed house for more than a year.
For the public, if not for the critics, this urbane drawing-
room comedy proved a refreshing change from the angry-
young-men social dramas that were just beginning to rage on
the English boards at this time.   Jack Minster directed Hugh
Williams (who co-authored along with his wife), as Victor,
Celia Johnson as Hilary, Edward Underdown as Charles, Joan
Greenwood as Hattie, and Moray Watson, who repeated the
role in the film, as Sellers.

Under Donen's supervision the Williams' own adaptation
expands the play's one set, an upstairs sitting room in the
manse's private section, to the entire estate, the village
chapel, a local restaurant, Lynley Station, the Savoy, Kew
Gardens, and a West End theater.   The particularly rainy
English summer of 1960, when the film was shooting, prevented the use of more outdoors scenes.   The authors likewise extended the play's temporal setting of eight days to
fourteen.

The quintet's backgrounds and the role of Sellers, whose
conversations with the master and interloper introduce three
of the play's four scenes, are whittled down, and the dialogue
is made more directly accessible to the American audience,
though there is still too much of it.

On the other hand, the film sharpens the dialectic of
the traditional (Victor) versus the modern (the quartet) and
extends the adults-as-children metaphor by means of the credits, the specks of tame farce, and the multiplication of white
lies, one even told to children by their parents, to get more
laughs.

As for the ending, the film replaces piquant ambiguity
(Hilary returns the mink, "It's a little too much for a house-
keeper to wear mink ... that's my position here for a little
while," as Hattie, curtseying to Charles, sinks to the floor)
with pat smugness.

If the heart of the comedy of manners is an outrageously imaginative conceit, then its soul must surely be repartee that is not so much spoken as shot. Here the conceit of husband's attempt to nip his wife's infidelity in the bud by inviting the lover for a weekend in the country à la Rules of the Game (Jean Renoir, 1938) and Smiles of a Summer Night (Ingmar Bergman, 1955) is staid and well-worn. The dialogue is curiously meditative, as if the characters were musing out loud instead of interacting, and platitudinous as well ("Marriage is not like a tray of hors d'oeuvres. You can't pick what you like. You must take the lot. The grass is always greener on the other side of the hedge").

Furthermore, the satire on the unromantic marital state and the romantic extramarital affair, as well as the civilized, honorable Tory and the upstart, dishonorable Yankee, is innocuously sedate and forgettable.

Finally, the script, along with its enactment, never generates any suspense about whether or not the wife will leave her husband. The film's cultural context and casting would hardly permit such a turn. (The American audience, at the end of the '50s, wouldn't have allowed a wife to walk away from her husband and two kids. Then, too, Kerr's eminent sensibleness--a persona that her From Here to Eternity Karen never obliterated--would always make her come round in the end, especially for someone like Grant.) As a result, we tend to overlook the flimsiness of Hilary's reason to stay put: habit.

Grant's lassitude throughout is due more to the laid-back, mellow role than to anything else. The character of the overly refined Victor does not come close to igniting the incandescence of this farceur extraordinaire. That would have required a character more cunning than contemplative, more antic than antiquated, more devilish than distingué. The business of putting on horn-rims to duel--so too with Mitchum --however, is a wonderful deflation of the stars and the romantic sentiment.

In their third time together--previously, Dream Wife (Sidney Sheldon, 1953) and An Affair to Remember (Leo McCarey, 1957)--Grant and Kerr again fail to set off sparks, probably because their physicality, personality, and characters are cut from the same cloth. Kerr's innately genteel Hilary-- and this gentility includes her Hardy Amies outfits--never allows us to see the passion for her lover. Oddly enough, she

The Grass Is Greener: Deborah Kerr and Jean Simmons re-
act to Moray Watson's pistols.   Copyright: Universal.

works up more steam for her purloined mink than for Charles
(Robert Mitchum).   Grass is also Kerr's third outing with
Mitchum.   Her novice and his marine (Heaven Knows, Mr.
Allison [John Huston, 1956]) and her domesticated wife and
his itinerant husband (The Sundowners [Fred Zinnemann,
1960]) exacerbated their antipodal personae and made their
playing touching.   Here Donen seems blinded to their con-
trariety and the possibilities therein.   Instead the Mitchum
character is not that different from that of Hilary's husband.
Accordingly we wonder about the reason for her infatuation
and, in addition, must confront a very uncomfortable Mitchum,
who, though a nonactor, can be very effective at times.

> I admired Mitchum very much.   I don't remember
> thinking of anyone else for the part.   Deborah and
> Jean were also first choices.   Anyway, I thought
> of Mitchum because he was the antithesis of every-
> thing English; you know, the typical American guy.
> His performance works for me.   As for working
> with him, it was very pleasant.

It is Simmons's apparently-dumb-but-actually-sharp Hattie and Watson's butler-novelist who save the day. For Simmons, the role of a classy and intelligent British bitch is a volte-face; so too her outré Dior creations, sparkling headband caricaturing a tiara, and green eye shadow. Watson's Sellers, continually fretting that he is "fundamentally happy and contented ... and normal" but that to be a successful writer, "one must have insecurity, frustration, despair, " is a decade ahead of misplaced neurosis.

Osterly Hall, the former ancestral home of the Earl of Jersey in Hampshire, England, seven miles from Shepperton Studio (exteriors were real, but interiors were duplicated on three sound stages) and various spiffy London environs comprise the film's scenery. Against such an august and sophisticated setting the quartet's games seem even more foolish, thus reinforcing the adult-child metaphor. Challis's sharp color and frequently static lensing in Technirama, still

The Grass Is Greener: Everyone, Cary Grant included, gets a dunking from Donen. Copyright: Universal.

another '50s anamorphic process that used wide film, [1] turns many shots into well-displayed tableaux, thereby giving the film a glossy, museum-souvenir-booklet look.

Binder's credits of babes playing at adults (with their antics matching the particular credit, as when they turn film stock into streamers for the editing credit) invert the film's central metaphor.

The globs of dialogue and mise-en-place more than anything else cause the film to hobble along, except during the montages and split-screen scene, when the film gracefully sprints by.

An aerial-tour montage of English castles, which settles down to a room-by-room description of Lynley Hall, provides a snappy opening. The items in Hilary's infatuation montage are all puckishly ironic; for example, her bizarre footwear (one black shoe, and other white) elicits laughter from a child (the central metaphor again made doubly ironic by having a child point it out). The affair montage is lyrically sly, with the camera a snoopy observer and shocked commentator.

The impish split-screen affair is played even faster. From his sitting room Victor, with Hattie leaning over his shoulder (left frame), places a call to Charles at the Savoy, with Hilary leaning over his shoulder (right frame). The mise-en-scène, business, and dialogue unfold identically. The topper has the couples, after hanging up, engage in a conversation that is just as much two-way as four-way.

Donen asked Noel Coward to compose a score to comment ironically on the situation. It consists of a new theme and adaptations of his most popular airs: "Mad About the Boy," "I'll Follow My Secret Heart," "Stately Homes of England," "The Party's Over Now," "Mad Dogs and Englishmen," "Sign No More," "Poor Little Rich Girl," and "Room with a View.

The critics split two-to-one against The Grass Is Greener. The marquee names did not lure the customers in.

> It wasn't a huge success, but you couldn't really call it a failure. One trouble was that the cast was too important. People thought, with such a

quartet of star names, they were going to see an epic, not a little bubble. I wasn't terribly pleased with it. I think it's very stagey.

A personally realized romantic comedy of manners, Indiscreet, and another superior musical adaptation (Damn Yankees) got this phase of Donen's career off to a flying start. But the period quickly sputtered with a farce (Once More, with Feeling) and a comedy of manners (The Grass Is Greener) and took a nose dive with the juggling of a Cowardese drawing room, Runyonesque caricatures, and a caper (Surprise Package). Though the pressures of branching out on one's own, divorce and family breakup, and courting a new wife, Lady Adelle Beatty, were enormous, the problem with the last three films was primarily due to the inferior quality of the material, the blame for which must in good measure be laid at Donen's door. He did, after all, choose the works and did have a hand in their adaptation. Even if he spent more time in preproduction, no silk purses could have been made from these sows' ears.

The rest of the decade, happily, finds his judgment on target once again and his career taking another memorable turn.

5. PRODUCER-DIRECTOR, PHASE II: 1961-1969

CHARADE (1963)

I always wanted to make a movie like one of my
favorites, Hitchcock's North by Northwest. What
I admired most was the wonderful story of the
mistaken identity of the leading man. They mis-
took him for somebody who didn't exist, so he
could never prove he wasn't somebody who wasn't
alive. So I searched to find some piece with a
wonderful story and the same idiom of adventure,
suspense, and humor. I found this short story,
"The Unsuspecting Wife," by Peter Stone and Marc
Behn, published in Redbook magazine. I bought
the story and went to work with Peter. Marc
Behn had nothing to do with the script. The short
story had a long history. It was first written as
a screenplay, which didn't sell and which I never
saw. Stone and Behn then turned it into a story.
Charade was going to be my third picture for
Columbia. After we prepared the script, I announced I wanted Cary and Audrey. Cary thought he
was going to do a picture with Howard Hawks
called Man's Favorite Sport [1963]. Hawks was
working on the script at this time, so Cary said
no to Charade. Audrey said yes. Columbia said,
get Paul Newman. Newman said yes, but Columbia wouldn't pay him his going rate. Then they
said get Warren Beatty and Natalie Wood. So I
got them and Columbia decided they couldn't afford
them or the picture. Columbia did this to me with

A Man for All Seasons,[1] which I owned for a long
time and Kingsley Amis's I Want It Now, which I
never got a good script for. So I said let's not
start another one. My contract was terminated.
So I sold Charade to Universal. In the meantime,
Cary had read Hawks's script and didn't like it.[2]
So he called me and said he would like to do
Charade.

In the '60s, many American filmmakers mixed genres
in an attempt to explode formulas. This particular hybrid--
the comic thriller--found a suitable climate to blossom in and
thrive throughout the decade because of the easing of censorship, the demythological drift, and the mass hunger for stylish intrigue during the Kennedy and early Johnson years.
The Big Steal (Don Siegel, 1949), Beat the Devil (John Huston, 1954), Big Deal on Madonna Street (Mario Monicelli,
1956), and Rififi (Jules Dassin, 1956); the host of light comedies of dark doings from the British in the '50s like The
Lavender Hill Mob (Charles Crichton, 1951) and The Ladykillers (Alexander MacKendrick, 1955); and of course North
by Northwest were the seeds.

The comic thriller, which works simultaneously on two
levels, must be distinguished from a parody of a thriller, as
say the essentially comedic High Anxiety (Mel Brooks, 1977).
While the thriller elements of adventure, suspense and mystery, fear and paranoia, violence, chaos, and romance are
heightened through comic contrast, thus eliciting more gasps,
they are inverted and raised by the comedy to a grotesque
and absurd surreality that makes for a good deal of giggles.

Such a symbiosis allows Donen to have the best of
both worlds--adventure without mindlessness and a comedy of
manners without static verbosity. Hitherto, it was more or
less a case of either back streets (Fearless Fagan, Surprise
Package) or drawing rooms (Love Is Better Than Ever, Kiss
Them for Me, Indiscreet, Once More, with Feeling, The
Grass Is Greener) and lately without much success.

The principle of alternation, more than anything else,
contributes to Charade's good bone structure and slam-bang
pace. Hideous scenes follow hilarious ones and vice versa,
and within each scene merriment spills over into mayhem,
fright into frolic. Camera and color movements, image size,
and the track, as we shall see later, also follow this principle.

<u>Charade</u>: George Kennedy hacking away at Cary Grant atop
the American Express. Copyright: Universal.

        <u>Charade</u> also possesses a circular structure that makes
the piece more humorous and, by effecting a contrary rhythm,
more tense.   The mystery commences and concludes with the
Lufthansa bag and the park.   Throughout, Reggie's flight from
danger always brings her back full circle to danger.   Reggie
starts out married to Charles, an older man with many identities, and in the end is united with another older man who
has relentlessly changed identities and been--just as she com-
plained of Charles--"all lies and deception."   She has in fact
come full circle from marriage with one professional liar
(a thief) to marriage with another (a spy).   And throughout
the film circular images and sounds enforce this structure:
the carousel, the credits' circular vectors coiling upon themselves, circular camera movements, and the ostinato pattern
lacing several musical passages.

        Repartee that is lickety-split, witty, and sustained is
the dialogue's most engaging characteristic, contributing to
the energy of the scenes and keeping us continually straining
forward so as not to miss anything, especially the clues.
And this repartee trips from the lips of all the players, not
just from those of the leads.

Everyone also indulges in off-the-wall remarks, which, besides being funny, are unsettling due to the sudden reversal and the tantalizing flow of information these comments effect. Mulling over the drowned Scobie during a walk along the Seine, for example, Reggie suddenly remarks to Peter, "Wouldn't it be nice if we could be like him?" Peter is perplexed: "Who, Scobie?" "No, Gene Kelly," she replies. "Remember when he danced down here by the river without a care in the world in An American in Paris?"

Everyone is a storehouse of ironic quips, most often delivered as asides. For example, Sylvie, observing Leopold sneezing over the corpse, theorizes, "He must have known Charles pretty well; he's allergic to him"; Scobie's drowned corpse elicits Tex's hope that "maybe now he'll meet up with his other hand someplace."

Charade is on another level a homage to Hitchcock's North by Northwest and to the Master of Suspense as well. Of course, the structure, dark and roseate by turns, and the casting of the male protagonist are replicated, as are the situation of his shifting identities, the window-ledge incident, and the shower scene. Peter's four roles echo Hannay's (Robert Donat) in The 39 Steps (1935). And Hitchcockian red herrings, single and double bluffs, and waiting games decorate Charade's script. Bartholomew's character, as written and played, carries on the maestro's tradition of humanizing the villian. The scene among the pillars where Reggie must choose between the two men is an exquisite example of suspense as a projection of an interior conflict, another Hitchcock ploy. And the real-life situation countered and paralleled by an illusory, theatrical one (Reggie and Peter watching Punch and Judy) dittos scenes from Sabotage (1936) and Stage Fright (1950) while the closeup of the charlady's scream upon discovering Scobie's body is right out of The 39 Steps (1935).

The physicalities of Grant and Hepburn mold their characters. His graying hair and frequently squinting eyes undercut the romance and make Peter a passive, put-upon partner; her bright, wide eyes and lithe frame turn Reggie into a teasing, prodding elf. Their being foils to each other adds a further tense irony to the piece.

Grant accomplishes the farcical chases and derring-do with his usual agility and panache. Charade adds one more portrait to his already crowded gallery of brilliant slapstick turns. As the nightclub's floor show, he must transport an

<u>Charade:</u>   The Colonnade at the Palais Royale provides the
backdrop for the finale frisson.   Copyright: Universal.

orange from the chin and neck of a buxom grandmom to that
of his partner by means of his own chin and neck.   Donen's
camera stays close, catching his every contortion and his
fretful brown eyes when the fruit runs down her mountainous
breasts along with his profile.   A clown never grows old, as
<u>Charade</u> which is Grant's film all the way, confirms.

        Despite a streak of forwardness, Hepburn's Reggie is
basically an ingenue.   It is a stale characterization and performance, a throwback to her early career.   By the '60s
she had wisely moved away from such parts, in films like
<u>The Nun's Story</u> (Fred Zinnemann, 1959), <u>Breakfast at Tif-
fany's</u> (Blake Edwards, 1961), and <u>The Children's Hour</u>
(William Wyler, 1962), to conquer new territory.   Donen's
overindulgence in facial dumbshows only aggravates the ingenue persona and playing.   Yet Donen's thematically ambigu-
ous introduction of his screen beloved is quite arresting.
After a 90° pan of skiers on the breathtaking slopes, the
camera pulls back to her face, with large sunglasses, in a
black medieval hood and a tan scarf wrapped around the collar
of a black snow jacket.   Wisely, neither the quantity nor

quality of her Givenchy clothes strains our credibility. She eats voraciously (a business that, besides being a refreshing visual gag, grounds her ethereality somewhat). The camera continues to fall back and stops at a yellow umbrella diagonally slashing the frame, from which a black gun peeks out. The changes in camera movement (horizontal to vertical), color (white to black to yellow), and content (star munching to being shot) equally disturb and delight.

> I liked Audrey in the role. I don't know of anyone else who could have done as well.

Cunningly written and enacted supports surround Grant and Hepburn. Walter Matthau's villain, despite all his folksy and cornball flourishes, never abandons shrillness. Besides their distinctively Grand Guignol entrances and exits, each of the ex-servicemen is decked out with distinctively bizarre personalities and physicalities. Ned Glass's Leopold is a dwarfish, bald, horn-rimmed timid soul afflicted with jitters and an allergy that has him sneezing constantly. Tex, portrayed by James Coburn, is a Southern redneck cock-of-the-walk with a diabolical sneer and a sadistic imagination. George Kennedy's Scobie, whose hook hacks away at wood as well as flesh and sends electric sparks flying in the night, is a volcanic bruiser. Jacques Marin's Grandpierre, with his bushy eyebrows and moustache, large droopy eyes, black fedora, and topcoat, striving at all costs to be serenely rational in the midst of chaos and frenzy, parodies the French detective. Paul Bonifas's incorruptible connoisseur is a welcome contrast to the film's passel of grubbers. Dominique Minot's sharp delivery of barbs never let us wonder why Sylvie is husbandless. And Thomas Chelimsky's Jean-Louis is endowed with the mysterious qualities of childhood that Wordsworth lauded. The child, remember, gives us the first clues in his remark about the stamps and his reply to where he would hide a treasure: "in the garden."

Except for the rear projection of the boat ride, Charade transpires against actual Parisian locales: Les Halles, Notre Dame, the Rue Scribe, the Seine, the Palais Royale, the Jardin de Champs Elysées, the Art Nouveau metro, as well as Megève, some four hundred miles from Paris in the shadow of Mont Blanc. Many of the film's interiors were photographed in real places. Whereas Funny Face's springtime Paris was enchantingly impressionistic, here Donen, cameraman Charles Lang Jr., and art director Jean d'Eaubonne's wintry city is sharp and prosaic. The location shooting and hard-

edged lighting invest the proceedings with a credibility and
immediacy.

> We didn't do the boat ride for real because we
> would have worked during the magic hours for
> at least a month and that would have been too
> expensive. Charade was only a moderately ex-
> pensive picture.

As we saw in Rain and Face and will see in Arabesque,
Two for the Road and Movie Movie, Donen's form is inex-
tricable from his content. In other words, his mise-en-
scène not only brings out and sharpens the piece's meaning
but also conveys it.

Donen assembles the film from many shots of short
duration, so short at times that we are just able to read,
but never savor, their content which keeps us on our toes.
Like pieces of a puzzle, we come to understand only after
everything is in place. The montage-built frissons that have
peppered the previous works--Town's car chase, Don's escape in Rain, the brothers purloining the gals and their papa's
pursuit in Seven Brides, Ted's slip in Weather, Hinesie's
flushing out Gladys in Game, Applegate's stampede to the
stadium in Yankees, and Package's shootings and robbery--
were, of course, his homework.

Donen throughout favors the extreme closeup, which
spatially suspends and disorients while its magnitude of detail jolts us, and the extreme long shot, which aggravates
the aloneness of people by separating them from other characters and ourselves and surrounding them with a vast amount
of space that seems to engulf and threaten them, thereby
adding a soupçon of paranoia to the brew. The former image
size usually prefaces a scene, thus dislocating us spatially
from what went on before while withholding knowledge of the
new site and transpiration therein.

His compositions, moreover, are continually disruptive, with canted angles, frame-slashing diagonals, and ob-
structed foregrounds, causing the tension of unclear sight.
And his unrelenting contrapuntal multidirectional movements
within and between shots also pull us this way and that, con-
firming Donen as a master of composing movement.

Equally startling is Donen's contrapuntal color flow,
as in the climax, where the metro's green-yellow melts into

the Colonnade's blue-black, which in turn dissolves into the Palais Royale's orange-scarlet.

Finally, Donen visually undermines matter, as when dazzling frames make important points difficult to hear or ironic contexts sabotage emotions, thus creating even more unrest.

Charade was Donen's first of three collaborations with composer Henry Mancini, who prefers a pop-music sound with heavy dependence on a theme song and prefers source music to underscoring.

> I loved Mancini's score for Hatari! [Howard Hawks, 1962], particularly the "Baby Elephant Walk." I wanted the same kind of sound for Charade....

With its shifting alternations, ironic counterpointings, proleptic placements, and exotic instrumentations Mancini's score also throws us off balance and helps Charade walk the precarious tightrope between dread and drollery. It also lifts the repartee and movements to lyrical and choreographic height, thus deepening the scene's emotional value.

Johnny Mercer, Mancini's partner on the 1961 Oscar-winner "Moon River," from Breakfast at Tiffany's (Blake Edwards), and the 1962 winner "The Days of Wine and Roses" (Blake Edwards), provided lyrics for "Charade," which was nominated for Best Song but lost to "Call Me Irresponsible" from Papa's Delicate Condition (George Marshall, 1963).

Charade also sports an expertly modulated effects track: a diesel's growling horn and clickety-clack wheels shatter the peace of a countryside; ever-louder footfalls, a door's creak, and a grating buzzer startle Reggie out of a daydream; shrill telephone rings interrupt love and sleep; sneezes dissolve to screams; and subways come screeching to a halt.

Summing up the film's narrative, visual, and aural styles and its consequent vision of life as a game of illusion are Binder's titles, perpetually moving graphic forms and colors undergoing constant transformations against black, white, or scarlet backgrounds. The felicitous title denotes an enigma in which a word or phrase has to be guessed by a representation of its separate syllables and parts, while connoting appearance, façade, and artifice, trick and game, obliquity and fragmentation.

> There are two moments in making movies that
> are fun: the beginning moment when you have
> either an idea or a story that gives you enough
> of a charge and carries you through in making it,
> as in Charade, and the editing.   The rest is sheer
> torture.   Throughout the production I laugh my
> head off, but I always laugh particularly when I'm
> suffering.   That's the only escape route I know....
> I generally shoot between 350,000 and 500,000 feet
> of film.   And the picture ends up approximately
> 10,000 feet.   It isn't all that much.   It includes
> everything, even the tests.   In the beginning, of
> course, I didn't use a 35-to-1 shooting ratio.   I
> used to expose about 120,000 feet then.   I suppose
> the turning point was Charade.

Most critics loved playing the game.   Pauline Kael
thought Charade the best American film that year.   The mayhem spiced with mirth did make a couple of the professionals
uneasy, however, but not the public, who adored it and turned
it into one of the season's top grossers.

> Charade's fun to see.   It's a good script, which
> is what I'm more interested in than anything else
> --always.

ARABESQUE (1966)

Charade's immense success and sudden paradigm status (every third or fourth film during the next couple of
years was a comic thriller, or so it seemed) pushed Donen
into the familiar Hollywood trap of reprise.   His decision to
make another Charade was the only time in his career that
he did not tackle a different comedic form.   The imitation,
which did not measure up to the original, was also the only
valley in an impressive stretch of peaks.

> Gregory Peck and Sophia Loren asked me to find
> a movie for them.   I desperately searched for a
> mystery story.   After I found something, it took
> two years for their available dates to coincide.
> Because of Charade's success, Universal wanted
> to do it.

Julian Mitchell, Stanley Price, and "Pierre Marton"

(a pseudonym for Charade's Peter Stone) are credited with
the script based on Alex Gordon's The Cipher (1961), a thriller with a dull but clean plot line and sharply limned characters. Donen and the three screenwriters retain the basic
situation--of a teacher who, while deciphering a code, stum-
bles upon a plot against a Middle East politician's life--and
send it through a series of convulsions that choke characterization and overlay it with Charade's glamour, titillation, and
humor.

        Most of the creators' perspiration and energy went
into the raveling and unraveling of the plot. Everyone, save
the professor, is engaged in double-dealing, all set against a
Middle East background that involves no fewer than three fac-
tions. This consumes a plentiful amount of screen time and
in some spots is pretty threadbare.

        The novel has as protagonist thirty-eight-year-old Philip
Hoag (he looks forty-five), a mousy, round-shouldered, asth-
matic, failed archaeologist-turned-teacher, recently abandoned
by his wife and child. In the movie he becomes handsome
exchange professor David Pollock at Oxford. In the book
Police Captain Docherty, a loner with a gnawing fear of mar-
riage, counterpoints and opposes Hoag every step of the way.
But in the film Yasmin, a luscious consort, tags along with
Pollock. And New York's West Side (Hoag's flat is redone
Salvation Army) is transformed into poshy London. While
Charade's glamour was just right, Arabesque's is a bit thick.

        Arabesque also overdoes the frissons, doubling
Charade's four, an excess causing an overall lack of modulation and an early weariness.

                I had a lot of ideas for sequences that I was deter-
                mined to put into the movie. And the only way I
                could work them out was to have two sets of vil-
                lains. I kept my sequences all right, but I ruined
                the movie.

        And as for the humor, there just is not enough to sup-
ply the needed gradation. Charade's repartee is not duplicated (nor is its romantic passages). The leads are given a
couple of waggish turns (the soccer match with the soap in
the shower, the Ascot mime, and Peck's drugged version of
"Let's Kiss and Make Up" on the turnpike), but they carry
them off rather feebly. Arabesque's few comic trumps are
in the hands of the supports.

<u>Arabesque</u>:   Reflections and shoe fetish, with Alan Badel and
<u>Sophia Loren</u>.   Copyright: Universal.

        Again Hitchcock's shadow, especially his <u>North by</u>
<u>Northwest</u>, looms over the enterprise.   The innocent sucked
into chaos recalls Thornhill and practically every Hitchcock
protagonist as well.   Yasmin is a replica of female double-
agent Eve Kendall (Eva Marie Saint), Beshravi of gentleman
villain Phillip Vandamm (James Mason).   (<u>Charade</u>'s Bartholomew is in the tradition of the buffoon villain.)   Even the agent
and villain's relationship in both films is similar.   The stabbing among the Royal Ascot crowd recalls the stabbing at the
United Nations Building.   Both Pollock (his name tag) and
Thornhill (his picture) turn up on the front page, indicted for
murders they did not commit.   Both don dark specs for camou-
flage.   When a bobby passes him in a phone booth, Pollock's
back arches in fear--fear of police is a Hitchcockian leitmotif.
The cornfield flight apes the crop-dusting sequence.   And action set against aquarium tanks echoes a similar scene in
<u>Sabotage</u> with a soupcon of <u>Lady from Shanghai</u> (Orson Welles,
1948), while the running against time to prevent the assassina-
tion of the Prime Minister evokes both versions of <u>The Man</u>
<u>Who Knew Too Much</u> (1934, 1956).

The script's unrealized characterizations do not completely exonerate Peck's and Loren's performances as David and Yasmin. He never allows his essentially grave and sincere persona to be warmed by the comic elements. And she is doing a somnambulistic turn; no matter the situation, she remains in a relaxed cheery state. She does, however, float through looking like an exotic painting in motion, with her face and figure made even more fabulous by Dior's outfits, a new one for each scene (which ploy, of course, spoofs Hollywood's star wardrobes). Her ravishing and mysterious entrance is a good example. A sky-blue coil fills the frame. Through its tiny circular center, her visage appears. (By not seeing her approach, her mystery is ensured.) Donen's dolly in then transforms the ebony bouffant, arched eyebrows, hazel orbs, and pink full lips into an exquisite azure-framed cameo. Donen, along with his American confreres, never really got beyond Loren's corporeality. Only on home soil, especially with the neorealistic De Sica, did her spirituality emerge. Needless to say, Peck and Loren together are about as exciting as a Friday night in a Benedictine abbey.

> I thought they were good. The picture was tailored to them. I didn't demand too much of them as artists.

The film's only performance comes from Alan Badel as Beshravi. Behind his soft-spoken voice, graceful walk, and unctuous manner, lurks a deadly menace, which that carnivorous falcon perched on his gloved left hand and an all-consuming shoe fetish only exacerbate. (Evidently, his fixation has rubbed off on Yasmin, who, recall, detects the fraud by Jena's slippers.)

While Arabesque's script and acting disappoint, its visual look ravishes us and is chiefly responsible for keeping us interested and making the film play fast. Donen, Challis, and art director Reece Pemberton render the queer happenings against actual London environs--interiors were done in Pinewood Studios--in bold, jolting op-art fashion, envisaging a freakish, devious, splintered, and, above all, inhuman world.

> The production was a little more expensive than Charade. Remember, I'd been trained to do things cheaply at Metro.

In addition to Yasmin's deliciously bizarre wardrobe, Arabesque's large Panavision frames are furbished with outré

<u>Arabesque:</u>   Donen's mobile mise-en-scène--Gregory Peck
at Ascot.   Copyright: Universal.

decor, which Donen invariably magnifies by foreground placement, thereby dwarfing the people in medium or back planes
and stabilizing the composition.   Furthermore, what we see,
more often than not, is a reflection of the real, like a chan-
delier's crystal lobe refracting an escape, or the real seen
through a transparent surface, like a jogger seen in the
Rolls's chromium trim.   Blurred, warped, shaky, and awry
frames are preferred, as are startlingly baroque color
schemes.   Also disequilibrating are Donen's withholding of
space by opening a scene upon a detail, the use of choker
closeups, which Panavision's generous horizontal plane renders even more grotesque, and especially his persistent use
of spatial movement in the countless shots of short duration
(even more than in <u>Charade</u>).

> I had hoped to avoid any sign of the studio manner
> this time, so I tried something like the "living
> camera" technique.   The hand-held camera had
> been used a lot lately, especially in Europe, but
> the trouble had been too much wobble because the
> operator has to carry the sheer weight of the cam-
> era while he's working.   One of our boys had the

idea of suspending the camera--sometimes in a
sort of ship's bo'sun's rig, sometimes just hung
from a pole--to give the operator all the mobility
of the hand camera without the weight.

Binder prefaces the escapade with a Vasarely-like
series of abstract designs that continually reform themselves
in size, shape and color.   Mancini's score, expertly fusing
England with the Middle East, adds further unease.

According to Webster, "arabesque" in its first meaning is "an ornament of style that employs flower, foliage, or
fruit and sometimes animal and figural outlines to produce an
intricate pattern of interlaced lines. "[1] It refers to a heavily
ornamented style, one that relies exclusively on the visual.
As such, the title perfectly describes the picture's structure
and method.

The word's second meaning, "a posture in ballet in
which the body is bent forward from the hip on one leg with
the corresponding arm extended forward and the other arm
and leg backward, "[2] is equally relevant.   The academician
and spy are pas de deux partners romping with grace and
poise, defying laws of balance.   Essential to balletists are
slippers, and the film contains a slipper motif.   Ballet, too,
is a dance of the upper class, which is the film's realm.
Finally, Donen's camera can be described as balletic.

The word "arabesque" also refers to Arabia.   This
meaning likewise suits the picture with its Middle East intrigue.   The title of the film is thus multileveled and sly,
itself an arabesque.

Accepted by some critics, spurned by others who felt
the film smelled of the lamp, Arabesque was accepted by the
audience but not by its maker.

> Because I had nothing of particular interest in
> Arabesque's script, I tried very hard, probably
> too hard, to keep the audience and myself amused
> with what they and I were looking at.   Arabesque
> is sort of going to the extreme until it almost makes
> you sick.   Granted, we did do some interesting
> photographic things.

Donen's next three masterworks continued to cross-

pollinate genres and exuded a distinct English flavor, plug-
ging into, as they did, the brazen mod humor and pyrotechnics of the new wave of British comedies in the mid-'60s. [3]
And this fusion of genres and national sensibilities, which
Donen's works largely contributed to, were two of the more
significant things about American movies in the Age of
Aquarius.

Viewed from the other side of the Atlantic, Donen's
films are part of the renaissance of the British film in the
late '50s and '60s. The first half of this springtime, known
as "Free Cinema," largely comprised the contributions of
directors like Lindsay Anderson, Karel Reisz, Tony Richardson, and Jack Clayton, as well as the Angry Young Men
school of writers like John Braine, Colin Wilson, Alan Silli-
toe, Harold Pinter, Shelagh Delaney, and David Storey. The
impact of foreign directors in London--France's Truffaut,
Italy's Antonioni, Poland's Polanski, and America's Losey
(who had been there since 1954), Kubrick, and Donen--as
well as the mod British comedies, were responsible for the
second half.

TWO FOR THE ROAD (1967)

> Freddie Raphael had written a movie called Nothing
> but the Best [Clive Donner, 1964]. It was a blackly
> comic variation of Room at the Top [Jack Clayton,
> 1959], in which a young, excessively ambitious
> English real-estate clerk climbs to the top of the
> social ladder. I didn't know him but I did know
> there was a very talented writer behind that movie.
> So I telephoned him. When we met, I told him I
> admired his work so much that I'd love to do a
> film with him. We sent each other novels back
> and forth for a while--nothing that either of us was
> really pleased with. Eventually he told me he had
> this one thought for a film. He and his wife had
> always gone on holiday in the south of France since
> they were childhood sweethearts. Going to the
> same places over and over again, he had often
> thought of passing himself going down the same
> road. Did it interest me, he asked, doing a movie
> about a personal relationship of a man and woman
> and telling the story of their life in five different
> time bands while they go down the holiday road?
> I said it sounded wonderful. So with that, we

started to work on Two for the Road. He wrote a
version. We discussed it. He went away and wrote
another version, which he sent to me. We worked
on it again. Universal was supposed to make the
picture, but when I cast Audrey they became dis-
enchanted. In the end Fox put up the money. The
casting of Albert Finney came after that. Paul
Newman was the first person I approached.

While the incidents in each of the five periods of the
couple's ten-year relationship evolve chronologically, the
periods are intercut on ironically contrasting visual, verbal,
or emotional rhymes.

This contextual structure never loses us along the
way and in fact makes the going humorous and suspenseful.
It also carries with it a couple of metaphysical implications:
the past's intrusion upon the present, the importance of memory or continuity in a relationship, which, though not one of
the strongest reasons in the world, does keep people together,
as the Fabians, Rhyalls, and Harry and Charlie (Staircase)
attest to.

With the appropriation of this Resnais-like narrative
form, Donen and Raphael at once introduced New Wave technique into the commercial Hollywood film and paid tribute to
D. W. Griffith, who pioneered this device as far back as
1916 with Intolerance.

The central metaphor of the road unifies the film.
Even at hotels and the beach we glimpse the road outside
the window or hear vehicles or talk of the road, a particularly
apt metaphor for a personal relationship, especially in our
day and age. Its rich connotation of advance and retreat,
growth and arrest, departure and arrival, beginning and end,
energy and fatigue, continuity and interruption, change and
repetition, is easily interchangeable with a metaphysical conception that vividly captures us as a people characteristically
on the move. In addition the road is an endemically filmic
metaphor, containing a built-in dramatic structure and having
an essence of space through time in common with film's. The
trope has much to do with the picture's solid construction and
fluent pace. [1]

Though the road remains the same in all five periods,
the suggestion of circularity or illusion of movement is absent. The semilinear structure and lack of departure and

arrival scenes see to that.   No, the film insists that the relationship changes even though the two people basically remain
themselves throughout.   After all, we meet Mark and Joanna
after their personalities are set.   The film expends no energy
in explaining these changes, but instead contents itself with
presenting the relationship's ranging moods, through which
we glean the inroads getting a little deeper, the cynicism a
bit bleaker, and the tolerance of each other a mite more expansive.   The film's view of a relationship rings true more
often than not.   It was extremely influential in bringing about
the demythological image of marriage in the American film
of the late '60s and early '70s, which refreshingly countered
Hollywood's pipe dreams.

     Various means of travel, hinting at the couple's eco-
nomic and emotional status in particular and the manners of
the nuclear family in general, also help stitch the pieces together while mirroring the changing relationship.   The steam-
er, their hitchhiking feet, and lifts in assorted trucks characterize the delirious blush of romance; the Manchesters' Ford
station wagon presages the suffocation of domesticity; the antique folding-top MG with a "donk" and the Dalbrets' Rolls
signify the first years together pregnant with exciting possibilities; their own new red Triumph Herald hints at the dan-
gers of intolerance, and their white Mercedes 230 and airplane, the pallor of the jet set.

     Raphael's dialogue is gorgeously crafted: sharply in
character, witty, fecund with Pinteresque pauses and silences
that mean as much as the words and are, above all, so
touching.

     Marriage, its togetherness and splintering, its passion
and coldness, its confrontations and games, is the target here.
And the Wallaces' coupling is paralleled and contrasted with
other pairs: the frightened, chubby newlyweds, the bickering
proprietors, the complacent Manchesters, sundry silent dining
partners (a running gag that ironically counters the Wallaces'
eating while chatting away during their courtship and early
married years), the bored and boring Dalbrets, and the Pat-
moses, forever on the make.   Howard's priggishness and need
for efficiency, his Jewish-princess-turned-Wasp wife, and
their bad seed, who has neither had nor ever will have one
unexpressed thought or gesture in her life, are also given
the once over.   The script goes on to sneer at jet-set philis-
tinism and vapidness.

This is Donen's most feeling effort since Indiscreet,
with glints of passion never disclosed before.   But lightening
the tenderness and pathos, while keeping the incisive satire
from turning cruel, are the farcical touches, verbal and visual jokes, and double entendres.   In the good old Sennett way,
for example, sexual appetite often climaxes in disaster.
Whenever the ripostes reach the scathing point, one turns the
other's words back on him- or herself and the exchange dwin-
dles to a teasing put-down.   (This trait springs from their
intimate knowledge of each other and their resentment of the
other's knowledge.) Occasionally Mark and Joanna pass each
other in different periods of their life in the same shot.
(This joke, too, is psychologically accurate in its depiction
of similar sights eliciting memory.) While the best double
entendre, which is also an allusion to A Letter to Three
Wives (Joseph Mankiewicz; 1949), takes the form of a train
that roars past the window and sends the bed quaking just
after Joanna's waking remark, "I dreamt that a train drove
slap bang through the room in the middle of the night. "

True, the light side does predominate, but not to the
extent of bleaching out the film's ambivalent portrait of marriage.   Road emerges as a gray, if not dark, comedy of romance and manners that consequently expands Donen's horizon.

Hepburn is as nifty as the script.   In her third and
best Donen round, her Joanna develops from a sharp-eyed
yet wistful girl into a hurt and hurting woman.   Visual clues,
such as clothes and hairstyles, help, but she manages the
transition mainly through facial expressions and voice inflec-
tions.   Though in this seesaw of the sexes her side is slanted
toward the sky, her teasing-turned-taunting does sting and her
comic timing is perfect.

While conveying Mark's stubborn, narcissistic, and
dominating ways, English actor Finney always makes us sense
the insecurity within.   As written and played, however, the
character lacks pastel shading.   This makes us favor Hepburn's Joanna although both characters are responsible for
their marriage problems.

> Albie really can't bear playing a man with pleasant
> charm.   He feels he's letting himself down as an
> actor if he tries to show charm.   He can't believe
> that that's a quality called for in acting.   He wants
> to play something more startling.   He doesn't like
> to come in and win you with his pleasant ways.

Nevertheless, Hepburn's and Finney's performances do
bring the characters to life, but it is the offbeat casting that
clinches for us this mutual attraction and volatility of oppo-
sites and makes the pairing downright entrancing. The back-
seat passengers never fail to divert. William Daniels's clipped
speech patterns and fussy movements as the efficiency consultant are terrifying hilarious. Everything that comes
from Eleanor Bron's haughty, upturned mouth and nasal voice
as Cathy is a sneer. Gabrielle Middleton, with Donen's painstaking help, etches a miniature Rhoda; the child's reading of
"now" appended to her every command sends shivers down
our spines. Claude Dauphin rests on his laurels as the
dreary, nebulous Gallic millionaire and in so doing delivers
a self-caricature. And Jacqueline Bisset as Jackie is, well,
luscious, while Georges Descrières as David gives the impression of being born old.

> We shot all the periods in one spot. Because most
> of Road occurs on a highway on which we had to
> turn the car around and travel hundreds of miles,
> I started using two cameras as a time and money
> saver. Previously, I used only one camera during
> filming. I found I was adept at this and so, from
> Road on, I used two cameras on a picture. There
> were exceptions, of course. For the TV sequence
> in Bedazzled, for example, I used eight to twelve
> cameras. ... As it was, Road was an expensive
> production.

More than anything else, Donen's razor-sharp cutting
on dialogue, directions of movement, objects, forms, colors,
and moods, which hones the ironic rhyme scheme, energizes
the film--a veritable textbook on editing. And the nimble
tripping through an entire decade, which this bravura editing
ensures, gives rise to still another motif, time's "swift and
winged feet."

Furthermore, since Donen regulates the dialogue, the
movement of vehicles and passengers, camera movement, shot
duration, and cutting to Mancini's lilting, melancholic, and
wry score, which never forsakes a traveling rhythm, the film
is lyrical and choreographic throughout: Mark and Joanna's
relationship is a pas de deux on wheels. This, along with
Challis's soft-focus location shooting in late spring and early
summer in Panavision, which mirrors the couple's emotional
states, is particularly responsible for the film's feeling.

<u>Two for the Road:</u>   Complications.   Copyright: Twentieth
Century-Fox.

> The score is done after the film.   After I hear the
> score, though, I go back and recut the film to make
> it work with the score.   It took me six months to
> edit <u>Road.</u>

In rhythm with Mancini's gently paced title ballad,
Binder's animated travel-emblem credits continually advance
and recede, move horizontally and vertically, crisscross each
other or extend and contract into something else against a
black background, which at times doubles for the road's as-
phalt.   When the Hepburn-Finney credit appears, the shape
of a rearview mirror expands to hold a fleeting closeup of
the actors--another arresting star entrée by Donen.   This
lovely sequence introduces us to the travelers, establishes
the film's central metaphor, and prepares us for its leaping
and rebounding structure as well as its mobile mise-en-scène.

Reviews of <u>Two for the Road</u> were mixed, although
they were more positive than negative.   Fox premiered the
film at Radio City Music Hall, where it died.   After a brief

three-week stay--the usual Hall run is six; five, if it is a
bomb--it moved uptown to an art house, where it did respect-
ably.   The film's shaky start resulted in the studio's insensi-
tive distribution.   It did go on to cop the Golden Shell for
Best Picture at the San Sebastian Film Festival.   The Writers
Guild of Britain voted the picture the Best British Comedy
Script and Best Original Screenplay.   The American Academy
stopped at a nomination.   Today Two for the Road is regarded
as one of the best romantic comedy-dramas to come out of
Hollywood and enjoys a cult status, viewed again and again
by film aestheticians, students, and enthusiasts.

> It's a good movie, but I don't think it should have
> been as sweet as it was.

BEDAZZLED (1968)

> I admired Peter Cook and Dudley Moore immensely.
> They had a weekly television show in London on the
> BBC.   I told them that I wanted to do a film with
> them.   We should try to find a subject, I suggested,
> and they told me they had written a script.   It was
> Faust.   I said if they wanted to do a movie based
> on Faust, I'd be happy to work on the script with
> them.   They agreed.   We discarded the original
> and started from scratch.   Only two or three things
> in the original and, of course, the Faust conception
> were kept.   Fox liked the script well enough to fi-
> nance it.

Save for the weak and uncharacteristic resolution of
the Devil returning a soul, the script is a lalapalooza.   Three
strands--the theological fantasy of man, Satan, and God; the
romantic fantasy of Stanley's seven wishes; and the mystery-
romantic fantasy of the Inspector's lust amid the search, all
the Devil's fabrications--are interwoven within the reality
frame of Wimpey's Burger bar.   The layering and framing
of an essentially cyclic structure give the script a solidity,
which is missing from the episodic revue-sketch form that
characterizes Cook and Moore's work on the BBC and stage
(Beyond the Fringe, 1961 in London, 1962 in New York, and
Behind the Fridge, 1972, renamed Good Evening when it
crossed the Atlantic the following year).

Bedazzled's satirical thrust is as sharp as it is expansive.   Its wary eye and ear and sentient mind catches

everything awry in the tormented '60s, especially organized
religion, with its dogmas (from motivation as a criterion for
morality to papal infallibility) and practices (the religious life,
in particular).

> While writing, I said to Cook and Moore that this
> is a movie about the Devil from the Christian side
> of things and I want it to be absolutely right from
> that point of view.   I had to use someone as my
> authority and that was C. S. Lewis and his book
> Mere Christianity. [1]

The second wish razzes intellectuals and tactile therapy of the Esalen ilk.   In the third wish the stiff-upper-lip
English temperament, the materialism of the monied class,
the English tax system, and English politics, with a nod to
the Profumo affair, are put over the coals.   The third wish
also has a go at marriage, as does the sixth wish.   The
fourth wish lambasts the rock scene.   And along the way pot
shots are taken at the police, the romantic sentiment, the
press, contests, business deals, fast-food chains, lawyers,
nymphomania, homosexuality, obesity, frugality, the teach-
yourself syndrome, advertising, contemporary morality, and
nylon underwear.

The film as a whole parodies Faust, turning the Marlowe, Goethe, and Gounod traditional tragic hero with a fatal
flaw into an antihero.   In particular, the tactile/intellectual
sequence lovingly spoofs the Mike Nichols and Elaine May
short Bach to Bach (Paul Lief, 1961) while roasting Le Bon-
heur (Agnes Varda, 1966) and Elvira Madigan (Bo Widenburg,
1967), where the lovers made it to Mozart, not Brahms.
The sixth wish burlesques Accident (Joseph Losey, 1967) and
the seventh The Sound of Music (Robert Wise, 1965), while
the Inspector-Margaret episode puts L'avventura (Michelangelo
Antonioni, 1961) on the block.   The personification of the
capital sins skewers the medieval morality plays.   And even
Zen conundrums come in for a fair share of abuse.   Donen's
exacting mise-en-scène, of course, contributes greatly to the
success of these lampoons.

While the satire is more bountiful here than in any
other Donen comedy and as dark as that in Kiss and Road,
it is still, in the end, friendly.   The film does not want to
change anything.   As a matter of fact, it roots for the status
quo: be content with what you have.

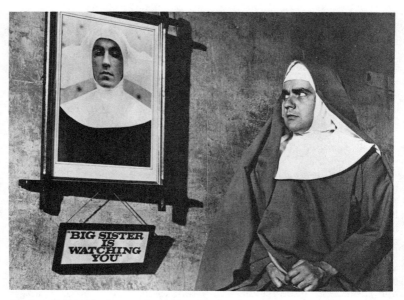

Bedazzled: A framed Peter Cook keeping an eye on Dudley
Moore.   Copyright: Twentieth Century-Fox.

     The farce, of which there's plenty, is ripsnorting
throughout; so are the masquerades.   The variety of Stanley's
and Margaret's personae cannot hold a candle, though, to the
diversity of George's lives.   He appears in every one of the
wishes (a blind beggar at the zoo collecting for the National
Society for the Preservation of Depraved Citizens, businessman Peter Bagshot, Drimble Wedge, a fellow fly, an Oxford
don, Sr. Domination) and doubles here and there as a gar-
dener, a bobby, a GPO telephone repairer, a Grooney Green
Eyewash man, and an underwater repairman.

     George perpetually perpetrates minor misfortunes,
another comic trick.   When not removing the last page of a
Christie mystery, for example, he is drilling ever so tiny
holes in oil tankers.

     Bedazzled is also festooned with comic reversals (the
trickle from a burst pipe), gags (acrophobic Stanley invariably
finds himself up on a height), and jokes ("Julie Andrews" but
not "Jackie Kennedy" is a magical name).

Finally, there is the film's wordplay, replete with puns, double entendres, and comic names.

"Bedazzled" is also a perfect name for all this lunacy, so chockablock with comic variety and invention.   Its primary meaning is "To confuse by a strong light: dazzle."   This succinctly defines the plot and subject, whereas its alternative meaning, "To impress forcefully: enchant,"[3] exactly expresses the film's effect upon us.

Cook and Moore made a promising movie debut as a pair of miscreants in The Wrong Box (Bryan Forbes, 1966). Bedazzled does more than just keep that promise.   Part of their flair as the snobbish instigator (George) and the sad little man (Stanley) respectively comes from their oneness with the material.   As with all great clowns, they say and do what they believe.   Their physicality helps too.   Cook is tall, lean, with piercing eyes; Moore, short, stocky, with cocker-spaniel eyes--the foil principle in practice.

Eleanor Bron, as Margaret, moves from the edges of Donen's canvas to its center, where her attractive features, vague smiling, and outward pose disguise an extremely ordinary mind and a snippity personality, which makes Stanley's quest more hilariously ironic.   So, too, their side-by-side stance, in which he comes up only to her eyebrows.

Critic Stanley Kauffmann's sensitive ear picked up the different dialects the trio use in their incarnations, which he lauded in his review: "Those who have even a rudimentary acquaintance with British accents will enjoy the skill with which the three leading performers range from lower class to lazy-tongued upper class, with various provincial and culturally pretentious waystops in between."[4]

The film's other jesters are equally standout.   Michael Bates's Inspector is a poker-faced, meat-and-potatoes, slightly creepy man, very much aware of his own importance.   In the service of Lillian Lust, Raquel Welch's physical endowments are finally given thematic value.   Robert Russell's Anger, the club's burly bouncer, is continually in a state of ill-contained fury.   Howard Goorney's Sloth sprawls over the nitery's membership booth in a deep coma.   No matter the situation, Alba as Vanity, in the white coat of a men's-room attendant, is mirror-fixated.   Barry Humphries, always with a touch of lime, highqueens it as Envy.   And Parnell McGarry's Gluttony, though eating constantly, still manages to look hungry, while Daniele Noel's Avarice, the thinnest ever, has a countenance wracked with worry over any monetary outlay.

Austin Dempster's location shooting in and around London enables us to go with the preposterousness. Most of the backdrops are drolly ironic, too, like the zoo's monkey cages, where a couple of the missing links fornicate with abandon behind Stanley's and Margaret's nature-civilization debate.

Below the physical realm is the crammed, dirty basement club, a representation of hell with its steps downward, fiery red walls, flashily hued denizens, and harshly lighted clubroom, done in early Hitler. Above, softly focused spacious green fields, lush vegetation, and a towering white greenhouse, all quite neat and clean, express heaven. Hell's mood is sluggish and depressing; heaven's tedious due to its solitariness and sameness of colors. The corny and dumb look of both metaphysical spheres is intentional, depicted in the way the good sisters and our parents had taught us. As such, the film's satirical jab at God-talkers is carried out in Terence Knight and Ted Tester's art direction as well. Also, the metaphysical dreariness contrasts with the world's teeming diversity, which, no matter how lowlife or mechanical it can be, is far preferable to either extreme. This visual contrast reiterates the film's main motif of reality (and this includes our own initiative, resources, and will) constituting our only given and therefore something that must be made the most of. This, too, is sound Christian doctrine, for Jesus did say "Let the day's own trouble be sufficient for the day."[5] And throughout, the color red is a structuring device, helping to unite the narrative strands.

Donen suspensefully builds each scene's beginning with a series of contextually funny details. This type of construction hearkens back, though in a less severe way, to the découpage-built Charade, Arabesque, and Road and heralds Donen's subsequent scene-structuring stylistic as one in which découpage has a decided edge over composition in depth. In Bedazzled Donen also frequently splinters the Panavision space, thus echoing the schizoid times. He exploits the medium's knack for magic, metamorphosis, and phantasmagoria just as he did in Yankees and will do in The Little Prince and Saturn 3, as when, through animation, friend and fiend become flies--the reverse of Anchors's reality within an animated context.

Behind Binder's black cutouts of the principal titles is a circular right-to-left swirl, so furious that figures are indistinguishable. Only colors are visible, which eventually push the cutouts away and become the background of the supered minor credits. It is as if we, at a carousel's center, where the operator works the amusement, were looking at a merry-go-round gone berserk. The image is an emblem for the film itself, with its outer and inner circular structures, driving pace, demented people and situations (the carousel as a metaphor for life's madness is a common one), and, of course, our godlike perspective given us by comedy's objective point of view.

> I just shot the background of the fair and gave Binder that sequence and said put some credits on it. We made the picture for thirty-two cents. ... The film unfolds furiously because in a fantasy, you mustn't give the audience time to niggle over anything, otherwise they'll fall out. ... I remember going through just agony on the editing. The picture went through three major changes in the editing.

Moore, also an accomplished musician, composed and directed the eclectic score: snycopated liturgical airs for the credits, riffing at Wimpey's, rock at the club, music hall for the theological discussion around the letter box, a jazz piano against lush romantic strains of a full orchestra at Oxford, pseudo-Gregorian chant and Palestrina polyphony at the nunnery, a Rolling Stones-ish monologue for Drimble to counter Stanley's Presleyesque "Love Me," an eerie chant, "Bedazzled," for the mesmerized girls, and an operettish "Leap in the Name of Beryl," a travesty of the Abbess's "Climb Every Mountain" from The Sound of Music.

Only a couple of critics played devil's advocate amidst the barrage of divine reviews. Fox, unfortunately, didn't give this darkly comic fantasy, quite easily one of the best comedies of this or any other decade, a first-class promotion, and thus most people never heard of it, let alone saw it, during its release. Today Bedazzled shares Road's cult status, a staple on the revival and college circuits.

> It's a very personal film in that I said a great deal about what I think is important in life.

STAIRCASE (1969)

> I saw the play <u>Staircase</u> in London with Paul Sco-
> field and Patrick Magee and it brought me to my
> knees. I asked Dick Zanuck, head of Fox at the
> time, to buy the rights and make it as a very low-
> budget picture with Scofield. Scofield didn't want
> to do it so I thought of Rex Harrison and Richard
> Burton.

The Royal Shakespeare Company presented Charles
Dyer's autobiographical play in November 1966 as part of a
series of "first new British plays" under Peter Hall's direction. (One of the characters bore the playwright's name
while the other character's name, Harry C. Leeds, like that
of every other character Charlie mentions, was an anagram
of "Charles Dyer.")   The New York version, helmed by Barry
Morse, with Eli Wallach (Charlie) and Milo O'Shea (Harry),
opened January 1968.   The London <u>Times</u> critic felt that
"the main excitement of the production is in its playing."[1]
Across the sea Clive Barnes opined that "the theme ...
is very acceptable, and the interplay between [the] two
characters is at the emotional level, honest and revealingly
dissected.   Yet the verbal means to the end are rather dead-
ening.   Queer conversation, with its calculated bitchiness, its
high camp, shrill exaggeration is funny ... only for a time,
because the method of its wit is too unvarying."[2]   By casting
the exchange in the stock vaudeville double act of comic and
straightman (Dyer was an old-time vaudevillian) and setting
the overnight banter (Act I, Scene 1, transpires late Sunday
evening; Scene 2, a half-hour later, Act II, early next morning) in the barbershop, the play emerged as an abstract, ab-
surdist duologue of a human relationship.

Dyer and Donen's adaptation--the director's first in
almost a decade--bursts the shop's three walls and fills the
new places with the day-to-day business of living that limns
character and setting, creates atmosphere, and deepens
mood, all the while respecting the realist tendency of the
medium.   And practically none of the activity chosen is special to gay coupling, which, no matter how sensitive the
handling, would have appeared sensational and lurid to a
straight audience in the '60s.[3]   Instead, Dyer and Donen stick
to the turf of our common humanity.

Dyer and Donen also people these additional contexts
and extend them for a period of ten days.

The two-character play, with the policeman's voice-
over, now makes room for their discomforting mothers; a
trick who utters not one solitary word; the neighbor, Miss
Ricard, who scolds Harry for leaving Mom alone; a constable
who does not even lower his voice at the sight of the cower-
ing couple; the gravedigger and acolyte unaware of Harry's
presence; the indiscreet couple petting before the shop window; an uncommunicative customer; a laundromat of absorbed
Pakistanis; the bus's supercilious female ticket collector;
Ricard's "John" stealing a peek at Charlie, most likely to
confirm the whore's juicy gossip about his peculiarity; the
officious cub mistress whose shrill whistle halts the game;
the Scouts who go off with not so much as a "thank you" to
Harry; the heedless sailor; the rest home's impatient nurse;
the Salvation Army engrossed in its hymn; the couples in the
park gazing at the bickering men as if they were freaks; the
gymnast too conceited to admit the couple's attention; the
teenagers fornicating insouciantly before Charlie and Harry;
and the angered customer turned away at the door.   All of
these, through inadvertence or hostility, exacerbate the pair's
aloneness.

Because of this spatial and temporal extension,
grounded by mundane activity and people, the film emerges
as a realistic document.   And given the room and time to
live with the two men, we come closer to them than we were
onstage, although the blistery comic tone still ensures our
distance.   This realism and black humor were new to Donen,
who had up to this time, stylized his worlds while observing
them with gently mocking eyes.

The adaptation undergoes some structural changes as
well in an effort to create suspense.   The staircase, a common symbol in literature and film from Homer to Hitchcock,
functions as a metaphor for Charlie and Harry's relationship
and for the universal predicament as well.   The image takes
on significance in the film, brilliantly organizing and synthe-
sizing its concerns and attitudes.   A staircase joins the
ground-floor salon to the second-story living quarters in
which Donen frequently sets the action.   Harry dreams of
himself climbing a staircase and, in his brothel tale, describes a man weeping on the staircase.   He upbraids Charlie for using him as a "staircase between flops" and consoles
him with "We'll build a staircase to the sky/We'll never be
lonely playing so high. "   Also, of course, there's the title,
the teaser in which Donen clinically observes two déclassé

Staircase: On the set Donen shows Harrison how to perform
the old cod routine.   Copyright: Twentieth Century-Fox.

drag queens braying out the sour song "Staircase" with re-
iterations of the word against a rickety staircase as well as
the credits in the form of a staircase.

I wanted to show the entertainers up close as I

> did the two men. There's something sad when you
> see people made up in such a bizarre way. A
> close look makes them even more bizarre. We
> get turned off and feel superior. But if we got to
> know them as we did the two men, I wanted to im-
> ply, we would see the similarities between them
> and us and realize our superiority was unfounded. ...
> Binder and I sat up weeks trying to solve the cred-
> its problem. Both Richard and Rex had contracts
> that demanded top billing. So Binder kept their
> names going up in multiple whereby you don't know
> which name is first or second since they keep mov-
> ing.

Except for the thinning of the East End patois and
some arch phrases, the barbed repartee, often at cross-
purposes, sometimes circular, is untouched. (The repartee
here is less stylized than Charade's, which is attuned more
to old screwball comedies than to life, and more vitriolic
and poignant than Road's.) Besides being the chief source
of the film's humor and violence (repartee is a battle between minds), the repartee serves as a continuity device
between scenes--the same conversation travels through several scenes--and is the main carrier of movement.

Harry, all kitchen sink and cleanser and soul, found
Burton in the post-golden period of his career. By the '60s
end Burton is walking through his roles. True, his verbal
expression of fidgetiness, pathological sensitivity to his appearance and moroseness, his memory flights, his self-
pitying wallows and vitriolic tongue, all are impeccable as
ever--his is a great voice. But as for his gestural expression, he seems to attack the workaday routines he is given
in every scene and conveys a "let's get this distasteful thing
over with as soon as possible" attitude.

> There were no rehearsals. Richard was going
> through a difficult time and he wasn't interested
> in doing it.

The image of pattering Pygmalion unfortunately hovered
over everything Harrison did after the role that turned this
leading man into a star--even here as Charlie, who's all
show biz and cologne.

> Harrison tried very hard, was really dedicated.
> Rex did a very good job in a difficult part.

The rest of the cast is admirable, each bringing home the sad-funny qualities of Dyer and Donen's conceptions. Cathleen Nesbitt as Mother Leeds is a watery-eyed vegetable with gnarled arthritic fingers. As Mother Dyer, Beatrix Lehman is a wiry Jeremiah with a thin, rasping voice, white hair stretched taut in a bun, veins bulging at the temples, false teeth, and a jaw that audibly clicks as she eats prunes. And Stephen Lewis is Jack, the soft trick whose loud and frequent laughter is about as sincere as a tap dancer's smile.

> Richard wouldn't work in England for tax reasons and I didn't want to make it in France. The play was about the East End of London, and the only way I could show what life was like there was to do it there. That compromise led to a lot of others. We did ten weeks of interiors at Paris' Studio Cinema at Billancourt, five weeks of location shooting on a replica of a London street built on the banks of the Seine, and one week of exteriors in London.

Nevertheless, art director Willy Holt, under Donen's direction, does invest the settings with the moldering, ramshackle feel of no man's land, which Challis, at Donen's behest, somberly underlights and occasionally relieves with slashes of lavender and pink--hues associated with gay men and old ladies--all in accordance with the film's motifs and moods.

Obstacles are frequent in Donen's Panavision mise-enscène, indicative of the couple's position of exile from society (the men are forever watching the world through windows) as well as their mutual estrangement. Prevalent, too, are mirror shots: Charlie attempting to remedy time's vehemence, Harry confronting it, and Mama Leeds staring at the couple through a distorting convex mirror outside her window, which, by the way, are Donen's most judgmental shots, condemning Mom, and through Mom, us.

As the film's principal cutting devices, the bitchy repartee and dismally trivial details (one shot starts on clothes swirling in a washer; another ends on false teeth sinking in a glass of water) are largely responsible for the brisk pace and harsh, staccato rhythm. In places, though, the piece is too rushed. Between the final draft and the finished film, Donen snipped items that would have grounded the context even more and smoothed out the narrative line.

Dudley Moore composed and selected the spare, down-
beat score.   In addition to the precredit and credit sequences,
the original thematic title tune is delivered over the radio,
by a vocalist reminiscent of Petula Clark, during Harry's
head-unwrapping.   A lad's treble intonation of the Protestant
hymn "All Things Bright and Beautiful" adds poignancy to the
graveyard scene and helps us share the director's perspective: "All creatures great and small/All things wise and
wonderful/The Lord made them all. "   A Dylanesque rock
rendition of two of Jesus's dicta, "Father, forgive them for
they know not what they do" and "Forgive us our trespasses
as we forgive those who trespass against us, " plays over the
delivery of the summons, revelatory of Charlie and Donen's
state of soul.   The Salvation Army's off-key ompahpahing of
the hymn "Yes Jesus Loves Me" speaks of religion's indif-
ference and encapsulates Harry's dilemma.   Hard rock from
Mother Leed's radio ironically underlines the commotion in
the room.   And cacophonous riffing under the couple's walk
to court suggests the world's crazy attitude toward these
marrieds.

Church bells are an occasional respite from the grating track of Mom's thunderous thumps, the tinny music from
the heterosexual couple's transistor, a chopping knife hitting
the board, the bobby's earsplitting knocks, garbage cans
crashing over, and so on.

Reviews of Staircase were mixed, with about twice as
many thumbs up as thumbs down.   Some critics believed the
film to be better than the play.   Others were happily surprised that a major studio, top actors, and a top director
would tackle such a subject in such an uncompromising way.
But the audience stayed away.

> Fox thought the picture was something like The
> Boys in the Band [Mart Crowley's '60s play in-
> volving the gamut of gay types at a Manhattan birth-
> day party, where they play a truth game].   I told
> them they didn't understand the picture.   Once the
> film opened and they saw what was what, they just
> walked away from it. ...   For what it was--a two-
> character picture, it was very expensive.

The '60s proved a creatively ambitious and rich time
for Donen.   His material, barring the clone Arabesque, was
for the first time multishaded and much more textured than

any of his other comedies. Staircase and, to some extent, Road pushed him into a realism that he had always turned his back upon, opting to fashion an imaginary world where lightness and grace prevailed rather than mirror the existing one. (Donen's work, as we have seen, is in the recreative rather than mimetic tradition of art.) Experimentation with narrative form was bold, sure, and always right for the story at hand. (In the '70s Movie Movie continues this experimentation with its trailer-separated double feature and its collapse of two entire movies into the length of one.) Also, Donen played around with the fusion of genres and national sensibilities.

It was at this time, too, that Donen perfected his cinematization of dialogue: stringing the phrases on a player's movement; investing them with some inventive, usually ironic business (another way of making the verbal visual); opening, closing, or having the frame stand still to enhance or undermine meaning or play variations on it; cutting on conversational rhythms; and often setting the lines to music to flavor them and connect them with what went before and what is to come and give them, and ultimately the entire piece, a flow. In addition new photographic and editing techniques were tried out.

This period also saw Donen's most elaborate interworkings of the score with the dialogue, visuals, and cutting. As a matter of fact, no other director working in film comedy, save Blake Edwards, paid such meticulous attention to the score as Donen did.

Of the five films made in this period four proved to be, along with Indiscreet, his most personal and accomplished comedies. And Staircase provided another model of stage-to-screen adaptation, as Indiscreet had a decade ago.

> My London base afforded me the advantage of being away from the Hollywood rat race. Just going your own way in spite of whatever anybody else is doing or in spite of what you've already done was satisfying. I also had the advantage of the European influence: their way of looking at life, of making movies. And it's cheaper to make movies in Europe than here. As far as my own personal reimbursements go, I don't suppose it's any better. I probably would have made more money if I had been here, probably would've made more movies too.

This second spring gave every indication that the '70s

would find Donen, just forty-five, making even further strides, but this just was not to be. So Staircase, instead of being a continuation of sorts, became somewhat of a climax.

AN ASSESSMENT OF THE DONEN COMEDY

Donen and company did not give the screen a distinct brand of comedy, as, say, Tashlin did with his cartoonization of American mores, nor did he continually work in and develop the same mold, as Wilder did with his dark comedy. Rather he plugged into existing popular forms, often mixing them. (The '70s will see the adventure comedy Lucky Lady and the parody Movie Movie.) On occasion Donen created the best examples of these types, such as four of the last five (Charade, Road, Bedazzled, and Staircase), the earlier Indiscreet, and the forthcoming Movie Movie.

Yet, despite the amazing range of subforms, which no other American comedy director can claim, distinct resonances mark the lot as Donen's: a relationship riddled with a straying-staying tension is at the heart of each work.

Donen's males, including those in Lucky Lady and Movie Movie, are adolescent, agitated, self-absorbed, evasive, and sometimes even crooked. All are professional men. The public sphere occupies a goodly amount of their time. Though basically self-sufficient, they seek the comfort of women from time to time, though a few have sublimated this need. They are philandering utilitarians who eschew domesticity, any long-term commitment to a woman, especially marriage. If they happen to be hooked, they are surly, cramped, and restless and make an unpleasant time for themselves as well as their mates. In Bedazzled's modification Stanley's lust for Margaret is repressed. He is actually afraid of her. His straying comes down to allowing George to arrange it with Margaret.

The fear of castration by women troubles some of them, more so when they run up against castrated victims: Jud seeing Stacy's father; Philip, the browbeaten Alfred and the bulldozed servant Carl; Victor, Mr. Wilbur Jr.; Mark, Howie; and Stanley, the Lord of the Manor.

Donen's females (of Lucky Lady and Movie Movie, too), on the other hand, are mature, steady, altruistic, and forthright. All except socialite Hattie have careers (Joanna

gives up her career when she marries) and are able to jug-
fle the public and private spheres gracefully.

They seek the security, stability, and comfort of a
permanent relationship, especially in marriate.   If married,
the females try to keep the relationship viable.   Their of-
fense is as energetic and resourceful as the men's defense,
and usually more persistent, and in the end carries the day.
As with their musical cousins, they stabilize their men's
lives.   (Even in a preliberation era, Donen's canvas--
including the musical side--admits of no condescension or
etherealization of the opposite sex.)

Donen's comedies are essentially a description of the
wooing, living together, and married ways of the contemporary American and English male and female.

Through Donen's satirical and farcical lenses, coupling emerges as a game of witty ripostes and rapier-like
shouts, elaborate stratagems and equally elaborate retaliatory
measures, crafty dodges and hypocrisies, and even surprise
attacks, sometimes erupting into skirmishes with limbs and
decor as weapons and targets.   But most of the bruises are
to egos and sensibilities and only occasionally to hearts.
Living rooms, hotel suites, bedrooms, restaurant bars, and
telephones are the usual battle stations.   (Donen never leaves
out violence in his comedies--or in his musicals, believing
firmly that violence, whether from repartee or slapstick, makes
for good drama.) Even when marriage or its repair is in sight,
there is no sign of the game's end.   These people, Donen implies, will remain the same until the day they die.   Consequently
there is very little, if any, character development.

Donen's satirical focus on his people's private sphere
always includes their public one as well in the frame's background or along its edges, thereby creating more density,
combustion, and humor.   Unlike the musicals' proletarian
contexts though, the comedies' straits are from upper middle
class to wealthy, except for Stanley and Margaret's reality,
the East End barbers', and Joey's and Betsy's (Movie Movie)
humble beginnings.   (Practically every comedy comes complete with at least one Rolls.)   The various professions and
their milieux Donen finds rife with codes of action, language,
and dress, in which accidents have replaced essences and
forms have denatured rather than enhanced reality, and as
a result contain a good deal of pretension and sham, if not
downright nonsense.

Some of the comedies' centers are shared by an adventure: securing a home for Fearless Fagan, Kiss Them for Me's shore leave, stealing the crown in Surprise Package, Charade's search for the loot, Arabesque's decoding, Bedazzled's seven wishes, Lucky Lady's rumrunning, and Movie Movie's accumulation of big bucks to have an eye operation and put on a show.

Adventure, in Donen's satirical and farcical way, is primarily an activity in which people indulge their finagling, larcenous, and acquisitive instincts and reveal their bumbling natures. Only secondarily, is it a test and expression of fealty--another overlap with the musicals.

Donen's method, in general, is lightly to skim the surface of both the romance and adventure, never pausing long enough to explore the inherent pathos of emotional involvement or an escapade's nasty implications, excepting Road, Bedazzled, and Staircase. Accordingly the romance and adventure, in spite of an occasional hurt or trouble, come off as contributing a good deal of fun and excitement to his peoples' lives, thus averting any trace of mawkishness or cynicism.

As in the musicals, Donen disavows any redemptive tone, barring Staircase. Our foibles are pointed out for the sheer fun of seeing how foolish and corrupt we are. Self-tormenting anxiety over our human condition, Donen implies, is for the birds; laughter is the only palliative.

To expose rather than explore helps Donen keep his distance from his characters, thus ensuring the situation's inherent humor. His creation of basically cerebral people who, no matter how silly or brutal the moves get, never lose their control or dignity, and his mapping out a farcical meeting ground for his couples enforces this distance.

> I don't think I'm afraid to show emotion on the screen if it seems to me real emotion. I don't like to see people crying a lot for themselves in pain. I owned the rights to A Patch of Blue for a while. [This story of a strident white mother enraged over her blind daughter's love for a black man was directed by Guy Green in 1965.] I just couldn't bring myself to do it. It was too anguished and, ultimately, sentimental and sloppy. I don't mind people crying for joy, however. And I don't mind showing people caring a lot for each other, but only when they really do.

Passages depicting an exchange of hearts and minds, when they occasionally occur, transpire usually at night near water, as in the musicals. As with countless other poets, the Old and New Testament writers, Shakespeare, and Hemingway, night is for Donen a time of serenity, a time when intimacies and secrets are shared, while water, with its connotations of refreshment, cleansing, and newness, is an appropriate site for the expression of understanding and love. Water, further, functions as a character icon depicting the males' adolescence in the comedies as it does the males' boyishness in the musicals.

Donen's preference of irony over sentiment, which chiefly characterizes his handling of the old battle-of-the-sexes chestnut, contributed to the intelligence and sophistication of American film comedy. In this regard Donen seems to have taken over from Lubitsch. And his methods, which came from the same toolbox as the musicals, gave the genre a look and a visual texture--both sorely lacking in American comedies--as well as a breeziness, even lyricism at times, and some unfadable performances: the playful Bergman and the shrewdly romantic Grant (Indiscreet);[4] the impish Kendall (Feeling) and Simmons (Grass); Grant's middle-aged grace (Charade); Hepburn's nuanced transition from sweet to snide, Bron's cagey bitchiness, and Daniels's anal fixation (Two for the Road); Bron's vacuousness that comes in seven shades, and Moore's Pierrot crossed with an Auguste (Bedazzled); Reynolds's smooth sailing (Lucky Lady); and Bostwick's brio (Movie Movie).

THE LITTLE PRINCE (1974)

About thirty translations and a startling number of re-
prints have marked The Little Prince's history since its publication in 1943. They say twenty thousand copies are sold
each year. Written in French by Antoine de Saint-Exupéry,
"a winged Hamlet" who was shot down while flying aircraft
during a World War II mission in 1944, this poetic-philosophic
fantasy of a pilot confronting the child within about the meaning of life has tantalized filmmakers from Walt Disney to
Orson Welles.

A. Joseph Tandet, a theatrical lawyer and occasional
producer bought the rights from Saint-Exupéry's widow and
Paris publisher Gallimard. Tandet then contacted Alan J.
Lerner, who in the mid-'60s was under contract to Paramount to produce a total of five mammoth musicals--Paint
Your Wagon (Joshua Logan, 1969) and On a Clear Day You
Can See Forever (Vincente Minnelli, 1970) were already in
production. Lerner completed a screenplay that Tandet sent
off to Frederick Loewe, Lerner's former collaborator, who
decided to end his retirement and write the music.

> My divorce from Adelle came through in '70 and I
> returned to the Coast looking for projects. [By
> this time, the British film renaissance of the last
> ten years was definitely at an end due to the severe
> financial crunch in the industry and the exodus of
> talent to America.] Bob Evans, veepee of produc-
> tion at Paramount, asked me if I would read The

Little Prince and listen to a few of the songs already written. I was very moved. [During the
film's preproduction, Donen married actress
Yvette Mimieux.]

After the score's completion Lerner left the project
as producer to concentrate on Coco (1969) and a Gigi revi-
sion (1973) for the stage.   Donen stepped into his shoes as
producer, thus putting an end to Tandet's interference.

Lerner's script wisely retains the author's narrative
form of the Pilot's first-person account and within that account, the Prince's first-person story--Lerner must have
felt at home with the rhyming scheme.   Saint-Exupéry's day-
night structure is also kept as well as the dialogic encounters.

Deleted are the Prince's parlays with the Conceited
Man, Tippler, Lamplighter, Geographer, Railway Switchman,
and pill-dispensing Merchant.

I did a sequence with the Lamplighter.   He was a
full-size puppet on a planet about six feet in diam-
eter.   There wasn't room on the planet for the
Prince so he hovered around it like a moon.   The
planet kept turning night and day.   I cut it because
the optical work wasn't to my satisfaction.

The book's Geographer becomes the film's Historian;
the Militarist is Lerner's and Donen's concoction, undoubtedly
in step with the '60s and '70s antiwar fervor.   The changes
in no way blur the fable's point that a child's heart is a better way of experiencing reality than an adult's mind.

In Lerner's version the Prince didn't die in the
end.   He just went back to the Snake, fell asleep
and then disappeared.   The title song was to be
the Pilot's lullaby to the Prince.   I told Lerner
that his version had no guts.   We came to blows
on that point....   The casting of the lead was another battle.   Nobody had given much thought to
who was going to be the Pilot.   Sinatra was a
neighbor of Loewe's in Palm Springs.   One evening
Loewe played the songs for him while adding: what
a great pity that you've retired because you'd be
wonderful as the Pilot.   And Sinatra was hooked.
The studio at first thought it was a terrible idea
but then wanted him.   Sinatra, they felt, would sell

tickets. In theory, I thought, he'd be wonderful
but I don't think he would have worked at it, and
I just wasn't going to risk it. It took me a year
to sort it out. Burton said that he wanted the part.
In the end, he realized that everybody was afraid
of how he would do the songs. Because he talked
a few songs in Camelot [1960], he assumed he could
talk the score. Well, the Pilot carries the musical
burden; besides that, the songs couldn't be talked.
I auditioned everybody under the sun: Richard Harris, Jim Dale, Nicol Williamson, Robert Goulet,
and more. Even Gene Hackman was considered.
Richard Kiley was a good choice.

Good actors and good singers are as plentiful as mush-
rooms in a forest after a fall rain. But good actors who can
sing well are scarce. Kiley, as credible a Joey Percival as
he was a Man of La Mancha (1965) on stage, is that rarity.
His enactment conveys the Pilot's disillusionment and joy
quite affectingly, while his rich baritone is a perfect vehicle
for the score.

I couldn't bear the idea of looking at any more
children so I chose Steven Warner, a six-year-old
unknown, for the Prince.

Under Donen's painstaking direction, Warner's appearance, eye movements, gestures, and stride are touching. So
is his unaffected line delivery when his diction is clear.

Donen cast the rest of the parts with as much concern
as the principals--something he has always done from Kiss
Them for Me on--and held out for people who could act.
Consequently the impressions made by the supports are in-
delible: the Snake, Bob Fosse (Joel Gray had been considered); the Fox, Gene Wilder, full of painful loneliness and
sprightly exuberance; Joss Ackland, the puffy King (Olivier
had been approached); Clive Reville, the ossified Businessman; Victor Spinetti, the absorbed and intolerant Scholar;
Graham Crowden, blustery and dotty as a British army general left over from the Great War; and Donna McKechnie,
keeping the Rose's guile this side of attractiveness. (Too
bad McKechnie, who danced magnificently as Kathy in Company (1970) and as Cassie in A Chorus Line (1975), is not
called upon to do what she does best.)

Included in Saint-Exupéry's text are some whimsical
watercolors that chiefly inspired the film's look.

I fought with the studio over financing.   Finally I
got to do it my way.   It was expensive ... A year
was spent in planning the film; a year filming on
location and at EMI-MGM studios.

After scouting locations in most of the North African
countries, Donen, his trusty Challis, and production designer
John Barry chose Tozeur on the very tip of the Sahara in
southern Tunisia as the film's major site, a refreshingly un-
common place for a musical film.

I did most of the night desert scenes on a sound
stage.   There's no way to photograph a real night
with stars because the stars are too far away.
Night photographs are simply black and therefore
you see no vistas, nothing.   I went through literally
seven or eight months of tests to get the approxi-
mation just right and match the studio stuff with
the location footage.

Beautifully blended into the locations and recreations
are the drawing-board animations and the Pilot's black-pencil
sketches on a white pad, which approximate the author's own.
The decor is kept uncluttered to preserve the adventure's
awesomeness and universality.   The frequently sudden and
stark color contrasts also reinforce the story's mythic sense,
as do Shirley Russell and Tim Goodchild's simple prototypical
uniforms, which continue the Pilot-Prince comparison of the
plot and narrative device.

Binder's farewell is a grand one indeed.   His coloring-
book figures that are not colored in, which float, twirl, and
somersault in and out of frame, clinch the man-child metaphor while synopsizing the odyssey ahead.   The outlines'
lyrical motions also adumbrate Donen's lyrical staging throughout, which more than anything else preserves the book's nu-
minous feeling.

The film's eighty-eight minutes drag during the Prince's
patches of dialogue--muddled diction rather than length being
the culprit here--and "You're a Child" due to the number's
lack of musical variation.

The Musical Sequences

The score, in addition to being derivative of Lerner

and Loewe's former successes (My Fair Lady, Gigi, Camelot), and anachronistic as well, fails to capture the simplicity
and profundity of Saint-Exupéry's prose, though it does express the Pilot's melancholia and the exhilaration of friendship. "A Matter of Consequence," the Pilot's recitative to
the Prince about what the world considers important, although
filmed, was excised since it did not play well.

Unlike Donen's other efforts, the musical contained
very little dancing. This is not surprising: Lerner and
Loewe wrote in the shadow of Rodgers and Hammerstein,
who used little dancing in their shows.

"It's a Hat/I Need Air": The first part is a quick-cut
montage of grown-ups' reactions to the child's sketch: an intellectual reading in a garden, a lady in a rowboat on a lake,
a baker selling bread to a nanny from his cart, tourists on
a two-decker Parc Monceau bus, a fat old hag's face, a
chauffeur fixing a motorcar, a lady playing croquet on a spacious lawn, and a barker before a horse-drawn kiddie carousel. This pallid reminiscence of On the Town's and Give a
Girl a Break's explosive openers climaxes with a rapid-fire
repetition of these images against a chorus's crescendo chant,
"It's a hat, it's a hat, It's a hat," countered by the Pilot's
sung narrative line, "I could see is wasn't worth/Spending
time with them on earth/There were fewer in the sky/I decided I would fly."

The Pilot in a tan Simoun Caudron monoplane, swirling
in the azure heaven on the expansive melody colored by the
engine's buzz, releases the unbearable tension. Long shots,
in which the camera's movements reinforce the plane's, then
alternate with tight shots of the driver, whom the camera
zeroes into and releases, pans across and tilts up and down
to. Donen's camera is the chief supplier of the scene's exhilaration. Are Kubrick's waltzing spaceship of 2001: A
Space Odyssey (1968) and Donen's cavorting craft the Astaire
and Kelly of musicals in the space age?

The number's second half is more successful than the
first, whose images, failing to specify the relation of the
child to the context, are more decorative than thematic and
whose melodic round echoes Gigi's "It's a Bore."

"I'm on Your Side": Anxiety and loneliness are the
keynotes of this twenty-shot montage of the Pilot shouting an

apology and support as he feverishly searches for the runaway
over desert sands, dunes, and ravines.

Conflicting screen directions between and within shots
are disturbing, as are the extreme changes of the Pilot's
form; the racing camera that traces the Pilot's frantic, even
schizoid, movements that backtrack on themselves; the shots'
short duration; and the pulsating melody, which approximates
running breathlessly. The engulfing space, made infinitesi-
mal by some telephoto shots, the ravine echo, the stark setting, and the color tedium of desert tan and Pilot khaki be-
speak a solitariness that borders on madness.

> Kiley wore a tiny hearing aid and we relayed the
> track to him on a radio lying on the ground. The
> camera car had a loudspeaker playing the same
> thing. When we did those musicals in the '50s,
> playbacks and tape weren't available. Then, we
> had to put the needle down on records.

"Be Happy": Over a magnified red rose that fills the
frame Donen superimposes a miniature of McKechnie, high-
heeled in a scarlet body stocking flecked with scarlet chiffon,
sensually posing and coyly waving her limbs. Though the
singsong yet lilting ditty that offers best wishes for the Prince's
plight perfectly captures the Rose's Gemini personality, the
business does not, since it conveys her silliness but not her
loveliness. Moreover, the juxtaposition of the woman, directed and dressed as a voluptuous go-go dancer in the spitting image of Bedazzled's Lillian Lust, and the child is unsettling.

> The first thought I had was that it should be a lit-
> tle girl, someone in the Prince's age group. But
> the more I thought of the part played by a child,
> the more it seemed like an Our Gang comedy. A
> little girl isn't vain, argumentative, possessive, or
> seductive as the Rose is supposed to be. So, then,
> it occurred to me to use a woman. And the only
> way I could get by with a woman was to miniaturize
> her on a rose. Dressing her up as a rose seemed
> ludicrous.

"You're a Child": The King, Businessman, Historian,
and General condescendingly reply to the Prince's questions
about the need to command, count the stars as their own property, make things up, and war. The melody is a weak varia-

tion of My Fair Lady's "A Hymn to Him" and Gigi's intro,
its attack on civilization's idiocies is blatant, and its quadru-
ple repetition is boring.   The art direction, however, is
somewhat arresting.

The first and last sections are played in a modern,
abstract stage set.   The Monarch resides on an enlarged ball
marked with borders, miniature houses and trees, and labels,
similar to Risk's gameboard, while the General lives on a
red globe, crossed with black-and-white directional vectors
and miniature flags.

An extreme wide-angle lens makes the figures and
props of the midsections bulge outwardly as if stuck to the
lens.   The frame's edges are matted out so that only a circular orb appears.   Tapes from an adding-machine wallpaper
the Businessman's abode and carpet his floor, while the Historian sits on a stool among millions of books, which comprise his earth and sky.

"I Never Met a Rose":   This wistful moonlit ballad of
sympathy is the movie's second completely achieved and innovative number.

The lyrics' ingenious flower conceit and a '20s jazz
orchestration keep the sentiment clear-eyed.   Also leavening
the moment are the flyer's self-mocking Rudy Vallee delivery
through a scratch-pad megaphone and two soft shoes: one on
the sand, the other involving his index and middle fingers
dressed in flower cutouts upon a tiny mound.   This digital
dance stirs the memory of the tramp's bun ballet in The Gold
Rush (Charles Chaplin, 1925).

"Why Is the Desert?":   The first part is a wipe montage of the couple hurrying in the afternoon desert in search
of water.   The song-commencing second part finds them silhouetted against a sunset and then a quarter moon.   The
third part comprises the Pilot's early-morning, spread-eagled
exhaustion, the lad's pointing to the cluster of palms, their
racing and leaping over the cliff, and a slow-motion lyrical
montage of their waterfall imbibing and frolicking.   Three
transitional normal-motion shots before the finale have the
duo kicking, stamping, and jumping in a shallow pool of
water--another salute to Kelly.

The passage invests the piece's pop-philosophic line
with more action and frequently illustrates its central theme:

The Little Prince: Steven Warner and Richard Kiley reveling
in "Why Is the Desert?"   Copyright: Paramount.

the existence and importance of the spiritual.   The lyrics
tell us that the desert hides a well and the sun; the body
hides water.   A ninety-foot ossified skeleton of a monster
fish standing upright in the desert, the sun slipping below the
horizon, the lane of dried-out but living palm trees, and the
couple sprawled out on a rock and satiated because of something inside them, image the theme.   Donen even ends on a
thematic note: the Pilot's gurgling stomach piercing the silence.

But the mounting is unimaginative. The first two
parts, recalling "I'm on Your Side," is a case of déjà vu,
while the third looks like a TV shampoo comercial. The
song, structured like a nursery rhyme or riddle with its
repetitious verse melodies with no contrasting bridge, is
tedious despite different tempos and orchestrations. And a
couple of its verses that celebrate H_2O stray from the point.

"A Snake in the Grass": Donen shrewdly cuts back
and forth from a real python wrapped around a branch of a
black-lacquered tree to Fosse in the same pose on the same
branch, until the latter image is firmly established in our
minds.

Fosse's slinky dance metaphor, adorned with a black
python-trimmed outfit and yellow-tinted specs, sibilant stressed
lyrics, and a tango heavily orchestrated with hisses, suggests
a drug pusher, thereby updating the Garden of Eden myth.

At first it is a soft-sell enticement around the tree
but soon the Snake adds pressure by strutting his slyness
all over the desert, rendered in a montage of quick cuts.
In one dazzling shot he comes sliding into right frame on
his knees with his face pointing right, twists his body and
finishes the slide on his stomach with his face now pointing
left. The slow motion so exaggerates his tortuousness, a
quality perennially associated with Satan, that the shot is
even spookier than Regan's gimmicky head twisting in The
Exorcist (William Friedkin, 1973).

His self-mocking words and ironic gestures, such as
pouring dust from inside his shirt pocket for a soft-shoe
snippet, make his sinisterness quite engaging.

> I wanted the Snake to be charming as well as dan-
> gerous. Besides being an instrument of death, the
> Snake is also the ancient symbol of healing. Poi-
> son taken in carefully small doses is medicine.[1]

"Closer and Closer and Closer": Donen brings on the
Fox as he did the Snake by alternately cutting from a real
animal to Wilder's personification, each poking their heads
from behind the same tree in a forest. The Fox's rust coat
and white-and-black streaked chest matches Wilder's rust
frizz and russet tweed suit over a white shirt and black tie.

Donen's wide-angle long shot emphasizes the enormous,

The Little Prince: The Prince waters his beloved Rose on
asteroid B-12. Copyright: Paramount.

awkward space between the teacher behind the tree and the
student on a stump, indicative of the strangeness and fear in
this and all relationships at the start. Eventually a normal-
lense camera dollies in as the Fox approaches the Prince,
connoting the burgeoning intimacy and stability. Other values
change also. The spare orchestration becomes full; the slow-
paced polka rhythm quickens and Wilder's business becomes
more and more animated. Extending his hand in a practice
touch, jumping, banging his head with his fist, stamping upon,
hurling and then rolling in leaves signal an elated spirit, albeit one still hard pressed to let go.

One of the most touching moments in all of Donen's
films occurs at the peripeteia. All the values return to this
initial ascetic moment. The Fox kneels before the boy (sotto
voce and almost recitativo): "And then one day/There'll come
a day/A Christmas Eve/Midsummer's Day/A moment when/
Right there and then/We're gonna' ..."--the Fox slowly puts
his hand on the boy's--"touch." The cut to an extreme closeup of the Fox's ever-less-fearful, ever-more-radiant countenance, as he glances down in the direction of the hands occupying the frame's right edge, against a silent track, and
the return to the original two-shot with the Fox's hand upon
the Prince's, who raises his free one to the Fox's cheek,
are indeed heartrending. Values return in an even higher
register than before. The camera circumscribes the couple,
briskly pans them horizontally, diagonally, and vertically and
then sharply cuts back and forth as they run into each other's
arms from opposite sides. The orchestration is rich. The
melody transposes itself through various rhythms. The business rises to the level of dance, in which choreographer
Ronn Forella seamlessly blends a potpourri of ballroom types
with children's games. This text on human relationships is
one of the film's highlights.

"The Little Prince": This plaintive waltz underlines
the Prince's wake. The hitherto intimate camera discreetly
cuts from the Pilot's weeping over the boy inside the cock-
pit to the Pilot's huddled back in the plane's doorway and
from there dollies out to a high-angle overview.

Critics loved or hated the film; there was no middle
ground. And they divided themselves evenly. The Academy
nominated the film in the "Best Scoring of an Original Song
Score and/or Adaptation," and "Best Song" (the title tune)
categories. The film was a commercial bust.

> I never felt that The Little Prince's financial fiasco
> --or that of any other film of mine--was the result
> of the way it was handled by a studio. [Paramount
> released the film during the Christmas season along
> with Francis Ford Coppola's The Godfather Part II,
> which it rallied behind 100 percent to fill the tills
> with greenbacks and the shelves with awards.] I
> don't think the picture has in it the elements that
> the audience likes in a movie. They like razzle-
> dazzle; they like flash. They are not very pleased
> about the whole musical form any longer. I always
> used to say I don't know for whom we are making

it.   I only know I like it. ...   There have been innumerable musicals that I have turned down in the
last ten years or so: The Sound of Music [Robert
Wise, 1965], Hello, Dolly! [Gene Kelly, 1969], and
Mame [Gene Saks, 1974] for starters.   I didn't like
them.   Making a movie is a slow process that requires the utmost care and attention over an extended
period of time.   To do that work a fierce dedication is
required.   That's about the sum total of direction--
to give a piece your undivided attention, actually to
love it for a very long time with no interruptions,
to make it the center of your universe.

Tom McLaughlin of Billy Jack fame telephoned
me about a musical he wrote about Santa Claus.
Disney called about a musical.   I said: you'd want
to control the movie and I would want the control
and since you'd have it, what would I do?   There
were, of course, musicals that I would have loved
to do but I never got the chance.   I wanted to do
Guys and Dolls [Joseph Mankiewicz, 1955], even
tried to get hold of it.   I wanted My Fair Lady
[George Cukor, 1964].   I loved Camelot [Joshua
Logan, 1966], but it was never offered to me.   I
loved Fiddler on the Roof [Norman Jewison, 1971].
I love Sondheim's work.   I can never stop playing
his scores, especially Company.   I've often talked
about Company as a movie.   I think it would make
a great movie and it could be quite a real movie. ...
Do I prefer doing musicals to comedies?   Yes, I
guess when the chips are down, I'm never happier
than when the playback is going.

LUCKY LADY (1975)

The young husband-and-wife writing team of Willard
Huyck and Gloria Katz (American Graffiti [George Lucas,
1973]) took their movie idea of Depression rumrunning, inspired by a magazine article, to producer Michael Gruskoff.
Gruskoff provided the seed money for the project and took
the finished script to Fox, where this one-time talent agent
had hit pay dirt producing Young Frankenstein (Mel Brooks,
1974).   The studio, fancying Graffiti's financially and critically bright future for this property, shelled out a phenome-
nal $450,000 for the script.   Fox's new president, Alan
Ladd, Jr., handpicked Donen to direct.

> Fox sent me a version of the script and asked if I
> liked it. I told them I liked it well enough to meet
> with the authors and to work with them. So the
> authors and I worked it through again and I got a
> script I liked very much. It took about ten weeks
> or so.... Gruskoff produced. He didn't interfere
> but he didn't help much either.... I did have the
> right of final cut.

Throughout its rewriting, production, and editing
phases, Lucky Lady, like Kiss Them for Me, experienced
conceptual turmoil. The Huycks' dark sensibility and Donen's
light one pulled this way and that, while the studio's block-
buster mentality tugged from yet another angle. So what we
get is a vessel veering off in different directions every ten
minutes or so, sailing a seemingly uncharted course. From
the opening scene, a frisson finely chiseled by ellipsis and a
camera roving over graveyard details in a black night, which
is the stuff of thrillers, we cut to Claire's number, more a
musical star-de-force than anything else, and continue on to
a Sennettesque border run. Most of the fanciful Coronado
sequences so transcends the film's undertow, which is felt
from the beginning, that it comes off as an excursion into
nostalgia. The Grand Guignol horror of McTeague's attack
bears no trace of the fun violence of the other sections.
Billy's death makes a bid for pathos, and a glib one at that
since the film never explores the relationship between him
and Walker. In the latter half, the Kibby-Walker duet gives
off the homosocial aroma of the then popular buddy genre,
while the wiping out of McTeague is a mini-disaster epic.
(As a matter of fact this maritime melee of sixty vessels
was coordinated by none other than the apocalyptic virtuoso
himself, Paul Strader.)[1] It is no wonder that after such a
climax as this, Lady runs out of steam before heading for
any port.

The film is more a series of set pieces than anything
else, too unrelated to each other ever to fuse into a subject
--luck, fate, friendship, or surviving in style--or, better yet,
a theme--say, shared danger is more exhilarating than security.

It seems funny to suggest that such an overly ambitious
film as this, which already contains too much for its own
good, needs something. But Lady can sure do with more
characterization of her passengers and their relationships,

Lucky Lady: A good deal of the doings occur on a cutter
afloat on the Pacific, as in this celebration with Burt Reynolds, Gene Hackman, Liza Minnelli, and Robby Benson.
Copyright: Twentieth Century-Fox.

which just might have given the voyage some modulation and
continuity and brought the girl safely home.   Even the film's
'30s setting is not really explored in terms of the Depression's
effect on the characters' lives.   Consequently the period setting throughout--and not just the Coronado sequence--seems
a mercenary flirtation with nostalgia and not a means of
characterization; so too the dialogue, full of those cute, brit-
tle, off-the-wall wisecracks that are good for a laugh or two
but do not bring us any closer to the characters, since
they're more revelatory of the writers' own cleverness and
affection for '30s movie jargon than a feel for the way people actually spoke then.

> I brought the picture in at 230 minutes.   The cut-
> ting lightened the picture....   The ending, that's
> a very long story.   When the script was given to
> me the first time, the two men were killed and you
> saw a scene where the woman had aged ten years,
> had a child by Charley and was remembering in a

very sad way her adventuresome life with those
two men. That brought tears to my eyes but at
the same time, even then, I felt that it didn't particularly satisfy me and for the next year or so,
we constantly niggled at trying to find a different
ending where the two men weren't killed. No particularly good ending was found and as many as we
tried the writers were not too pleased with trying
to get anything new. So when we filmed it, we
filmed the original ending. But when the picture
was finished, it seemed even less right, for the
picture had taken on a much lighter tone in the rewriting and in the making. For example, the Coast
Guard Captain, who was the villain in the original
script, written as a true psychotic bent on killing
the rumrunners, was played almost as a buffoon.
He became a light farcical villain and he was very
funny. In doing that and a host of other things
like that with the script, the serious side of the
picture was even lessened, so that the ending really
seemed totally wrong to me. Also the picture,
during its making, replaced Claire at the center
and now focused on the trio. After the first preview, in October, I knew I had to change the ending. At subsequent previews I tried several end-
ings, including a happy one that came down to chopping off the film's last ten minutes or so. In mid-
November, a month before the movie's release, the
Huycks, after great protestation, finally agreed to
write a concluding scene in which the characters
live. By that time the studio also favored a happy
ending. This ending was a funny, light ending that
had the three mouthing the same dialogue in the
dark with only the lighted ends of three cigars and
smoke visible. As the lights come on, you see
that they were all three in bed together and they
were 75-year-olds. That was actually a very funny idea. I called Gene and Burt and read it to
them. They loved it and agreed to do it gratis.
Since Liza was on location in Rome [doing A Matter of Time, Vincente Minnelli, 1976], Gene, Burt,
and I went over to Rome to spend one Saturday in
late November shooting the new ending. It just
didn't work because of the poor makeup jobs for
them. Since I couldn't get Liza again, I couldn't
do a retake. I couldn't fix it, so I discarded it.

Despite all the rumors concerning the kaleidoscopic casting--Paul Newman, Warren Beatty, Robert Redford, and Barbra Streisand were all in and out of the picture at one time or another--the film underwent one cast change.   Hackman, a hot property since his Oscar rendition of the sadistic cop Popeye (The French Connection [William Friedkin, 1971]) replaced George Segal.

As the grifter Kibby, Hackman physically and metaphysically is out of joint with Donen's confection.   Overweight and balding, Hackman does not cut a romantic adventurer figure even in nautical blues and whites or evening clothes. And his movement and timing are not comicly precise.   Furthermore, his persona of an introspective soul whose inner torture bursts through the surface in bold, violent strokes and caustic tongue-lashings curdles Kibby's foolhardiness.

Claire was Minnelli's first screen appearance since her role in Cabaret (Bob Fosse, 1972).   As written, the tough, wily cynical chanteuse in search of Easy Street who initiates the action is a strong female role, which in the mid '70s was a rarity.   Minnelli, however, plays her--and Donen directs her--as a pigeon-toed, carrot-topped cupie doll.   Her lack of any warm sensuality and ruttish sexuality with Hackman and Reynolds hurts the film immeasurably. Had there been less Bow and more Dietrich, we would have been spared that gnawing impression that Kibby is too intelligent and Walker too dapper for this kook.

>Liza was the first person I sent the script to.... I liked her in the role.

The few times Lady does stay on keel is due to Reynold's smooth-talking, snappily dressed, bumbling high roller Walker.   With dues paid up, he had developed into a clown somewhere between the classy and breezy Grant and the rough-and-tumble Gable.   As they did, he rolls with a part.

Geoffrey Lewis's Mosely gets caught between two interpretations, which also holds true of John Hillerman's sinister gentleman-gangster McTeague, while the humanity of Robby Benson's shy, resourceful mascot seems to be from another movie.

A good deal of Lady's doings take place on a sixty-three-foot, thirty-five-ton racing cutter, afloat on the aqua Pacific.

> There weren't really any rehearsals.... During
> the five-month shoot we experienced every kind of
> weather and calamity.... Trying to match up shots
> against an endless sea when there was nothing to
> match them to was like working in a fifth dimension.

Lady's other haunts include Guaymas, a drowsy sea-
port on the Gulf, Mexico City's opulent Gran Hotel (which
French and Italian architects built in 1910 and shipped to
Central America in prefabricated sections) substituting for
Del Coronado, and a suburban house in Sierra Vertientes re-
furbished as the Aquarium Club with red-velvet-lined walls,
tubular steel furniture, a row of fish tanks set into the wall
behind the bar, and the newest of inventions, neon lighting,
in keeping with the '30s trend of decorating speakeasies with
the latest colors, materials, and inventions to attract the
young and affluent.

While the Gran, with its central salon rising through
four gilded galleries topped by cupola domes of stained glass,
provided an ideal setting for the fortune-hunters' arrival,
there wasn't a suite in the 120-room hotel that afforded enough
space coupled with a sense of intimacy for their bain-à-trois.
So production designer John Barry and his aide Norman Reynolds rebuilt the suite--the film's only hothouse set--at Mexico City's Cherebusco Studio.

Cinematographer Geoffrey Unsworth, through the frequent use of on-screen light sources, bright reflections within the frame, and dense filters, paints these picturesque locales so softly, almost impressionistically, that it takes
about a reel or so to realize that the picture is not out of
focus. Donen's explanation, "It was a romantic movie that
needed a soft focus," seems misplaced simply because the
film does not manage the feel of romantic love or romantic
adventure, while his evaluation, "I thought it was attractive,"
is not astutely critical. Had the authors' original memory
structure been retained--and during the shooting it was--the
gossamer look might have made sense.

In the costume department Donen's judgment is on target with Minnelli's wardrobe fashioned from 1929 originals
found on the racks of LA's hand-me-down shops.

For the titled Dan Perri created a kinestasis of Art
Deco cartoon flappers (Binder was overbooked). Arranged
and cut to the film's peppy original tunes, the titles set an

exhilarating, topsy-turvy tone, which the film as a whole never lives up to.

The pace is skipping throughout; in places, though, Lady steps too lightly and quickly. The film's agility is especially the result of Donen's rich, atmospheric score (from Bessie Smith's torchy blues to the jazzy "Varsity Drag"), which provides flow, continuity, and ironic bite. The two Kander and Ebb originals, more Broadwayese than Bahaesque, are essentially vehicles for Liza from her pet composers. Yet, for the performed "Get While the Getting's Good," with its sectional intro and comic cutaways, as well as the voiced-over title tune, which mortars a montage, Donen keeps the show-off quality in low profile.

Time's Jay Cocks, likening Lady to MGM's comic adventures of the '30s with Gable, Tracy, and Harlow, was just about the only positive voice. [2]

> I really cared about it and gave three years of my life to it.... I saw it forty times.... I've never understood why so many critics were incensed by it. Maybe it was the feeling we all sometimes get about why such a big amount of money was spent on such a picture. The script's good and well realized. I think it's a very good movie.

Lady was commercially unlucky too. The way-over-budget picture, which according to some sources cost $13 million, was not as successful as the studio had hoped.

It had made its money back and then some.

MOVIE MOVIE (1978)

> Larry Gelbart had this double-feature concept during his TV days. He even brought it to Universal, who didn't want to do it. After writing the script he let producer Marty Starger see it. Marty was associated with Gelbart on Sly Fox. [1] Starger liked it. Both thought George C. Scott was perfect for the lead roles. Lord Lew Grade [emperor of ITC Entertainment] decided to put up the money. They brought me the script. I was their first choice to direct. [The nostalgic air of Singin' in the Rain

and Lucky Lady as well as the movie allusions and
spoofing throughout his work undoubtedly influenced
their choice.] I thought the script was very funny
and euphoric. I dropped the Shields and Yarnell
biography called Show Biz that I was working
on.... On this one the script was totally finished.
I contributed no more than ten percent.... Other
than certain financial limits, which were set at the
beginning and were certainly fair, Grade left me
to my work, Starger was a lovely man, too, who
didn't interfere.... Warners distributed.

Movie Movie, of course, was part of the cycle of
genre-parody that plagued American film comedy in the late
'60s and '70s. [2] Here, such liniment-soaked melodramas as
Kid Galahad (Michael Curtiz, 1937), Golden Boy (Rouben
Mamoulian, 1939), and City for Conquest (Anatole Litvak,
1940); The Dawn Patrol-type of aerial film (Howard Hawks,
1930); and the Berkeley backstager, particularly 42nd Street
(Lloyd Bacon, 1933)--three types of movie fare churned out
by Warners--are given an affectionate kick in the pants. By
combining the pieces in a double feature separated by a
breathless coming attraction and two title cards and utilizing
the same players, sets, costumes, and mise-en-scène in the
different fare, the film concomitantly teases movie format
and house style as well.

The script is clever. The targets are new (Ken Russell's The Boy Friend [1971], which traversed part of the territory, was more burlesque than parody) and the tone is sure.
Gelbart, Sheldon, Keller, and Donen know very well that
parody loves what it sends up, which love, by the way, implies an astute sense of how far to go.

When I first came to Hollywood, I had a personal
antagonism toward Busby Berkeley musicals. I
thought them trite, stilted, limited. My impetus
was a reaction against those backstage musicals.
But today, I love them, and I see their inventive-
ness, variety, cinematic quality. I guess I appreciate them because I don't have to fight them. [3]

The use of three different parodies in one film and
the short scene construction are also shrewd moves on the
creators' parts. Genre-parody's fuse is short, since its
point, being singular and depending upon audience familiarity
with the subject, is perceived immediately. The film

scampers along so that we aren't given time to think and
feel, for with genre-parody there is not really anything to
mull over and digest unless it reveals something new about
the form: what made the elements popular, where did they
come from, how and why did they change, etc. , which Movie
Movie does not attempt. Genre-parodies are movies about
movies, not life; they are movies that feed on their own en-
trails. It is surface art in which formulae and techniques--
not people and situations--are what we respond to.

> I also tried to make this film a little bit real.
> I wanted people to be moved by the situation de-
> spite the obvious parody.

The intentional fallacy rears its head again. Despite
the teller's very words, nowhere in the tale is there evidence
of this. Whereas in Rain, Charade, and Bedazzled parody
was only one level of the film--and not the most important
one either--here, as in Arabesque, it is the only one.

The script's a caboodle of clichés: situations, character types, monickers telegraphing personalities, business,
and lines. "Dynamite Hands" dialogue is chock-full of those
daffy metaphors, straight and mixed, tautologies, synecdoches
and metonymies that were part of movie lingo back then,
while "Baxter's Beauties" delightfully dishes up a banquet of
maxims, wise-crackese, and period slang that gave the backstager a language all its own.

> I wanted to call it Movie Movie as in going to a
> movie-movie. That's the kind of film it was. I
> worried that George C. Scott in Double Feature
> [the film's original title] would cause people to
> think they were going to see Patton [Franklin J.
> Schaffner, 1970] and Islands in the Stream [Frank-
> lin J. Schaffner, 1977].

The cast of veterans and newcomers perform with such
teamwork that even Stanislavsky would have been impressed.
Not since The Pajama Game has the Donen ensemble been as
jim-dandy. Moreover, Donen never allows any player to slip
into caricature, which would have threatened the tone.

Scott's manager, with a tuft of white hair sprouting
around a bald pate, chicken-wire specs on his nose, cigar
stub, and potbelly, is a crusty marshmallow whose every
breath conveys a world-weariness. His big-chested, well-

dressed producer is down-to-earth flamboyance.   Whenever
he experiences a twinge of Spencer's disease, Scott manages
to turn the affected portion of his anatomy into a comic
floor show.   In the preview he plays a stiff-upper British
World War I ace.

> Scott was totally supportive.   It was a very pleas-
> ant experience.   I frankly didn't expect it'd be
> easy to work with him.

Trish Van Devere, in her first comic role since
Where's Poppa? (Carl Reiner, 1971), is inspired as the
spic-and-span librarian who speaks in hushed, cultivated
tones.   In her volte face as the tanked, raven-haired bitch
she amazingly lets the superstar's charm and beauty cut
through her supercilious airs.   Barbara Harris, as a heart-
of-gold chorine of the Rogers-Farrell persuasion, brings off
some wry postures--for shame the film doesn't make more
of her awesome talents.   Whether as a punchy "Slapsie"
Maxie Rosenbloom second with a towel around his neck, a
Q-tip behind his ear and a cold in his nose, or the harassed
creative dynamo, or the "nice" aviator, Red Buttons continually bustles on the sidelines.   Versatile Eli Wallach is a
cold, slimy underworld king whom we hiss (his squinting is
truly malefic) and a heart-on-his-sleeve stage-door guardian
whom we love, while in the coming attraction we feel ambivalent about his aviator, all business with a yellow streak.
Art Carney, bringing the same brand of paternalism with
nary a nuance to his roles as ophthalmologist, GP, and
priest, is a monument to studio typecasting and the player's
type-acting.   And Michael Kidd's dour puss and bland delivery
of one-liners as the Hungarian papa is, unlike his Weather
performance, just right.

And on the original side, things are equally fortunate.
What keeps Scott from blowing Harry Hamlin (from the American Conservatory Theater) off the screen as the fighting lawyer is the novice's animal magnetism, which, while recalling
Garfield's and the young Brando's, is riddled with Clift sensitivity.   Barry Bostwick, Broadway's Grease (1972) and The
Robber Bridegroom (1974) lead, displays enormous plasticity
and impeccable timing, whether spilling down tenement steps
as the gangster's oily henchman or nervously bumbling as
the Powellesque tunesmith.

> Bostwick was the first choice for Dick.   He wanted
> to play the gangster Marlowe.   He came to my

Movie Movie: Ann Reinking's "Torchin' for Bill." Copyright: Warner Bros.

office one day in a chauffeured limo dressed like
a Mafioso and took me for a ride.   I did want
the same male to play the lead in both parts but
I felt that though Hamlin was too perfect for Joey
he couldn't sing and dance the way Bostwick could.

As the ingenue, Rebecca York, from the musical stage, has
Keeler, Temple, and Kane always in the back of her mind.
During her "Yes Sir, That's My Baby" audition, for example,
Donen has her pantomiming the lyrics as a further indication
of her artlessness, which even the selection of the song, a
1925 composition, hints at.

"What a Cutie" was written as her audition song.
I wanted a real one.

And Ann Reinking, the chorus-girl understudy who became

the sensational lead of Fosse's Dancin' revue (1978), is
equally sensational here, fusing Harlow and Dietrich.

In casting a couple of minor roles Donen had the
good sense to use the original players in the parts that made
them famous: earnest, skinny, spectacled Charles Lane as
the judge and lawyer, and Madie Norman as Gussie the maid.
The director himself appears in two cameos: the bleary-
eyed emcee announcing "Miss Troubles Moran" and the cabbie with several days' growth on his face who tells Spats he
doesn't have change for a ten.

As an insurance policy taken out by the creators,
George Burns, after the Movie Movie credits, introduces
the concept of the double feature and screen fare of the '30s.

> Initially the writers had newsreel footage from the
> '30s with a narration track written by them.   A
> preview audience didn't think it was funny that way.

The film's look seconds its parodic premise.   High-
contrast black-and-white, recalling at times Curtiz's work
at Warners, mark Charles Rosher Jr.'s photography for
"Dynamite Hands."   Rosher should have gone further, though,
by duplicating Curtiz's arabesque shadows and reflection shots
as well.   The trailer is in scratchy black-and-white.   Bruce
Surtees, on the other hand, bathes "Baxter's Beauties" in
rich, velvety color tones, a throwback to Fox's technicolor
musicals of the '40s.

> The black-and-white and color combination played
> better at the previews then either an all-black-and-
> white or all-color version.

Art director Jack Fisk and set decorator Jerry Wun-
derlich must have taken a crash course in art history of the
'30s and watched every Warners boxing saga and backstager,
for their work is not only period but period as interpreted
by Warner Bros.

> Filming was done both in studios and on location.
> The Warners street and the Fox street were both
> used.   The big musical number was shot on Bur-
> bank's large sound stage.   The fight sequence was
> shot in the Olympic Auditorium.   The courtroom
> scene was shot in an actual courtroom in Orange
> County.

Patty Norris's sleeveless argyle sweaters, jazzbows, ruffled blouses, watch lapels, and silk camisoles are at once nostalgic and satiric, as are the bee-stung lips and penciled eyebrows of Winnie D. Brown, Del Acevedo, Ed Butterworth, Joseph McKinney and Michael Germain and Renate Leuschner's and Hazel Catmuel's patent leather and platinum marceled tops.

Dan Perri, who displayed a period eye in <u>Lucky Lady</u>, designed the titles, which never stray from the tone, either. For "Dynamite Hands" white credits dissolve over a pair of spotlighted black boxing gloves hanging in the frame's left center against a gray backdrop. For "Baxter's Beauties" colored cardboard curtains go up with white titles on them.

Donen did his homework too, for his mise-en-scène is part of the parodic whole. Some memorable samples: the film opens with second-unit location work--a tilt down from "E. 50th Street/Park Ave. " street sign to a brass plate on a building front, which becomes stock footage when used again in the backstager; the movement of people riding in cars is created solely by lighting; Joey climbs the corridor steps to his apartment and as he enters the camera moves sideways across the invisible wall of the studio set to pick him up inside the living room; the killing of Gloves is off screen with the camera focusing on a blank wall upon which a gangster's shadow is cast; montages take us through Joey's rise to fame, Dick and Isobel's affair, and opening night. And Donen's editing exaggerates the '30s syntax of dissolves, vertical and horizontal wipes, flipflops, iris outs, rhyme cuts, and plot-reinforcing form-mattes.

A few times, though, Donen chucks this stylistic. When Joey, hearing the shots, rushes back into the corridor, a hand-held camera follows hard on his heels. This touch of cinéma vérité is as out of place as the suspenseful sectional introduction of Scott as the producer and the diagonal split-screens in Joey's rise-to-fame montages. (The script is not entirely free of the '70s either, as when Dr. Blaine asks Angela to put her blouse back on after the eye exam.)

The track, too, is a careful imitation of yesteryear's. Slugs and taps are magnified. The booming voice-over narration of "Zero Hour" echoes that of Westbrook Van Voorhis. The "Spencer" piano sets off a verbal memory of Spats's disease: "It attacks show people ... it attacks show people ... it attacks show people. " Ralph Burns's music is appro-

priately obtrusive at critical moments, tautologically telling
us what is happening and making sure we feel what we are
supposed to feel.

Burns supplied music, with Buster Davis assisting in
"Baxter's Beauties"; Gelbart and Keller wrote lyrics for the
songs.   Donen himself choreographed Reinking's high-kicking
"Torchin' for Bill" and Bostwick's spastic "I Just Need the
Girl"; Michael Kidd choreographed the other numbers with
an assist from Donen.

Although "Torchin' for Bill"'s conceit of the supposedly
bruised blonde, who is actually a kinkily sadistic bruiser,
seems to twit Las Vegas's Ann-Margret more than Von Sternberg's Blonde Venus Dietrich, it is still winsome.

Dick's audition "I Just Need the Girl," with roots in
"Make 'Em Laugh" and "The Bombo Audition," teases the
razzmatazz, get-up-and-git song found in every musical, the
"june/moon/croon/spoon" school of songwriting, the cockeyed
way a song happened on the spot in these backstagers and
was suddenly accompanied by a full studio orchestra, and the
desperation of kids to please the old man producer and get
the job.   At one breathtaking point he jumps from his knees
on the floor to the piano bench, where he lands on his feet
and bends over to play with nary a missed beat.

"Just Shows to Go Ya" is Dick and Kitty's love duet
(and what musical did not have one or two or three back
then?) set at night atop a roof furnished with a piano.   The
loaded symbolism of the girl providing the one line the composer is missing, and the sentimentality of the tenants climbing out of their windows onto their fire escapes to look on
lovingly (would it have been too much to have had the neigh-
bors sing along?), are as smartly parodic as the complication-
designating end with its billowing sheet on the line pushing the
image of the couple's approaching lips off and that of Isabel
on.

The show montage's illogical plot, made even more
so by the vast amount of deleted footage, its death-in-the-
wings counterpoint, preposterous spectacle, positioning at the
picture's close and mathematically precise abstract design
recall Berkeley's musical montages.   Once in a while, though,
the sequence gets a little too smart for its own good, as in
the startling split-second cuts of the speeding bicyclists'
counter movements against metallic streamers or the split
screens in "Lucky Day."

> "The Bicycle Number" didn't work originally and
> so I decided to edit out every other frame. I
> then added a different music track to go with the
> speeded up number.... The composers had origi-
> nally written "Beauty Is" for the finale. I wanted
> a big up-song. So they countered with "Lucky
> Day. "

The critical verdict on Movie Movie was about 75
percent favorable, 25 percent unfavorable. After a spectacular showing in New York, where it premiered on the East
Side during the Thanksgiving holidays, the film died everywhere else.

> It's a good script, a well-made film with good
> performances. I like it a lot.

SATURN 3 (1980)

> While working on Lucky Lady my production de-
> signer, John Barry [who had also worked on The
> Little Prince and would create the looks of Star
> Wars (George Lucas, 1977) and Superman (Richard
> Donner, 1978)], came to me with a story he had
> written, which I thought was a fairly good idea.
> Barry eventually turned it into a script. When
> Lord Grade was in Hollywood visiting the Movie
> Movie set, I gave him the work. He liked it well
> enough to finance it. Barry was supposed to di-
> rect it and I was just going to produce, but it didn't
> work out. Barry was unable to direct a movie.
> He couldn't organize the script. Actors were walk-
> ing all over him. He couldn't stage anything. It
> was a nightmare. So after some weeks of shooting,
> Grade asked me to take over. Only a tiny bit of
> what Barry shot ended up in the finished film....
> Associated Film Distribution released the film.
> [One of the most ambitious among the new film
> firms of the '70s, AFD, the joint venture of Lord
> Grade's ITC Entertainment and Sir Bernard Del-
> font's EMI Ltd. , folded on February 26, 1981,
> after a series of financial failures. Only The
> Muppet Movie (James Frawley, 1979) made
> money. Universal now markets AFD's products.]

Unfortunately, Martin Amis's screenplay does very little to circumvent the triteness or to flesh out the flimsiness of Barry's extraterrestrial variations of Frankenstein and the romantic triangle. Otherwise, the sketch of the Captain could have become a chilling Hawthornian villain, the stuff that nightmares are made of, while that of the Major, an expatriate of earth who creates his own little world on the Saturnian moon, could have been turned into an intriguingly ambivalent character. The "traditional" Major versus the "modern" Captain dialectic also might have been explored in the light of the next millennium with witty results--perhaps too, the May-December aspect of the coupling. Amis is certainly capable of wit as the Captain's conclusion upon his arrival, "I guess you don't get many droppings on Saturn 3, " attests to. A pervasive drollery might have been another way to give the piece distinction. But instead the script concentrates on a lot of exciting actions that are not clearly related, uses figures not to confront difficult moral problems but to get in and out of scrapes, and rests content with silly lines to such an extent that there is a slapdash, scrambling quality about the enterprise, as if all that it really has on its mind is to cash in as quickly as possible on the lucrative science-fiction market of the late '70s. As a matter of fact the nods, perhaps unintended, to 2001: A Space Odyssey (Stanley Kubrick, 1968), Silent Running (Douglas Trumbull, 1972), and Alien (Ridley Scott, 1979) confirm this suspicion.

> After Grade decided to back the project, we took Barry's script to Evan Hunter for a rewrite. We didn't like his version and threw it out. I had recently read the futuristic fantasy Dead Babies by the young novelist Martin Amis [son of novelist Kingsley Amis] and suggested he do a version. Of course, as director, Barry had worked on Amis's version. When I took over, I had either to follow through or close down. And it was too expensive to close down. The overall schema of the picture and tone were established. I was locked into them. I was able to inject only a few ideas, such as the robot transmitting the Captain's most guarded thoughts on the screen [which incidentally is a very witty scene].

Thematically the film is more an expansion of than departure from Donen territory. The man-woman relation-

Saturn 3: Donen's witty mise-en-scène of the robot and Farrah Fawcett parodies that of the ape and Fay Wray. Copyright: Associated Film Distribution.

ship (even to the extent of Charade's May-December twist) and adventure, though assuming a different hierarchical order and tone, are familiar; so also, are the suspense-thriller mold (Charade and Arabesque) and horror element (Damn Yankees, Bedazzled, and The Little Prince's devils), though these had been brightened by satire and farce. Even the extraterrestrial geography recalls that of The Little Prince.

And here Donen holds up to nature a lamp rather than a mirror, and in doing so creates another stylized rather than real realm.

Kirk Douglas's enactment of Adam is, too, more familiar than not. He clenches his teeth, exposes his top-heavy frame, and races up and down the set, as he has done in over sixty films.

Whether the situation is serene or threatening, the mood frolicsome or glum, Farrah Fawcett's lines are un-changingly monotoned, her eyes consistently glazed, her body unalterably posed. The renegade angel in her third feature is still the celluloid equivalent of elevator music, which merely washes over us without ever getting under our skins. Why did not Donen, who appreciates an irony more than most, use her face and figure as an emblem of the plastic future or turn her into a robot? Either choice would have secured the picture a specialness. Donen instead only aggravates the situation by stooping to calendar art at times, as when he has a white sheet unfurl before her Rembrandt-lighted nude body.

Harvey Keitel, an Actors Studio alumnus whose impression of contemporary angst and neurosis in Scorsese's and Schrader's worlds has the power to disturb, manages a brooding menace with his curt, almost monosyllabic, speech pattern, long dark wig brailed into a pigtail, and intense brown eyes glaring out under lowered brows.

> On his flight back to England, Lord Grade handed Barry's script to Farrah, who was the first role to be cast. For the male leads the script was submitted to many people--Bill Holden for the Major; Jeff Bridges, Martin Sheen, Michael Douglas for the Captain--before Kirk and Harvey came aboard. Yes, I directed Farrah's lines and didn't allow her to go off on her own. I guess her performance was as good as we--she and I working together--could get it.... Because of all the noise on the set, the original dialogue track had to be looped. Harvey wouldn't come back to do the loops. So I had to dub his voice with that of Roy Dotrice.

The movie's true stars (as is usually the case in this genre) are, however, Stuart Craig's production design, Norman Dorme's art direction, Colin Chilvers's special effects,

and Roy Field, Wally Veeveres, and Peter Park's optical
effects, all given a terrifyingly beautiful cast by Billy Williams's photography.

Once past the establishing views of Saturn and the
surface of its satellite, which look like drawing-board illus-
trations, the images never cease to astonish and delight.
Blue-lit serpentine corridors, which look like they have been
hewn from black lava, connect the work areas with the living
quarters of the subterranean space station. (Despite advanced
technology, Craig shrewdly reasoned, space stations would
still have to be prefabricated on earth, so he constructed the
set with paneled sections, leaving the lava rock of Saturn's
exterior poking through here and there.) The lab's concate-
nation of tubes, pipes, vials, and dials--reshaped from London junkyards, computers, and communication systems--
conveys the menacing glitter of space-age high-tech. Despite
the lighting that simulates earth's day-night cycle, the suede
covering that softens the walls, the plants kept alive with artificial light and hydroponics, and the contemporary overstuffed
chairs bolted down airplane-style (today's "modern" after all
is tomorrow's "antique" or so it would seem), the living
quarters are alarmingly antiseptic. And exposing the work-
ings of the mighty eight-foot-tall monster, whose body resembles Da Vinci's anatomical paintings and head a mantis, has
the same effects as nails on a blackboard.

> We shot at Shepperton Studio Center outside London.
> The set covered the full area of its two largest
> sound stages. The film came in around $10 mil-
> lion.

Donen's mise-en-scène is expressive throughout, witty
sometimes, as in the lateral pan of the Captain checking the
robot's parts list, but terrifying most of the time. Constant
in Donen's direction here is the use of the frame's edges to
create shock. Also, the extraterrestrial future allows Donen
to indulge his penchant for film-within-film and the split-
screen.

> Crosscutting and montages especially kept things
> moving. I cut about twenty minutes from the
> completed film--no large hunks--mostly just ex-
> tension of scenes.

White titles burning in and out of a black background
against a silent track seems to be the only technical departure.

Composer Elmer Bernstein is as empathic as ever and obviously had committed 2001's score to heart. The opening sequence's track is exceptionally unnerving, with its overlapping dialogue at varying decibels (among them, the director's urgent, elliptical "Captain James, your presence requested urgent pad 73 immediate launch"), beeps, clicks, and somber musical stirrings.

The critical reaction to Saturn 3 ranged from pans to reserved acceptance. Despite a heavy sales pitch of the movie's hardware (Farrah's name meant nothing commercially since her first two features were turkeys), the public did not buy.

> I didn't want to put my name on it, but Lord Grade couldn't sell the movie without a name. I tried to do my best with it for Grade's sake.

What went wrong for Donen in the '70s was easy to see and was in part an index of the general malaise in the American film scene during that time.

The Little Prince just about sidestepped Donen's strengths. Though holding out for the importance of friendship and the child within the adult, themes close to his heart, the story was basically meditative and did not lend itself particularly to dance, while the score was derivative and old-fashioned. Except for the score, however, it must be noted that The Little Prince, unlike Donen's next three efforts, and the decade's output in general, struck out in a new direction rather than backtracked upon a familiar path.

A clash of intentions sent Lucky Lady reeling. (One cannot help wondering whether the commercial fiascoes of Donen's overcast Road, Bedazzled, Staircase, and Prince made him chase the writers' clouds away?) Lady's nostalgic overlay was the only impression this adventure comedy made --unfortunately, since nostalgia is about as substantial and nourishing as junk food. Nostalgia results in a formal sophistication at the expense of a thematic one.

Donen's genre-parody, Movie Movie, admittedly gorgeously crafted, was less a movie than an exercise in movie conventions and techniques, a reflection upon a reflection. And as for Saturn 3, his rescue attempt, the effort was not worth it, since the material was penny dreadful and a spinoff

as well. Genre-parodies and spinoffs, like nostalgia trips,
sequels, and remakes, all of which infected American movies of the '70s, are safe and conservative, backward and
redundant (if not mindless), formalistic, and, in the end,
superficial approaches to filmmaking.

That Donen made only four films in the last ten years,
as opposed to fourteen in the '50s and eight in the '60s, further signals the sorry state of the art in the '70s, which
saw far fewer features than any other comparable time span.
Inflation, which doubled the cost of an average film by the
decade's end (to $9 million), was far less responsible for
this tapering off than the conglomerates that presently run
the industry, corporations interested more in making money
than in creating entertainment. Investments, for these busi-
nessmen, must be well nigh certain; therefore the familiar
and proven are chosen over the experimental and dicey.
(The influences of film schools upon the new directors and
writers of the '70s and, in Donen's case, the influence of
growing up with film, aggravated this rear-view mirror situation.) And most productions were thrashed out of a block-
buster mentality, which, among other things, homogenizes
content.

Yet in all these misses Donen's visually expressive
manner, inimitable sense of timing, and above all his enthusiasm were as sure as ever. It is to be hoped that his
undiminished talent and desire to please will be put to better
use in the '80s.

> After Saturn 3 I worked very hard on adapting
> Stephen King's Dead Zone [1979], a novel about
> precognition. Lorimar owned the property, and I
> made a deal with them to produce and direct. Af-
> ter getting the adaptation to a point where Lorimar
> and I were satisfied, Lorimar decided it didn't
> have the money to make it. Then I worked with
> Larry Gelbart on a comedy that didn't materialize.
> Right now I'm adapting an old French romantic
> comedy set in Brazil called Love Rio.

The next chapter--not that there need be one, since,
as the premier builder of the musical and a distinct contrib-
utor to comedy, Donen's place in American film history is
secure--will, for now, just have to wait.

The University of Southern California's DKA banquet, November 1975, and the two honorees: Astaire and Donen.

Preface

1. Unless otherwise indicated, all of Donen's words throughout the text are taken from a series of interviews recorded on tape July 20, July 27, August 2, and August 9, 1976, October 18, 1979, and April 16, 1980 in Los Angeles and preserved in the Special Collections of the Cinema Library, University of Southern California.

Chapter I

1. Since its shaky debut Pal Joey has been revived frequently. The 1950 revival at the Broadhurst featured Harold Lang as Joey, Vivenne Segal reprising Vera, Pat Northrop as Linda, David Alexander's direction, Robert Alton's dances, Oliver Smith's sets, and Miles White's costumes. Hailed by the critics, it played 540 performances, a record for a musical revival at that time.

Its 1961 renaissance at the City Center had Bob Fosse as Joey, Carol Bruce as Vera, Christine Matthews as Linda, Gus Schirmer's direction, Ralph Beaumont's dances, Howard Bay's sets, and Frank Thompson's costumes. Critics were as enthusiastic as the public.

Joey aged a little in the 1963 revival, also at the City Center, with Fosse encoring the lead, Viveca Lindfors as Vera, Rita Gardner as Linda, Schirmer's direction, George and Ethel Martin's choreography, Bay's sets, and Thompson's costumes.

No version was as ill fated as the bicentennial mounting at the Circle in the Square. Director Theodore Mann

released New York City Ballet's Edward Villella from his
singing and acting debut as Joey and screen actress Eleanor
Parker as Vera and went along with their understudies, Christopher Chadman and Joan Copeland.   Mann retained Boni En-
ton as Linda.   Margot Sapping choreographed.   John J. Moore
did the sets; Arthur Boccia, the costumes.
      Pal Joey 1978, which opened in the spring at the Ah-
manson Theatre in Los Angeles, never made it to Broadway,
although it intended to.   In this incarnation the musical became a star vehicle for Lena Horne as Vera.   Clifton Davis
played Joey; Marjorie Barnes, Linda.   Jerome Chodorov and
Mark Bramble revamped the book.   Michael Kidd directed.
Claude Thompson choreographed.   Robert Randolph designed
the sets; Robert Fletcher, the costumes.
      In 1957 Columbia Pictures presented Dorothy Kingsley's
bowdlerized edition with Frank Sinatra as Joey, Rita Hayworth
as Vera, and Kim Novak as Linda, George Sidney's direction,
Harold Lipstein's photography, Hermes Pan's dances, Walter
Holscher's art direction, and Jean Louis's costumes.   The
public turned out in droves.

      2.   In the mid-1950s Lemuel Ayers, respected set de-
signer and producer of Kiss Me, Kate (1948), hired Sondheim
to musicalize his property Front Porch in Flatbush, written
by Hollywood's Julius J. and Philip G. Epstein.   Jack Cassidy,
Alice Ghostley, and Arte Johnson were inked to play in the
Epsteins' biographical account of their third brother and his
pals, who, in Flatbush of 1928, invested in the stock market.
Half the money was raised for the show, now retitled Saturday
Night, but with Ayers's death, Joseph Kipness's attempt to
resuscitate the piece with Bob Fosse as director-choreographer
was in vain.

      3.   For a survey history of the musical genre from
its beginnings to the Freed-Minnelli dispensation at MGM, see
this author's "Traditions: The Film Musical," Vincente Minnelli and the Film Musical (South Brunswick, N.J., and New
York: Barnes, 1977), pp. 21-32.

      4.   This is the first of Kelly's dances with children.
"Ring Around the Rosie: Children's Medley" from Living in
a Big Way (Gregory La Cava, 1947), "I Got Rhythm" from
An American in Paris (Vincente Minnelli, 1951), and "Sinbad
the Sailor" from his personally directed Invitation to the
Dance (1956) are to follow--an inevitable conceit for him,
since he did teach dancing to children in his parents' school.

      5.   A distinct Latin American strain pervaded Holly-

wood films in the first half of the 1940s. With Europe in
turmoil since September 1939, the industry's chief overseas
market was wiped out, except for England and some neutral
countries. Other markets had to be expanded, particularly
Latin America. And the MGM musical, at least in parts,
began to move to the south-of-the-border beat.

6. The influence of Douglas Fairbanks's swashbuckler
on the screen persona and dancing style of Kelly cannot be
overestimated. In a dream sequence in his third feature,
Dubarry Was a Lady (Roy del Ruth, 1943), he dances "The
Black Arrow," leader of the lower classes who fights Louis
XV's tyranny. Here, in Anchors Aweigh, his dances as the
gob, the Pomeranian sailor, and the bandit chief bear the
Fairbanks signature. His playing and dancing in The Pirate
(Vincente Minnelli, 1948) is on one level a parody of Fairbanks's The Black Pirate (Albert Parker, 1926). He reprised
Fairbanks's role as D'Artagnan in The Three Musketeers
(George Sidney, 1948). As navy man Gabey in On the Town
he dances a modern buccaneer. Kelly's Don Lockwood screen
image in Singing' in the Rain is Fairbanks through and through.
He danced and directed himself as Sinbad the Sailor in Invitation to the Dance (1956). And then there are the Fairbanksian
bits in "The Chase Ballet" in Brigadoon (Vincente Minnelli,
1954) and in "The Binge" in It's Always Fair Weather.

7. Among them were Hey Rookie (Charles Barton,
1944), about a theatrical producer (Larry Parks) who nabs a
star (Ann Miller) for his show benefiting the induction center;
Jam Session (Charles Barton, 1944), highlighting the big-band
scene with Ann Miller; and Kansas City Kitty (Del Lord, 1944),
about a song-plugger (Joan Davis) who is tricked into buying
a publishing firm.

Chapter 2

ON THE TOWN

1. The 1942 Paramount movie musical The Fleet's In
(Victor Schertzinger) gave Robbins the idea for his ballet.

SINGIN' IN THE RAIN

1. Betty Comden and Adolph Green. Singin' in the
Rain (New York: Viking, 1972).

2.   Before Rain, Showgirl in Hollywood (Robert Lord, 1930) sported scenes detailing how early sound films were made.   Since Rain, Goldilocks (1958), Fade-Out Fade-In (1964), and Mack and Mabel (1974) have used a similar backdrop.

3.   "Broadway Melody, " "You Were Meant for Me, " and "The Wedding of the Painted Doll" were lifted from The Broadway Melody (Harry Beaumont, 1929); "Should I?" from Lord Byron on Broadway (William Nigh and Harry Beaumont, 1929); "Singin' in the Rain" from Hollywood Revue of 1929 (Charles Reisner, 1929); "Beautiful Girl" from Going Hollywood (Raoul Walsh, 1933) and Stage Mother (Charles Brabin, 1933); "Fit as a Fiddle" from College Coach (William Wellman, 1933); "Temptation" from Going Hollywood; "All I Do Is Dream of You" from Sadie McKee (Clarence Brown, 1934); "I Got a Feelin' You're Foolin' " and "You Are My Lucky Star" from Broadway Melody of 1936 (Roy del Ruth, 1935); "Would You?" from San Francisco (W. S. Van Dyke, 1936); and "Good Mornin' " from Babes in Arms (Busby Berkeley, 1939).   Freed and Brown wrote "Make 'Em Laugh" for Rain.

4.   Not strictly a dance, the tableau is an expression of an object, idea, emotion, or event in terms of decor, costumes, a male and/or female chorus, their movement and positioning, accompanied by instrumental and/or vocal music. Florenz Ziegfeld crystallized this type of number in his series revues on Broadway during the 1910s and 1920s; Berkeley made the tableau cinematic.

5.   Stanley Kubrick obliquely pays tribute to the passage's lyricism in his chilling futuristic foray A Clockwork Orange (1971), when he used the "Singin' in the Rain" track against a scene of excessive violence.   Paul Mazursky in his comedy Next Stop, Greenwich Village (1975) also honors the number by duplicating its situation, content, and, most particularly, its denouement.   Late at night protagonist Larry Lepinski (Lenny Baker) has just seen his girl home and walks to the Brooklyn El.   On the platform he creates his own little world in which he pretends at being Brando and other famous actors and even thanks the Academy for his Oscar, for which an empty beer can substitutes.   An incredulous cop on the beat eventually interrupts and ends the fantasy.   Moishe Mizrahi in Madame Rosa, the Academy's Best Foreign Film for 1977 from France, also pays tribute in the scene in which the fourteen-year-old male protagonist goes to the park with

his puppet creation to perform and is enthralled by a large
string puppet manipulated to sing and dance to the original
cast recording of Kelly's vocal. So, too, Masuto Harada in
Goodbye, Flickmania (1979) and Alan Parker in Fame (1980)
who have their protagonists mimic Kelly's antics in the rain.

FEARLESS FAGAN

1. Eventually turned over to Pasternak, Jumbo was
made in 1962 with Charles Walters directing Doris Day and
Stephen Boyd.

GIVE A GIRL A BREAK

1. Champion later became a sought-after Broadway
choreographer-director--Three for Tonight (1955), Bye, Bye
Birdie (1960), Carnival (1961), Hello, Dolly! (1964), The
Happy Time (1968), Sugar (1972), Irene (1973), Mack and
Mable (1974), Rockabye Hamlet (1976), and 42nd Street (1980);
he also went on to direct a caper film, The Bank Shot (1974).

2. After choreographing and playing a role in Columbia's My Sister Eileen (Richard Quine, 1955) Fosse returned
East and became a notable Broadway choreographer--The
Pajama Game (1954), Damn Yankees (1955), Bells Are Ring-
ing (1956), and New Girl in Town (1957)--and an even more
notable choreographer-director--Redhead (1959), How to Succeed in Business Without Really Trying (1961), Little Me
(1962), Sweet Charity (1965), Pippin (1972), Chicago (1976),
and Dancin' (1978). Out West again, he directed Sweet Charity (1969), Cabaret (1971), for which he won the Best Director
Oscar, Lenny (1975), and All That Jazz (1979).

SEVEN BRIDES FOR SEVEN BROTHERS

1. For example: High, Wide and Handsome (Rouben
Mamoulian, 1937), The Harvey Girls (George Sidney, 1946),
Annie Get Your Gun (George Sidney, 1950), Calamity Jane
(David Butler, 1953), Red Garters (George Marshall, 1954),
and The Second Greatest Sex (George Marshall, 1955), the
Universal-International answer to Seven Brides that western-
ized the Lysistrata legend. Remember, it was Joshua Logan's
mise-en-place and his nonmusical casting (Lee Marvin, Clint
Eastwood, and Jean Seberg) that shackled Paint Your Wagon
(1969).

2. Kidd, who trained at the American Ballet Theatre,

where he danced one of the original roles in Fancy Free and
choreographed the wry and tender one-act ballet On Stage,
eventually graduated to a first-rank Broadway choreographer--
Finian's Rainbow (1947), Guys and Dolls (1950), and Can Can
(1953)--and then unleashed his birr and boldness in Hollywood
--Where's Charley? (David Butler, 1952), The Band Wagon
(Vincente Minnelli, 1953), and Knock on Wood (Melvin Frank,
1954).   Between It's Always Fair Weather and Movie Movie
Kidd's credits are equally impressive: choreographer-director
on Li'l Abner (1956), Destry Rides Again (1959), Wildcat
(1960), Subways Are for Sleeping (1961), Ben Franklin in
Paris (1964), The Rothschilds (1970), and Cyrano (1973) on
the stage and choreographer on Guys and Dolls (Joseph Mankiewicz, 1955), Merry Andrew (which he also directed in
1958), Star! (Robert Wise, 1968), and Hello, Dolly! (Gene
Kelly, 1969) in the movies.

3.   In the summer of 1978 Larry Kasha, Norman and
Gayle Sedawie, Barry Brown, Fritz Holtz, and David Landay
prepared a stage production.   Powell and Keel reprised their
original roles.   Kasha directed, Jerry Jackson choreographed,
and Kasha and Landay adapted the book.   Al Kasha and Joel
Hirschhorn, Best-Song Oscar-winners for "The Morning After"
from The Poseidon Adventure (Ronald Neame, 1972) and "We
May Never Love Like This Again" from The Towering Inferno
(John Guillermin, 1974), wrote about half a dozen new songs.
"Bless Yore Beautiful Hide," "Wonderful, Wonderful Day,"
"Go'in Co'tin', " and "Sobbin' Women" were retained.   The
show shuttered in Miami in the winter of 1979 during its pre-
Broadway national tour but was revived in the spring of 1982
in San Diego and Los Angeles with Debby Boone and David-
James Carroll and died on Broadway that summer.

DEEP IN MY HEART

1.   "Leg of Mutton," a pop tune written for the cafe's
dancing customers, was published in 1913.   "Auf Weidersehen"
came from The Blue Paradise (1915); "The Road to Paradise"
and "Will You Remember?/Sweetheart" from Maytime (1917);
"I Love to Say Hello" from Poor Little Ritz Girl (1920); "The
Very Next Girl I See" from Bombo (1921); "Fat, Fat Fatima"
and "I Love to Go Swimmin' with the Wimmin' " from Love
Birds (1921); "Girls Goodbye" and "Mr. and Mrs." from The
Blushing Bride (1922); "Deep in My Heart, Dear, " "Drink,
Drink, Drink" (bkgd.), "Golden Days" (bkgd.), and "Serenade"
from The Student Prince (1924); "The Desert Song," "It, "
"One Alone, " and "The Riff Song" from The Desert Song (1924);

"Your Land and My Land" from My Maryland (1927); "Lover
Come Back to Me," "One Kiss," "Softly, As in a Morning
Sunrise," and "Stouthearted Men" from The New Moon (1928);
"You Will Remember Vienna" from the film Viennese Nights
(Alan Crosland, 1930); and "When I Grow Too Old to Dream"
from the film The Night Is Young (Dudley Murphy, 1934).

IT'S ALWAYS FAIR WEATHER

1. As You Like It, Act II, Scene 7, Line 181.

Chapter 3

FUNNY FACE

1.   The film was eventually made in 1963.   George
Marshall directed Jackie Gleason in the Astaire part.

2.   "Funny Face" had already been used as the title
of a 1927 Gershwin musical that starred Astaire and his sister, Adele.   Fred played Jimmy Reeves, guardian of Frankie
(Adele), who possesses a valuable string of pearls that Jimmy
insists on keeping locked away in a safe.   Frankie encourages
her boyfriend, Peter (Allen Kearns), to try to steal the jewelry.   While penetrating the safe, Peter tussles with two
blundering crooks who are also after the pearls.

3.   Arthur Knight's essay "Choreography for Camera:
Funny Face," in Dance Magazine (May 1957), 16-22, contains
an insightful comment on Avedon's style: "If architecture can
be described as 'frozen music,' then Avedon's photographs
might well be called 'frozen dance.'   Nor is this relationship
purely adventitious.   Avedon, who took up photography as a
hobby on wartime service in the Merchant Marine, also spent
many hours of his shore leave studying modern dance.   Inevitably, once he had returned to civilian life he sought to
merge these two prime interests.   His early photographs of
dancers and ballets, in fact, were among the first pictures
that he sold.   Later, when he turned to fashion photography,
he found that he could work best by laying out his shots in
advance with the aid of dancers like his friends John Butler
and Tanaquil LeClercq.   He would plan those poses for each
of his models with them.   The plasticity of dance, the grace
of its positions--at once fixed and fluid--gave him an approach
to photography that has since become his characteristic."

4. "Clap Yo' Hands" was lifted from Oh, Kay (1926); "Funny Face," "He Loves and She Loves," and "Let's Kiss and Make Up," from the show Funny Face (1927). "How Long Has This Been Going On?," written for Funny Face but axed on the road, went unused until Rosalie (1928).

5. Webster's 8th New Collegiate Dictionary (Springfield, Mass., Merriam, 1977), p. 92.

6. The review cited was written by David Vaughan and appeared in Vol. 27, No. 1 (Summer 1957), p. 40. The previous year the British journal joshed Donen for practically the same thing when, in an interview, he said, "I happened to look at a copy of Sight and Sound and, you know, it's terribly highbrow." That quote and the response, "Moanin' Critics," to be sung to the tune of "Sobbin' Women," was written by Anthony Brode and appeared in Sight and Sound, 26, 2 (Autumn 1956), p. 74.

THE PAJAMA GAME

1. The experience of adapting a bestseller to a hit musical provided Bissell with the material for another novel, Say Darling, which became a comedy with musical interludes on Broadway in 1958.

2. Jean Narboni and Tom Milne, eds., Godard on Godard (New York: Viking, 1972), pp. 86-87.

KISS THEM FOR ME

1. Lewis Nichols, "Review of Kiss Them for Me," New York Times, March 21, 1945, p. 27.

Chapter 4

INDISCREET

1. Krasna's piece, retitled Let's Make Love, was eventually directed by George Cukor in 1961 with Marilyn Monroe and Yves Montand.

2. Brooks Atkinson, "Review of Kind Sir," New York Times, November 5, 1953, p. 41.

3. Webster's New Collegiate Dictionary, p. 58.

4.   Arthur Knight interview with Stanley Donen recorded on tape July 6, 1958, in Los Angeles and preserved in the Special Collections of the Cinema Library, University of Southern California.

5.   Richard Corliss, ed., The Hollywood Screenwriters (New York: Avon, 1972), pp. 263-64.

6.   Derek Hill, "Indiscreet," American Cinematographer, 39, 4 (April 1958), p. 230.

DAMN YANKEES

1.   Billy Wilder, film's genius name-giver and dropper, christened Ginger Rogers's hick from the sticks in The Major and the Minor (1942) "Susan Applegate."

2.   The waning of the film musical had much to do with this.   Broadway, however, continued to stand on its feet for her and her partner-husband Fosse's work in New Girl in Town (1957), Redhead (1959), Sweet Charity (1965), and Chicago (1976).

AN ASSESSMENT OF THE DONEN MUSICAL

1.   The Pirate was Kelly's finest hour; The Unsinkable Molly Brown (Charles Walters, 1964), Reynolds's; and When My Baby Smiles at Me (Walter Lang, 1948), Dailey's.

2.   Mary Jane Hungerford in her unpublished dissertation "Dancing in Commercial Motion Pictures" (Columbia University, 1946) coined the term "cine-dance," which she identified in four ways: the unreproducibility of the dance on the stage, a series of shots of dance movements adding up to an entity, the camera's collaboration in the composition, and the dance's dramatic and technical connection with the story.

ONCE MORE, WITH FEELING

1.   Brooks Atkinson, "Review of Once More, with Feeling," New York Times, October 2, 1958, p. 39.

THE GRASS IS GREENER

1.   In James Limbacher's Four Aspects of the Film (New York: Brussel and Brussel, 1969, p. 129), William E. Snyder, cinematographer for Escapade in Japan (Arthur Lubin, 1957), one of the first films in Technirama, explains the pro-

cess developed by the Technicolor Company from a Dutch process: "Basic to the system is a mirror-prism anamorphic lens which squeezes the image fifty percent in shooting, as against Cinemascope's hundred percent. An additional squeeze of fifty percent is accomplished in printing. The positive prints can be projected in any of the various ratios. Technirama is photographed on a double-width negative and the process is noted for its very sharp image and depth of focus and is especially good in outdoor films.... The versatility of the process and its large negative photography is that it can present standard, anamorphic or "road show" widescreen prints all from one original negative...."

Chapter 5

CHARADE

1. The film was eventually made by Fred Zinnemann in 1966 and by Columbia.

2. Rock Hudson stepped into Grant's shoes.

ARABESQUE

1. Webster's New Collegiate Dictionary, p. 57.

2. Ibid.

3. This new wave included expatriate Richard Lester's surreal romps The Knack (1965), How I Won the War (1967), The Bed Sitting Room (1969); the comedies of disillusionment Only Two Can Play (Sidney Gilliat, 1961) and The Family Way (Roy Boulting, 1966), and the stud comedies like Clive Donner's Nothing but the Best (1964), What's New Pussycat? (1965), Here We Go Round the Mulberry Bush (1968), and Alfie (Lewis Gilbert, 1966).

TWO FOR THE ROAD

1. The five-star status of It Happened One Night (Frank Capra, 1934), Grapes of Wrath (John Ford, 1940), Sullivan's Travels (Preston Sturges, 1941), The Bicycle Thief (Vittorio De Sica, 1948), La Strada (Federico Fellini, 1954), Il Grido (Michelangelo Antonioni, 1956), Wild Strawberries (Ingmar Bergman, 1957), Lolita (Stanley Kubrick, 1962), Tom Jones (Tony Richardson, 1963), Weekend (Jean-Luc Godard, 1968), Easy Rider (Dennis Hopper, 1969), Five Easy Pieces

(Bob Rafelson, 1970), O Lucky Man (Lindsay Anderson, 1973), and Alice Doesn't Live Here Anymore (Martin Scorsese, 1975) is due, in no small part, to their use of the road metaphor.

BEDAZZLED

1.   London: Bles, 1952.

2.   Webster's New Collegiate Dictionary, p. 99.

3.   Ibid.

4.   Stanley Kauffmann, "Bedazzled," Film 67/68: An Anthology by the National Society of Film Critics, eds. Richard Schickel and John Simon (New York: Simon and Schuster, 1968), pp. 155-56.

5.   Matthew, 6:34.

STAIRCASE

1.   "Review of Staircase," Times (London), November 3, 1966.

2.   Clive Barnes, "Review of Staircase," New York Times, January 11, 1968, p. 41.

3.   For example: The Fox (Mark Rydell, 1968) and The Boys in the Band (William Friedkin, 1969).

4.   Curiously, Indiscreet completely skips Pauline Kael's mind in her essay on Cary Grant, "The Man from Dream City," in When the Lights Go Down (New York: Holt, Rinehart and Winston, 1980), pp. 3-32.

Chapter 6

THE LITTLE PRINCE

1.   Bridget Byone, "Making Magic from 'No No No,'" Los Angeles Herald Examiner, December 22, 1974, sec. E-1, p. 3.

LUCKY LADY

1.   Strader was responsible for the cataclysms in

The Poseidon Adventure (Ronald Neame, 1972) and The Towering Inferno (John Guillermin, 1974).

    2.   Jay Cocks, "Review of Lucky Lady," Time, 106
(December 22, 1975), p. 72.

MOVIE MOVIE

    1.   Gelbart's Barbary Coast version of Ben Jonson's
Volpone with George C. Scott and Trish Van Devere was directed by Arthur Penn for the 1976 Broadway season.

    2.   Cat Ballou (Elliot Silverstein, 1965), Lonesome
Cowboys (Paul Morrissey, 1967), Blazing Saddles (Mel Brooks,
1974), and The Villain (Hal Needham, 1979) ribbed the western.   Brooks went on to jab at the horror film in Young
Frankenstein (1974), silent slapstick in Silent Movie (1976),
and Hitchcockian thrillers in High Anxiety (1977).   Woody
Allen spoofed Antonioni-like dramas of ennui and the horror
film in Everything You Wanted to Know About Sex (1972) and
science fiction in Sleeper (1973); Gene Wilder, the detective
film in Sherlock Holmes' Smarter Brother (1976) and Valentino
romances in The World's Greatest Lover (1977); Marty Feld-
man, the adventure film in The Last Remake of Beau Geste
(1977).   Robert Moore and Neil Simon sent up screen detec-
tives and the mystery film in Murder by Death (1976) and
film noir in The Cheap Detective (1978).   Film noir was
given the once over in The Blackbird (David Giler, 1975),
while The Big Bus (James Frawley, 1976) and Airplane!
(Jim Abrahams, 1980) played havoc with the disaster flick
and Wholly, Moses (Don Weis, 1980), the biblical epic.

    3.   Clarke Taylor, "A Junket, Junket to Movie Movie,"
Los Angeles Times Calendar (December 16, 1978), p. 67.

1924   Born April 13, Stanley Isaac Donen, the first child of Mortie and Helen Donen (pronounced 'Dän-en--ä as in bother, cot) in Columbia, South Carolina. (Mortie, of Russian-Jewish extraction, was a first-generation American. His parents emigrated to the United States at an early age. Helen, of German-Jewish extraction, was second-generation. Her parents were born in the United States; her grandparents emigrated from Germany.)

1948   Marries Jeanne Coyne, New York dancer, in Santa Monica.

1951   Divorces Jeanne Coyne.

1952   Marries Marion Marshall, actress, in Los Angeles.

1953   Son, Peter, born to Stanley and Marion Donen.

1955   Son, Joshua, born to Stanley and Marion.

1959   Divorces Marion Marshall.

1960   Marries Lady Adelle Beatty, British socialite, in Henley, England. (Oklahoma-born Adelle Dillingham, former hostess of the Ocean House in Santa Monica and former wife of Los Angeles attorney William O'Connor, wed David, Earl of Beatty, in 1951.)

1962   Son, Mark, born to Stanley and Adelle Donen.

1970   Divorces Lady Adelle Beatty.

1972   Marries Yvette Mimieux, actress, in Los Angeles.

FILMOGRAPHY

ON THE TOWN (1949) [with Gene Kelly]

Production Company: MGM. Producers: Arthur Freed, Roger Edens (associate). Script: Betty Comden, Adolph Green, from their musical play based on an idea by Jerome Robbins. Director of Photography: Harold Rosson, in Technicolor. Special Effects: Warren Newcombe. Editor: Ralph E. Winters. Art Directors: Cedric Gibbons, Jack Martin Smith. Set Decorators: Edwin B. Willis, Jack D. Moore (associate). Costumes: Helen Rose. Choreographers: Gene Kelly, Stanley Donen. Musical Director and Conductor: Lennie Hayton. Orchestrations: Conrad Salinger. Sound Recordists: Douglas Shearer, John A. Williams.
Numbers: "Come Up to My Place," "New York, New York," by Leonard Bernstein (composer), Betty Comden, Adolph Green (lyricists). "A Day in New York Ballet," "Miss Turnstiles Ballet," by Leonard Bernstein (composer). "Count on Me," "Main Street," "On the Town," "Pearl of the Persian Sea," "Prehistoric Man," "That's All There Is Folks," "You're Awful," by Roger Edens (composer) Betty Comden, Adolph Green (lyricists).
Cast: Gene Kelly (Gabey), Frank Sinatra (Chip), Betty Garrett (Brunhilde Esterhazy), Ann Miller (Claire Huddesen), Jules Munshin (Ozzie), Vera-Ellen (Ivy Smith), Florence Bates (Mme. Dilyovska), Alice Pearce (Lucy Shmeeler), George Meader (Professor), Bea Benaderet (Brooklyn Girl), Eugene Borden (Walter), Hans Conried (François).
Production Dates: March 28-July 2, 1949.
Running Time: 98 min.
Release Date: December 1949.

ROYAL WEDDING (1951) [WEDDING BELLS in Europe]

Production Company: MGM. Producer: Arthur Freed.
Script: Alan Jay Lerner, from his story. Director of
Photography: Robert Planck, in Technicolor. Special Ef-
fects: Warren Newcombe. Editor: Albert Akst. Art Di-
rectors: Cedric Gibbons, Jack Martin Smith. Set Decorators: Edwin B. Willis, Alfred E. Spencer. Costumes:
uncredited. Choreographer: Nick Castle. Musical Director:
Johnny Green. Orchestrations: Conrad Salinger, Skip Mar-
tin. Sound Recordist: Douglas Shearer.
Numbers: "Every Night at Seven," "The Happiest Day of My
Life," "How Could You Believe Me When I Said I Loved You
When You Know I've Been a Liar All My Life?," I Left My
Hat in Haiti," "Open Your Eyes," "Sunday Jumps" (instru-
mental), "Too Late Now," "What a Lovely Day for a Wed-
ding," "You're All the World to Me," by Burton Lane (com-
poser), Alan Jay Lerner (lyricist).
Cast: Fred Astaire (Tom Bowen), Jane Powell (Ellen Bowen),
Peter Lawford (Lord John Brindale), Sarah Churchill (Anne
Ashmond), Keenan Wynn (Irving Klinger/Edgar Klinger), Al-
bert Sharpe (James Ashmond), Viola Roache (Sarah Ashmond),
Henri Letondal (Purser), James Finlayson (Cabby), Alex
Frazer (Chester), Jack Reilly (Pete Cumberly), William Ca-
banne (Dick), John Hedloe (Billy), Francis Bethancourt
(Charles Gordon), Andre Charisse (Steward), Bess Flowers
(Women Guest).
Production Dates: July 6-October 5, 1950; October 17, 1950.
Running Time: 93 min.
Release Date: March 1951.

LOVE IS BETTER THAN EVER (1952)
[THE LIGHT FANTASTIC in Europe]

Production Company: MGM. Producer: William H. Wright.
Script: Ruth Brooks Flippen. Director of Photography: Harold
Rosson. Editor: George Boemler. Art Directors: Cedric Gib-
bons, Gabriel Scognamillo. Set Decorators: Edwin B. Willis,
Keogh Gleason. Costumes: Helen Rose. Musical Director:
Lennie Hayton. Sound Recordist: Douglas Shearer.
Cast: Larry Parks (Jud Parker), Elizabeth Taylor (Anastacia
"Stacy" Macaboy), Joseph Hutchinson (Mrs. Macaboy), Tom
Tully (Mr. Macaboy), Ann Doran (Mrs. Levoy), Elinor Dono-
hue (Pattie Marie Levoy), Kathleen Freeman (Mrs. Kahrney),
Doreen McCann (Albertina Kahrney), Alex Gerry (Hamlet),
Dick Wessel (Smittie), Gene Kelly (Himself).

Production Dates: November 27, 1950-week of January 22, 1951.
Running Time: 81 min.
Release Date: March 1952.

SINGIN' IN THE RAIN (1952) [with Gene Kelly]

Production Company: MGM. Producers: Arthur Freed,
Roger Edens (associate). Script: Betty Comden, Adolph
Green. Director of Photography: Harold Rosson, in Techni-
color. Special Effects: Warren Newcombe, Irving G. Ries.
Editor: Adrienne Fazan. Art Directors: Cedric Gibbons,
Randall Duell. Set Decorators: Edwin B. Willis, Jacques
Mapes. Costumes: Walter Plunkett. Choreographers: Gene
Kelly, Stanley Donen. Musical Director: Lennie Hayton.
Sound Recordist: Douglas Shearer.
Numbers: "All I Do Is Dream of You, " "Beautiful Girl, "
"Broadway Melody/Broadway Rhythm, " "Good Mornin', " "I've
Got a Feelin' You're Foolin', " "Make 'Em Laugh, " "Should
I, " "Singin' in the Rain, " "Temptation, " "Wedding of the
Painted Doll, " "You Are My Lucky Star, " "You Were Meant
for Me, " by Nacio Herb Brown (composer), Arthur Freed
(lyricist). "Fit as a Fiddle, " by Al Goodhart, Al Hoffman
(composers), Arthur Freed (lyricist). "Moses, " by Roger
Edens (composer), Betty Comden, Adolph Green (lyricists).
Cast: Gene Kelly (Don Lockwood), Donald O'Connor (Cosmo
Brown), Debbie Reynolds (Kathy Selden), Jean Hagen (Lina
Lamont), Millard Mitchell (R. F. Simpson), Rita Moreno
(Zelda Zanders), Douglas Fowley (Roscoe Dexter), Cyd Cha-
risse (Dream Ballet Dancer), Madge Blake (Dora Bailey),
King Donovan (Rod), Kathleen Freeman (Phoebe Dinsmore),
Jimmie Thompson (Beautiful Girl Singer), Patricia Denise,
Jeanne Coyne (Girl Dancers), Bill Chatham, Ernest Flatt,
Don Hulbert, Robert Dayo (Male Dancing Quartet), David
Kasday (Kid), Julius Tannen (Man in Talking Picture).
Production Dates: June 18-November 21, 1951; December 26,
1951.
Running Time: 103 min.
Release Date: April 1952.

FEARLESS FAGAN (1952)

Production Company: MGM. Producers: Edwin H. Knopf,
Sidney Franklin Jr. (associate). Script: Charles Lederer,
from an adaptation by Frederick Hazlitt Brennan, based on a
story by Sidney Franklin Jr. and Eldon W. Griffiths. Direc-

tor of Photography: Harold Lipstein. Special Effects: A.
Arnold Gillespie. Editor: George White. Art Directors:
Cedric Gibbons, Leonid Vasian. Set Decorators: Edwin B.
Willis, Fred MacLean. Costumes: uncredited. Musical
Director: Rudolph G. Kopp. Sound Recordist: Douglas
Shearer. Song: "What Do You Think I Am?," by Hugh Mar-
tin and Ralph Blane (composers-lyricists).
Cast: Janet Leigh (Abby Ames), Carleton Carpenter (Pvt.
Floyd Hilson), Keenan Wynn (Sgt. Kellwin), Richard Anderson
(Capt. Daniels), Ellen Corby (Mrs. Ardley), Barbara Ruick
(Nurse), John Call (Mr. Ardley), Robert Burton (Owen Gill-
man), Wilton Graff (Col. Horne), Parley Baer (Emil Tauch-
nitz), Jonathan Cott (Cpl. Geft).
Production Dates: February 11, 1952-week of March 17,
1952.
Running Time: 78 min.
Release Date: September 1952.

GIVE A GIRL A BREAK (1953)

Production Company: MGM. Producer: Jack Cummings.
Script: Albert Hackett, Frances Goodrich, from a story by
Vera Caspary. Director of Photography: William C. Mellor,
in Technicolor. Special Effects: Warren Newcombe, Irving
G. Ries. Editor: Adrienne Fazan. Art Directors: Cedric
Gibbons, Paul Groesse. Set Decorators: Edwin B. Willis,
Arthur Krams. Costumes: Helen Rose (for the women),
Herschel (for the men). Choreographers: Stanley Donen,
Gower Champion. Musical Directors: Andre Previn, Saul
Chaplin. Orchestration: uncredited. Sound Recordist:
Douglas Shearer.
Numbers: "Applause," "Give a Girl a Break," "In Our United
State," "It Happens Every Time," "Nothing Is Impossible," by
Burton Lane (composer), Ira Gershwin (lyricist). "Challenge
Dance," by Andre Previn, Saul Chaplin (composers).
Cast: Marge Champion (Madelyn Corlane), Gower Champion
(Ted Sturgis), Debbie Reynolds (Suzy Doolittle), Helen Wood
(Joanna Moss), Bob Fosse (Bob Dowdy), Kurt Kasznar (Leo
Belney), Richard Anderson (Burton Bradshaw), William Ching
(Anson Pritchett), Lurene Tuttle (Mrs. Doolittle), Larry
Keating (Felix Jordan), Donna Martel (Janet Hallson).
Production Dates: October 14-December 22, 1952; March 31,
1953.
Running Time: 82 min.
Release Date: December 1953.

SEVEN BRIDES FOR SEVEN BROTHERS (1954)

Production Company: MGM. Producer: Jack Cummings.
Script: Dorothy Kingsley, Frances Goodrich, Albert Hackett,
based on the story "The Sobbin' Women, " by Stephen Vincent
Benét. Director of Photography: George Folsey, in Ansco
Color and Cinemascope. Special Effects: A. Arnold Gillespie,
Warren Newcombe. Editor: Ralph E. Winters. Art Directors:
Cedric Gibbons, Urie McCleary. Set Decorators: Edwin B.
Willis, Hugh Hunt. Costumes: Walter Plunkett. Choreog-
rapher: Michael Kidd. Musical Directors: Adolph Deutsch,
Saul Chaplin. Orchestrations: Alexander Courage, Conrad
Salinger, Leo Arnaud. Sound Recordist: Douglas Shearer.
Numbers: "Barnraising Ballet, " "Bless Yore Beautiful Hide,"
"Goin Co'tin', " "June Bride, " "Lonesome Polecat, " "Sobbin'
Women, " "Spring, Spring, Spring, " "When You're in Love, "
"Wonderful, Wonderful Day, " by Gene de Paul (composer),
Johnny Mercer (lyricist).
Cast: Howard Keel (Adam), Jane Powell (Milly), Jeff Rich-
ards (Benjamin), Russ Tamblyn (Gideon), Tommy Rall (Frank),
Marc Platt (Daniel), Matt Mattox (Caleb), Jacques d'Amboise
(Ephraim), Julie Newmeyer (Dorcas), Nancy Kilgas (Alice),
Betty Carr (Sarah), Virginia Gibson (Liza), Ruta Kilmonis
(Ruth), Norma Doggett (Martha), Ian Wolfe (Rev. Elcott),
Howard Petrie (Peter Perkins), Earl Barton (Harry), Dante
DiPaolo (Matt), Kelly Brown (Carl), Matt Moore (Ruth's Un-
cle), Dick Rich (Dorcas' Father), Marjorie Wood (Mrs. Bix-
by), Russell Simpson (Mr. Bixby).
Production Dates: November 30, 1953-February 1, 1954.
Running Time: 102 min.
Release Date: August 1954.

DEEP IN MY HEART (1954)

Production Company: MGM. Producer: Roger Edens.
Script: Leonard Spiegelgass, from the novel by Elliot Arnold. Director of Photography: George Folsey, in Eastman
Color. Special Effects: Warren Newcombe. Editor: Adrienne Fazan. Art Directors: Cedric Gibbons, Edward Car-
fargo. Set Decorators: Edwin B. Willis, Arthur Krams.
Costumes: Helen Rose (for the women), Walter Plunkett (for
the men). Choreographer: Eugene Loring. Musical Director: Adolph Deutsch. Orchestrations: Hugo Friedhofer,
Alexander Courage. Sound Recordist: Wesley C. Miller.
Numbers: "Auf Wiedersehen, " by Sigmund Romberg (com-

poser), Herbert Reynolds (lyricist). "Deep in My Heart,"
"Drink, Drink, Drink," "Golden Days," "Serenade," "Your
Land and My Land," by Sigmund Romberg (composer), Doro-
thy Donnelly (lyricist). "Desert Song," "It," "One Alone,"
"The Riff Song," by Sigmund Romberg (composer), Oscar
Hammerstein II, Otto Harbach (lyricists). "Mr. and Mrs.,"
by Sigmund Romberg (composer), Cyrus Wood (lyricist).
"Road to Paradise," "Will You Remember?/Sweetheart," by
Sigmund Romberg (composer), Rida Johnson Young (lyricist).
"The Very Next Girl I See," Sigmund Romberg (composer),
Harold Atteridge (lyricist).
Cast: José Ferrer (Sigmund Romberg), Merle Oberon (Doro-
thy Donnelly), Helen Traubel (Anna Mueller), Doe Avedon
(Lillian Romberg), Walter Pidgeon (J.J. Shubert), Paul Hen-
reid (Florenz Ziegfeld), Tamara Toumanova (Gaby Deslys),
Paul Stewart (Bert Townsend), David Burns (Lazar Berrison
Sr.), Isobel Elsom (Mrs. Harris), Jim Backus (Ben Judson),
Douglas Fowley (Harold Butterfield), Russ Tamblyn (Berrison
Jr.), Cyd Charisse, Rosemary Clooney, Jane Powell, Vic
Damone, Howard Keel, Tony Martin, Gene Kelly, Fred Kelly,
Ann Miller, Joan Weldon, William Olvis, James Mitchell.
Production Dates: May 3-August 3, 1954.
Running Time: 132 min.
Release Date: December 1954.

IT'S ALWAYS FAIR WEATHER (1955) [with Gene Kelly]

Production Company: MGM. Producer: Arthur Freed.
Script: Betty Comden, Adolph Green. Director of Photog-
raphy: Robert Bronner, in Eastman Color and Cinemascope.
Special Effects: Warren Newcombe, Irving G. Ries. Editor:
Adrienne Fazan. Art Directors: Cedric Gibbons, Arthur
Lonergan. Set Decorators: Edwin B. Willis, Hugh Hunt.
Costumes: Helen Rose. Choreographers: Gene Kelly, Stan-
ley Donen. Musical Director: Andre Previn. Orchestrations:
Andre Previn. Sound Recordist: Wesley C. Miller.
Numbers: "Baby, You Knock Me Out," "Blue Danube," "I
Like Myself," "March, March," "Once I Had a Friend,"
"Situation Wise," "Stillman's Gym," "Thanks a Lot but No
Thanks," "Time for Parting," by Andre Previn (composer),
Betty Comden, Adolph Green (lyricists). "Music Is Better
Than Words," by Andre Previn, Roger Edens (composers),
Betty Comden, Adolph Green (Lyricists).
Cast: Gene Kelly (Ted Riley), Dan Dailey (Doug Hallerton),
Cyd Charisse (Jackie Leighton), Dolores Gray (Madeline Brad-
ville), Michael Kidd (Angie Valentine), David Burns (Tim),
Jay C. Flippen (Charles Z. Culloran), Steve Mitchell (Kid
Mariacchi), Hal March (Rocky Heldon), Paul Moxie (Mr.

Fielding), Peter Leeds (Mr. Trasker), Alex Gerry (Mr.
Stamper), Madge Blake (Mrs. Stamper), Wilson Wood (Roy),
Richard Simmons (Mr. Grigman), Almira Sessions (Lady),
Eugene Borden (Chef).
Production Dates: October 13, 1954-March 15, 1955; April 6,
1955.
Running Time: 101 min.
Release Date: September 1955.

FUNNY FACE (1957)

Production Company: Paramount. Producer: Roger Edens.
Script: Leonard Gersche, from his musical play Wedding
Bells. Director of Photography: Ray June, in Technicolor
and Vista Vision. Special Effects: John P. Fulton. Editor:
Frank Bracht. Art Directors: Hal Pereira, George W.
Davis. Costumes: Edith Head, Hubert de Givenchy (for Aud-
rey Hepburn in Paris). Titles Designer: Richard Avedon.
Choreographers: Eugene Loring, Fred Astaire. Musical Di-
rector: Adolph Deutsch. Orchestrations: Conrad Salinger,
Van Cleave, Alexander Courage, Skip Martin. Sound Record-
ists: George and Winston Leverett.
Numbers: "Clap Yo' Hands, " "Funny Face, " "He Loves and
She Loves, " "How Long Has This Been Going On?, " "Let's
Kiss and Make Up, " " 'S Wonderful, " by George Gershwin
(composer), Ira Gershwin (lyricist). "Basal Metabolism, "
"Bonjour, Paree!, " "On How to Be Lovely, " "Think Pink!, "
by Rober Edens (composer, Leonard Gersche (lyricist).
"Marche Funebre, " by Roger Edens (composer).
Cast: Audrey Hepburn (Jo Stockton), Fred Astaire (Dick
Avery), Kay Thompson (Maggie Prescott), Michael Auclair
(Prof. Emile Flostre), Robery Flemyng (Paul Duval), Dovima
(Marion), Virginia Gibson (Babs), Suzy Parker (Special Danc-
er), Sunny Harnett (Special Dancer), Sue England (Laura),
Ruta Lee (Lettie), Jean Del Val (Hairdresser), Alex Gerry
(Dovitch), Iphigenie Castiglioni (Armande).
Production Dates: April 7-July 16, 1956.
Running Time: 103 min.
Release Date: April 1957.

THE PAJAMA GAME (1957) [with George Abbott]

Production Company: Warner Bros. Producers: Stanley
Donen, George Abbott, Frederick Brisson (associate), Robert
E. Griffith (associate), Harold S. Prince (associate). Script:
George Abbott, Richard Bissell, from their musical play,

based on the novel $7\frac{1}{2}$ ¢, by Richard Bissell. Director
of Photography: Harry Stadling, in Warner Color. Editor:
William Ziegler. Art Directors: Malcolm Bert, Frank
Thompson (assistant). Set Decorator: William Kuehl. Cos-
tumes: William and Jean Eckart. Choreographer: Bob
Fosse. Musical Director: Ray Heindrof. Orchestrations:
Nelson Riddle, Buddy Bregman. Sound Recordists: M. A.
Merrick, Dolph Thomas.
Numbers: "Hernando's Hideaway," "Hey There," "I'll Never
Be Jealous Again," "I'm Not at All in Love," "Once a Year
Day," "The Pajama Game," "Racing with the Clock," "$7\frac{1}{2}$¢,"
"Steam Heat," "There Once Was a Man," by Richard Adler,
Jerry Ross (composers-lyricists).
Cast: Doris Day (Babe Williams), John Raitt (Sid Sorokin),
Carol Haney (Gladys Hotchkiss), Eddie Foy Jr. (Vernon Hines),
Reta Shaw (Mabel), Barbara Nichols (Poopsie), Thelma Pelish
(Mae), Jack Straw (Prez), Ralph Dunn (Hasler), Owen Martin
(Max), Jackie Kelk (First Helper), Ralph Chambers (Charlie),
Mary Stanton (Brenda), Buzz Miller, Kenneth LeRoy (Fea-
tured Dancers), Jack Waldron (Salesman), Ralph Volkie (Sec-
ond Helper), Franklyn Fox (Pop Williams), William A. Fores-
ter (Joe), Peter Gennaro (Dancer), Elmore Henderson (Waiter),
Fred Villani (Headwaiter), Kathy Marlowe (Holly), Otis Grif-
fith (Otis).
Production Dates: November 28, 1956-January 15, 1957.
Running Time: 101 min.
Release Date: August 1957.

KISS THEM FOR ME (1957)

Production Company: 20th Century-Fox. Producer: Jerry
Wald. Script: Julius Epstein, based on the play by Luther
Davis, based on the novel Shore Leave, by Frederic Wakeman.
Director of Photography: Milton Krasner, in Deluxe Color
and Cinemascope. Special Effects: L. B. Abbott. Editor:
Robert Simpson. Art Directors: Lyle R. Wheeler, Maurice
Ransford. Set Decorators: Walter M. Scott, Stuart A. Reiss.
Costumes: Charles Lemaire. Musical Director: Lionel New-
man. Orchestrations: Pete King, Skip Martin. Sound Re-
cordists: Charles Peck, Frank Moran. Title Song: Lionel
Newman (composer), Carroll Coates (lyricist).
Cast: Cary Grant (Andy Crewson), Jayne Mansfield (Alice
Kratchna), Suzy Parker (Gwynneth Livingston), Leif Erickson
(Eddie Turnbill), Ray Walston ("Mac"/J. G. McCann), Larry
Blyden (Mississip' Hardy), Nathaniel Frey (C. P. O. Ruddle),
Werner Klemperer (Commander Wallec), Jack Mullaney (En-

sign Lewis), Harry Carey Jr. (Roundtree), Frank Nelson
(Neilson), Caprice Yordan (Debbie), Ann McCrea (Lucille),
Bill Phipps (Lieutenant Hendricks), Richard Deacon (Hotch-
kiss), Kathleen Freeman (Nurse Wilinski), Maudie Prickett
(Chief Nurse), Rachel Stevens (Bit Wave), Nancy Kulp (Bit
Wave at Switchboard).
Production Dates: April 29-week of June 24, 1957.
Running Time: 103 min.
Release Date: December 1957.

INDISCREET (1958)

Distribution Company: Warner Bros.   Production Company:
A Grandon Production.   Producers: Stanely Donen, Sydney
Streeter (associate).   Script: Norman Krasna, from his play
Kind Sir.   Director of Photography: Fredrick A. Young, in
Technicolor.   Editor: Jack Harris.   Art Director: Don Ash-
ton.   Costumes: Christian Dior, Pierre Balmain, Lanvin-
Castillo (for Ingrid Bergman), Quintino (for Cary Grant).
Titles Designer: Maurice Binder.   Musical Directors: Rich-
ard Bennett, Ken Jones.   Sound Recordists: Winston Ryder
(sound editor), Richard Bird, Len Shilton.   Title Song: James
Van Heusen (composer), Sammy Cahn (lyricist).
Cast: Cary Grant (Philip Adams), Ingrid Bergman (Anna
Kalman), Cecil Parker (Alfred Munson), Phyllis Calvert
(Margaret Munson), David Kossoff (Carl Banks), Megs Jen-
kins (Doris Banks), Oliver Johnston (Finleigh), Middleton
Woods (Finleigh's clerk).
Production Dates: November 18, 1957-February 7, 1958.
Running Time: 100 min.
Release Date: July 1958.

DAMN YANKEES (1958) [with George Abbott]
[WHATEVER LOLA WANTS in Europe]

Production Company: Warner Bros.   Producers: George
Abbott, Stanley Donen, Fredrick Brisson (associate), Robert
Griffith (associate), Harold Prince (associate).   Script:
George Abbott, from his and Douglass Wallop's musical play,
based on the novel The Year the Yankees Lost the Pennant,
by Douglass Wallop.   Director of Photography: Harold Lip-
stein, in Technicolor.   Editor: Frank Bracht.   Art Director:
Stanley Fleischer.   Set Decorator: John P. Austin.   Cos-
tumes: William and Jean Eckart.   Titles Designer: Maurice
Binder.   Choreographer: Bob Fosse.   Musical Director:

Ray Heindorf.   Sound Recordists: Stanley Jones, Dolph
Thomas.
Numbers: "A Little Brains--a Little Talent," "Goodbye, Old
Girl," "Shoeless Joe from Hannibal, Mo," "Six Months Out
of Every Year," "Those Were the Good Old Days," "Two
Lost Souls," "Whatever Lola Wants," "Who's Got the Pain?,"
You've Got to Have Heart," by Richard Adler, Jerry Ross
(composers-lyricists).   "An Empty Chair," by Richard Adler
(composer-lyricist).
Cast: Tab Hunter (Joe Hardy), Gwen Verdon (Lola), Ray
Walston (Applegate), Russ Brown (Van Buren), Shannon Bolin
(Meg), Nathaniel Frey (Smokey), Jimmy Komack (Rocky), Rae
Allen (Gloria), Robert Shafer (Joe Boyd), Jean Stapleton (Sis-
ter), Albert Linville (Vernon), Elizabeth Howell (Doris).
Production Dates: April 16, 1958-May 29, 1958.
Running Time: 110 min.
Release Date: September 1958.

ONCE MORE, WITH FEELING (1960)

Distribution Company: Columbia.   Production Company:
Stanley Donen Productions.   Producers: Stanley Donen, Paul
B. Radin (associate).   Script: Harry Kurnitz, from his play.
Director of Photography: Georges Perinal, in Technicolor.
Editor: Jack Harris.   Art Director: Alex Trauner.   Cos-
tumes: Hubert de Givenchy.   Titles Designer: Maurice
Binder.   Musical Director: Muir Mathieson.   Sound Re-
cordist: Joseph De Bretagne.
Cast: Yul Brynner (Victor Fabian), Kay Kendall (Dolly Fa-
bian), Geoffrey Toone (Dr. Hilliard), Maxwell Shaw (Grisha
Gendel), Mervyn Johns (Mr. Wilbur Jr.), Martin Benson
(Bardini), Harry Lockhart (Chester), Gregory Ratoff (Max-
well Archer), Shirley Ann Field (Angela Hopper), Grace New-
combe (Mrs. Wilbur), C.S. Stuart (Manning), Colin Drake
(Doctor), Andrew Paulds (Interviewer), C.E. Joy (Sir Austin
Flapp), Barbara Hall (Secretary).
Production Dates: April 6, 1959-week of June 29, 1959.
Running Time: 92 min.
Release Date: February 1960.

SURPRISE PACKAGE (1960)

Distribution Company: Columbia.   Production Company:
Stanley Donen Productions.   Producer: Stanley Donen.
Script: Harry Kurnitz, based on the novel A Gift from the

Boys, by Art Buchwald. Director of Photography: Christopher Challis. Editor: James Clark. Art Director: Don Ashton. Costumes: Mattli. Titles Designer: Maurice Binder. Musical Director: Benjamin Frankel. Sound Recordist: John Cox. Title Song: James Van Heusen (composer), Sammy Cahn (lyricist).
Cast: Yul Brynner (Nico March), Mitzi Gaynor (Gabby Rogers), Noel Coward (King Pavel II), Eric Pohlmann (Stefan Miralis), George Coulouris (Dr. Hugo Panzer), Guy Deghy (Tibor Smolny), Warren Mitchell (Klimatis), Lyndon Brook (Stavrin), Man Mountain Dean (Igor Trofin), Bill Nagy (Johnny Stettina), Lionel Murton, Barry Foster (U.S. Marshalls).
Production Dates: October 19-week of December 28, 1959.
Running Time: 99 min.
Release Date: November 1960.

THE GRASS IS GREENER (1960)

Distribution Company: Universal-International. Production Company: Grandon Productions, Ltd. Producers: Stanley Donen, James Ware (associate). Script: Hugh and Margaret Williams, from their play. Director of Photography: Christopher Challis, in Technicolor and Technirama. Editor: James Clark. Art Director: Paul Sheriff. Set Decorator: Vernon Dixon. Costumes: Hardy Amies (for Deborah Kerr), Christian Dior (for Jean Simmons). Title Designer: Maurice Binder. Musical Directors: Douglas Gamley, Len Stevens from the music by Noel Coward. Sound Recordist: John Cox.
Cast: Cary Grant (Victor Rhyall), Deborah Kerr (Hilary Rhyall), Robert Mitchum (Charles Delacro), Jean Simmons (Hattie), Moray Watson (Sellers).
Production Dates: April 4-week of August 1, 1960.
Running Time: 104 min.
Release Date: December 1960.

CHARADE (1963)

Distribution Company: Universal. Production Company: Stanley Donen Productions. Producers: Stanley Donen, James Ware (associate). Script: Peter Stone, from the short story "The Unsuspecting Wife," by Peter Stone and Marc Behm. Director of Photography: Charles Lang Jr., in Technicolor. Editor: James Clark. Art Director: Jean d'Eaubonne. Costumes: Givenchy (for Audrey Hepburn). Titles Designer: Maurice Binder. Musical Composer and

Director: Henry Mancini. Sound Recordists: Jacques Car-
rere, Bob Jones. Title Song: Henry Mancini (composer),
Johnny Mercer (lyricist).
Cast: Cary Grant (Peter Joshua), Audrey Hepburn (Regina
"Reggie" Lambert), Walter Matthau (Hamilton Bartholomew),
James Coburn (Tex Penthollow), George Kennedy (Herman
Scobie), Ned Glass (Leopold Gideon), Jacques Marin (Insp.
Edouard Grandpierre), Paul Bonifas (Felix), Dominique Minot
(Sylvia Gaudet), Thomas Chelimsky (Jean-Louis Gaudet).
Production Dates: October 22, 1962-week of February 11,
1963.
Running Time: 113 min.
Release Date: December 1963.

ARABESQUE (1966)

Distribution Company: Universal. Production Company:
Stanley Donen Enterprises. Producers: Stanley Donen, Denis
Holt (assistant). Script: Julian Mitchell, Stanley Price,
Pierre Marton, from the novel The Cipher, by Alex Gordon.
Director of Photography: Christopher Challis, in Technicolor
and Panavision. Editor: Fredrick Wilson. Art Director:
Reece Pemberton. Costumes: Christian Dior (for Sophia
Loren). Titles Designer: Maurice Binder. Musical Com-
poser and Director: Henry Mancini. Sound Recordists:
John W. Mitchell, Colin Le Mesurier.
Cast: Gregory Peck (David Pollock), Sophia Loren (Yasmin
Azir), Alan Badel (Beshravi), Kieron Moore (Yussef), Carl
Duering (Hassan Jena), John Merivale (Sloane), Duncan La-
mont (Webster), George Coulouris (Ragheeb), Ernest Clark
(Beauchamp), Harold Kasket (Mohammed Lufti).
Production Dates: April 20-week of September 12, 1965.
Running Time: 105 min.
Release Date: July 1966.

TWO FOR THE ROAD (1967)

Distribution Company: 20th Century-Fox. Production Com-
pany: Stanley Donen Films, Inc. Producers: Stanley Donen,
James Ware (assistant). Script: Frederic Raphael. Direc-
tor of Photography: Christopher Challis, in DeLuxe Color
and Panavision. Special Effects: Gilbert Manzow. Editors:
Richard Marden, Madeleine Gug. Art Directors: Willy Holt,
Marc Frederix (assistant). Set Decorator: Roger Volper.
Costumes: Sophie Rochas, Ken Scott, Michele Rosier, Paco

Rabanne, Mary Quaint, Foale Tuffin (for Audrey Hepburn), Hardy Amies (for Albert Finney). Titles Designer: Maurice Binder. Musical Composer and Director: Henry Mancini. Sound Recordist: Jo De Bretagne.
Cast: Audrey Hepburn (Joanna Wallace), Albert Finney (Mark Wallace), William Daniels (Howie Maxwell Manchester), Eleanor Bron (Cathy Maxwell Manchester), Claude Dauphin (Maurice Dalbret), Nadia Grey (Francoise Dalbert), Georges Descrières (David), Gabrielle Middleton (Ruthie), Kathy Chelimsky (Caroline), Carol Van Dyke (Michelle), Karyn Balm (Simone).
Production Dates: May 2-week of October 10, 1966.
Running Time: 112 min.
Release Date: July 1967.

BEDAZZLED (1968)

Distribution Company: 20th Century-Fox. Production Company: Stanley Donen Enterprises. Producer: Stanley Donen. Script: Peter Cook, from a story by Peter Cook, Dudley Moore. Director of Photography: Austin Dempster, in Deluxe Color and Panavision. Editor: Richard Marden. Art Directors: Terence Knight, Ted Tester (assistant). Costumes: Yvonne Caffin, Clare Rendlesham, Jean Muir (for Eleanor Bron), Cue at Austin Reed (for Peter Cook), Mr. Risk (for Dudley Moore). Titles Designer: Maurice Binder. Animation: Bailey Pettengal Design, Ltd. Musical Composer and Director: Dudley Moore. Sound Recordist: John Purchese, Doug Turner.
Cast: Peter Cook (George Spiggot), Dudley Moore (Stanley Moon), Eleanor Bron (Margaret Spencer), Raquel Welch (Lillian Lust), Michael Bates (Insp. Clarke), Bernard Spear (Irving Moses), Parnell McGarry (Gluttony), Howard Goorney (Sloth), Alba (Vanity), Barry Humphries (Envy), Daniele Noel (Avarice), Robert Russell (Anger), Peter Hutchins(P. C. Roberts), Max Faulkner (Priest), Martin Boddy (Cardinal), John Steiner (TV Announcer), Robin Hawdon (Randolph), Eric Chitty (Seed), Michael Trubshawe (Lord Dowdy), Evelyn Moore (Mrs. Wisby), Lockwood West (St. Peter).
Production Dates: June 1-August 22, 1967.
Running Time: 107 min.
Release Date: December 1967.

STAIRCASE (1969)

Distribution Company: 20th Century-Fox. Production Company: Stanley Donen Films, Inc. Producer: Stanley Donen. Script: Charles Dyer, from his play. Director of Photography: Christopher Challis, in Deluxe Color and Panavision. Editor: Richard Marden. Art Director: Willy Holt. Costumes: Clare Rendlesham. Titles Designer: Maurice Binder. Musical Composer and Director: Dudley Moore. Sound Recordists: Alex Pront, Jean-Louis Ducarme.
Cast: Richard Burton (Harry Leeds), Rex Harrison (Charlie Dyer), Cathleen Nesbitt (Harry's Mother), Beatrix Lehmann (Charlie's Mother), Gordon Heath (Postman), Stephen Lewis (Jack), Jake Kavanagh (Choirboy), Dermot Kelly (Gravedigger), Avril Angers (Miss Ricard), Neil Wilson (Policeman), Shelagh Fraser (Cub Mistress), Gwen Nelson (Matron), Pat Heywood (Nurse), Rogers and Starr (Opening Song).
Production Dates: September 2-week of December 23, 1968.
Running Time: 96 min.
Release Date: August 1969.

THE LITTLE PRINCE (1974)

Production Company: Paramount. Producers: Stanley Donen, A. Joseph Tandet (associate). Script: Alan Jay Lerner, based on the novel by Antoine de Saint-Exupéry. Director of Photography: Christopher Challis, in Technicolor. Special Effects: John Richardson. Editors: Peter Boita, John Guthridge. Art Director: Norman Reynolds. Production Designer: John Barry. Costumes: Shirley Russell, Tim Goodchild. Choreographers: Bob Fosse ("Snake in the Grass"), Ronn Forella. Titles Designer: Maurice Binder. Musical Director: Frederick Loewe. Orchestrations: Angela Morley. Sound Recordists: John Willis, John Richards, Bill Rowe. Numbers: "A Snake in the Grass," "Be Happy," "Closer and Closer and Closer," "I Never Met a Rose," "I'm on Your Side," "It's a Hat/I Need Air," "Little Prince," "Why Is a Desert?," "You're a Child," by Frederick Loewe (composer), Alan Jay Lerner (lyricist).
Cast: Richard Kiley (The Pilot), Steven Warner (The Little Prince), Bob Fosse (The Snake), Gene Wilder (The Fox), Joss Ackland (The King), Clive Revill (The Businessman), Victor Spinetti (Historian), Graham Crowden (The General), Donna McKechnie (The Rose).
Production Dates: January 30-August 6, 1973.
Running Time: 88 min.
Release Date: December 1974.

LUCKY LADY (1975)

Production Company: 20th Century-Fox. Producer: Michael
Gruskoff. Script: Willard Huyck, Gloria Katz. Directors of
Photography: Geoffrey Unsworth, Rico Browning (the battle
sequence), in Deluxe Color. Editors: Peter Boita, George
Hively, Tom Rolf (the battle sequence). Production Designer:
John Barry. Art Director: Norman Reynolds. Costumes:
Lilly Fenichel. Titles Designer: Dan Perri. Musical Di-
rector: Ralph Burns. Sound Recordist: Theodore Soderberg.
Title Song and "Get While the Gettin's Good," by Fred Ebb
(composer), John Kander (lyricist).
Cast: Gene Hackman (Kibby), Liza Minnelli (Claire), Burt
Reynolds (Walker), Geoffrey Lewis (Capt. Aaron Mosely),
John Hillerman (Christy McTeague), Robby Benson (Billy
Weber), Michael Hordern (Capt. Rockwell), Anthony Holland
(Mr. Tully), John McLiam (Rass Huggins), Val Avery (Dolph),
Louis Guss (Bernie), William H. Bassett (Charley), Emilio
Fernandez (Ybarra), Raymond Guth (Brother Bob), Duncan
McLeod (Auctioneer), Milt Kogan (Supercargo), Suzanne Zenor
(Brunette), Richard Caine (Young Bootlegger), Richard Arm-
bruster (Hanson), Doyle Baker (Gene), Michael Greene (Tur-
ley).
Production Dates: February 22-week of July 14, 1975.
Running Time: 117 min.
Release Date: December 1975.

MOVIE MOVIE (1978)

Distribution Company: Warner Bros. Production Company:
Lord Lew Grade. Executive Producer: Martin Starger.
Producer: Stanley Donen. Script: Larry Gelbart, Sheldon
Keller. Director of Photography: Charles Rosher Jr. ("Dy-
namite Hands"), Bruce Surtees ("Baxter's Beauties of 1933").
Special Effects: Cinema Research Corp. Editor: George
Hively. Art Director: Jack Fisk. Costumes: Patty Norris.
Titles Designer: Dan Perri. Choreographer: Michael Kidd.
Songs: Ralph Burns (composer with Buster Davis for "Bax-
ter's Beauties of 1933"), Larry Gelbart, Sheldon Keller (lyri-
cists). Arrangements: Buster Davis. Sound Recordist:
James Webb Jr.

"Dynamite Hands"

Cast: George C. Scott (Gloves Malloy), Trish Van Devere
(Betsy McGuire), Red Buttons (Peanuts), Eli Wallach (Vince
Marlowe), Harry Hamlin (Joey Popchik), Ann Reinking (Trou-

bles Moran), Jocelyn Brando (Mama Popchik), Michael Kidd
("Pop" Popchik), Kathleen Beller (Angie Popchik), Barry Bost-
wick (Johnny Danko), Art Carney (Dr. Blaine), Clay Hodges
(Sailor Lawson), George P. Wilbur (Tony Norton), Peter T.
Stader (Barney Keegle), James Lennon (The Announcer).

"Baxter's Beauties of 1933"

Cast: George C. Scott (Spats Baxter), Barbara Harris (Trixie
Lane), Barry Bostwick (Dick Cummings), Trish Van Devere
(Isobel Stuart), Red Buttons (Jinks Murphy), Eli Wallach (Pop),
Rebecca York (Kitty), Art Carney (Dr. Bowers), Maidie Nor-
man (Gussie), Jocelyn Brando (Mrs. Updike). Charles Lane
(Mr. Pennington), Barney Martin (Motorcycle Cop), Dick
Winslow (Tinkle Johnson), Sebastian Brook (Fritz).
Production Dates: October 10, 1977-week of May 6, 1978.
Running Time: 105 min.
Release Date: December 1978.

SATURN 3 (1980)

Distribution Company: Associated Film Distribution. Produc-
tion Company: Lord Lew Grade in association with Elliot
Kastner. Executive Producer: Martin Starger. Producer:
Stanley Donen. Script: Martin Amis, from a story by John
Barry. Director of Photography: Billy Williams. Special
Effects: Colin Chilvers. Editor: Richard Marden. Produc-
tion Designer: Stuart Craig. Art Director: Norman Dorme.
Costumes: uncredited. Musical Composer and Director:
Elmer Bernstein. Orchestrations: Christopher Palmer.
Cast: Farrah Fawcett (Alex), Kirk Douglas (Adam), Harvey
Keitel (Benson/James), Douglas Lambert (Real Capt. James),
Ed Bishop (Harding), Christopher Muncke (2nd Crewman).
Production Dates: January 17-week of June 20, 1979.
Running Time: 95 min.
Release Date: February 1980.

DISCOGRAPHY OF SOUNDTRACKS

The Musicals:

Damn Yankees. RCA Victor, LOC-1047.

Deep in My Heart. MGM records, 2-SES-54ST.

Funny Face. STET, a Division of Out-Take Records, Inc., DS-15001.

It's Always Fair Weather, Polydor Records LTD. for MGM Records, MGM SELECT 2353-036.

The Little Prince. ABC Records, ABDP-854.

On the Town. Show Biz, 5603.

The Pajama Game. Columbia, OL 5210.

Royal Wedding. MGM Records, 2-SES-53ST.

Seven Brides for Seven Brothers. MGM Records, 2-SES-41ST.

Singin' in the Rain. MGM Records, 2-STS-40ST.

The Comedies:

Arabesque. RCA Victor, LSP--3623.

Bedazzled. London, MS-82009.

Charade. RCA Victor, LPS-2755.

Lucky Lady. Arista, AL-4069.

Songs from Movie Movie. Filmscore Records, FS--7914 (not a soundtrack)

Two for the Road. RCA Victor, LSP-3802.

BIBLIOGRAPHY

Books

Abbott, George. Mister Abbott. New York: Random House, 1963.
_____, and Richard Bissell. The Pajama Game. New York: Random House, 1954.
Arnold, Elliott. Deep in My Heart: A Story Based on the Life of Sigmund Romberg. New York: Duell, Sloan and Pearce, 1949.
Astaire, Fred. Steps in Time. New York: Harper, 1959.
Bassinger, Jeanine. Gene Kelly. New York: Pyramid, 1976.
Benét, Stephen Vincent. "The Sobbin' Women," in Twenty-Five Short Stories. Garden City, N. Y.: Sun Dial, 1943.
Bentley, Eric. The Life of the Drama. New York: Atheneum, 1967.
Bergman, Ingrid, and Alan Burgess. Ingrid Bergman: My Story. New York: Delacorte, 1980.
Buchwald, Art. A Gift from the Boys. New York: Harper, 1958.
Burrows, Michael. Gene Kelly: Versatility Personified. London: Primestyle, 1972.
Casper, Joseph Andrew. Vincente Minnelli and the Film Musical. South Brunswick, N.J., and New York: Barnes, 1977.
Comden, Betty, and Adolph Green. Singin' in the Rain. New York: Viking, 1972.
Corliss, Richard, ed. The Hollywood Screenwriters. New York: Avon, 1972.
_____. Talking Pictures: Screenwriters on the American Cinema. New York: Penguin, 1975.

266

Crawley, Tony. The Films of Sophia Loren. London: LSP,
    1974.
Croce, Arlene.   The Fred Astaire and Ginger Rogers Book.
    New York: Dutton, 1972.
Davis, Luther. Kiss Them for Me.   Copyright 1944 and
    1970 by Luther Davis under the title Uncle Sugar, Acting
    Edition, Kiss Them for Me, copyright 1945 and 1970 by
    Luther Davis.
De Saint-Exupéry, Antoine. The Little Prince (trans. Kather-
    ine Woods). New York: Harcourt, Brace and World, 1943.
Deschner, Donald. The Films of Cary Grant. Secaucus,
    N.J.: Citadel, 1973.
Eames, John Douglas. The MGM Story: The Complete His-
    tory of Fifty Roaring Years. New York: Crown, 1976.
Epps, Preston H., trans. Aristotle: The Poetics. Chapel
    Hill: University of North Carolina Press, 1942.
Fordin, Hugh. The World of Entertainment: Hollywood's
    Greatest Musicals. Garden City, N.Y.: Doubleday, 1975.
Freedland, Michael. Fred Astaire. London: Allen, 1976.
Golden, Leon, trans., and O. B. Hardison Jr., commentary.
    Aristotle's Poetics: A Translation and Commentary.
    Englewood Cliffs, N.J.: Prentice-Hall, 1968.
Gordon, Alex. The Cipher. New York: Simon and Schuster,
    1961.
Green, Stanley, and Burt Goldblatt. Starring Fred Astaire.
    New York: Dodd, Mead, 1973.
Harbage, Alfred, ed. William Shakespeare: The Complete
    Works. London: Penguin, 1969.
Hart, Dorothy. Thou Swell Thou Witty: The Life and Lyrics
    of Lorenz Hart. New York: Harper and Row, 1976.
Hirschhorn, Clive. Gene Kelly: A Biography. Chicago:
    Regnery, 1974.
_____. The Warner Brothers Story. New York: Crown,
    1979.
Kael, Pauline. I Lost It at the Movies. New York: Bantam,
    1966.
_____. Kiss Kiss Bang Bang. New York: Bantam, 1969.
_____. When the Lights Go Down. New York: Holt,
    Rinehart and Winston, 1980.
Krasna, Norman. Kind Sir. New York: Dramatists Play
    Service, 1954.
Kurnitz, Harry. Once More, with Feeling. New York:
    Random House, 1959.
Larkin, Rochelle. Hail, Columbia. New Rochelle, N.Y.:
    Arlington House, 1975.
Limbacher, James L. Four Aspects of the Film. New
    York: Brussel and Brussel, 1969.

McVay, Douglas. The Musical Film. New York: Barnes,
    1967.
Martin, Tony, and Cyd Charisse, as told to Dick Kleiner.
    The Two of Us. New York: Mason/Charter, 1976.
Morris, George. Doris Day. New York: Pyramid, 1976.
Narboni, Jean, and Tom Milne, eds. Godard on Godard.
    New York: Viking, 1972.
Pasternak, Joe, as told to David Chandler. Easy the Hard
    Way. New York: Putnam, 1956.
Peary, Dan, ed. Close-ups. New York: Workman, 1978.
Quirk, Lawrence. The Films of Ingrid Bergman. New
    York: Citadel, 1973.
Raphael, Fred. Two for the Road. New York: Holt, Rine-
    hart and Winston, 1967.
Sennett, Ted. Warner Brothers Presents. New Rochelle,
    N.Y.: Arlington House, 1971.
Shipman, David. The Great Movie Stars: The International
    Years. New York: St. Martin, 1972.
Taylor, John Russell, and Arthur Jackson. The Hollywood
    Musical. New York: McGraw-Hill, 1971.
Thomas, Tony. The Films of Gene Kelly: Song and Dance
    Man. Secaucus, N.J.: Citadel, 1974.
_____, and Aubrey Solomon. The Films of 20th Century
    Fox. Secaucus, N.J.: Citadel, 1979.
Webster's New Collegiate Dictionary. Springfield, Mass.:
    Merriam, 1980.
Williams, Hugh and Margaret. The Grass Is Greener. New
    York: French, 1959.
Young, Christopher. The Films of Doris Day. Secaucus,
    N.J.: Citadel, 1977.
Zadan, Craig. Sondheim & Co. New York: Macmillan,
    1974.

Articles

Atkinson, Brooks. "Kind Sir." New York Times, November
    5, 1953, p. 41.
_____. "Once More with Feeling." New York Times,
    October 2, 1958, p. 39.
Barnes, Clive. "Staircase." New York Times, January 11,
    1968, p. 41.
Bell, Joseph N. "On Location in Mexico with Liza and
    Friends." New York Times, July 29, 1975, Arts and
    Leisure Section, p. 15.
Bitsch, Charles, and Jacques Rivette. "Recontre avec Gene
    Kelly." Cahiers du Cinema, 15, 85 (July 1958) 24-31.

Byone, Bridget. "Making Magic from 'No No No.'" Los Angeles Herald-Examiner December 22, 1974, Section E-1, pp. 1-3.

Causson, Jean-Louis. "Entrez dans la danse; elements pour histoire du film musical." Cinema, 11, 11 (May 1956), 27-43.

Champlin, Charles. "Saturn 3." Los Angeles Times Calendar, February 14, 1980, pp. 1, 6.

Clark, James. "Giving Life an Up Beat." Films and Filming, 4, 10 (July 1958), 7, 32.

Cocks, Jay. "Lucky Lady." Time, 106 (December 22, 1975), 72.

Donen, Stanley. "Musical Talent Shortage Poses Problem-- Donen." Hollywood Reporter, 133, 46 (March 23, 1955), 5.

_____. "What to Do with Star Quality." Films and Filming, 6, 11 (August 1960), 11.

Farber, Stephen. "Perfect Imperfection: 'That's Donen.'" Los Angeles Times Calendar, August 25, 1974, p. 23.

_____. "Why Couldn't This Lady Have a Happy Ending?" New York Times, December 14, 1975, Arts and Leisure Section, pp. 1, 15.

Gavin, Arthur E. "Novelty and Originality Mark Photography of Damn Yankees." American Cinematographer, 39, 10 (October 1958), 618-619, 646-648.

Gelbart, Larry. "Movie Movie--Why? Why?" New York Times, September 11, 1978, Arts and Leisure Section, pp. 1, 17.

"The Grass Is Greener." Times (London), 54, 324 (December 3, 1958), 14.

Grenier, Cynthia. "Playing Once More, with Feeling in Paris." New York Times, July 19, 1969, Section II, p. 5.

Harvey, Stephen. "Stanley Donen." Film Comment, 9, 4 (July-August 1973) 4-9.

Hill, Derek. "Indiscreet." American Cinematographer, 39, 4 (April 1958), 230-231, 240.

Hillier, Jim. "Interview with Stanley Donen." Movie, 24 (Spring 1977), 26-35.

Johnson, Albert. "The Tenth Muse in San Francisco." Sight and Sound, 26, 1 (Summer 1956), 46-50.

Knapp, Dan. "Henry Mancini--A Winner in Scoring Motion Pictures." Los Angeles Times Calendar, July 12, 1969, p. 26.

Knight, Arthur. "Choreography for Camera: Funny Face." Dance Magazine, 28 (August 1954), 21-23, 66.

Kyrou, Adlo. "Notes sur l'erotisme des films danses."

Positif, 12 (December 1954), 33-36.

Lawson, Carol. "Lionizing MGM in Retrospect." New York Times, June 24, 1977, Section III, p. 12.

Lightman, Herb A. "The Photography of Charade." American Cinematographer, 45, 5 (May 1964), 254-55, 282-86.

McVay, Douglas. "Moanin' for Donen." Film, 27 (January-February 1961), 20-25.

Murphy, Mary. "Lucky Lady Filming Just Plain Unlucky." Los Angeles Times Calendar, June 29, 1975, pp. 1, 39-43.

Myrsine, Jean. "Gene Kelly: Auteur de films et homme-orchestre." Cahiers du Cinema, 3, 14 (July 1952), 34-38.

Nichols, Lewis. "Kiss Them for Me." New York Times, March 21, 1945, p. 27.

Perez, Michel Raymond. "Sur trois films de Gene Kelly." Positif, 2, 12 (November-December 1954), 47-50.

Power, James. "Henry Mancini Seminar." American Film, 3, 3 (January 1974), 2-22.

Raines, Halsey. "Film Package on a Grecian Isle." New York Times, November 8, 1959, Section II, p. 7.

"Staircase." Times (London), 56, 779 (November 3, 1966), 7.

Tavernier, Bertrand and Daniel Palas. "Entretien avec Stanley Donen." Cahiers du Cinema, 24, 143 (May 1963), 1-25.

Tavernier, Colo and Bertrand. "Talking in the Sun: Entretien avec Stanley Donen." Positif, 111 (December 1969), 33-47.

Taylor, Clarke. "A Junket, Junket to Movie Movie." Los Angeles Times Calendar, December 16, 1978, pp. 65-67.

Thomas, Kevin. "Stanley Donen: After Singin' in the Rain, a Flood of Elegant Films." Los Angeles Times Calendar, March 10, 1968, pp. 16-17.

Vaughan, David. "After the Ball." Sight and Sound, 26, 2 (Autumn 1956), 84-91, 111.

Warga, Wayne. "Double Feature: Revisiting the '30s." Los Angeles Times Calendar, January 29, 1978, pp. 52, 55.

Watts, Stephen. "A More Stately Sophia." New York Times, August 22, 1965, Section II, p. 7.

_____. "Focus on Amour in a Stately Home." New York Times, June 26, 1960, Section II, p. 7; revised December 24, 1960, Section II, p. 8.

_____. "Indiscreet Goes Before the Camera in Britain." New York Times, January 28, 1958, Section II, p. 5.

Wolf, William. "The Careful Retelling of a Children's Classic." Los Angeles Times Calendar, May 27, 1973, p. 16.

_____. "Stanley Donen: Movie Maker from Carolina." Atlanta Journal and Constitution Magazine, April 9, 1967, pp. 29-30.

Wood, Thomas. "The Uncasting Coup of Donen's The Little Prince." Los Angeles Times Calendar, August 26, 1973. pp. 1, 26.

Interviews

Casper, Joseph Andrew. Interviews with Stanley Donen recorded on tape July 20, July 27, August 2, and August 9, 1976, October 18, 1979, and April 16, 1980, in Los Angeles and preserved in the Special Collections of the Cinema Library, University of Southern California.

Fordin, Hugh. Interviews with Stanley Donen recorded on tape May 19 and May 21, 1972, in London and preserved in the Special Collections of the Cinema Library, University of Southern California.

Knight, Arthur. Interviews with Stanley Donen recorded on tape July 6, 1958, and November 30, 1978, in Los Angeles and preserved in the Special Collections of the Cinema Library, University of Southern California.

Dissertations

Charness, Casey. "Hollywood Cine-Dance: A Description of the Interrelationship of Camerawork and Choreography in Film by Stanley Donen and Gene Kelly." New York University, 1977.

Delameter, Jerome Herbert. "A Critical and Historical Analysis of Dance as a Code of the Hollywood Musical." Northwestern University, 1978.

Hungerford, Mary Jane. "Dancing in Commercial Motion Pictures." Columbia University, 1946.